The Self and Its Emotions

If there is one value that seems beyond reproach in modernity, it is that of the self and the terms that cluster around it, such as self-esteem, self-confidence, and self-respect. It is not clear, however, that all those who invoke the self really know what they are talking about, or that they are all talking about the same thing. What is this thing called 'self', then, and what is its psychological, philosophical, and educational salience? More specifically, what role do emotions play in the creation and constitution of the self? This book proposes a realist, emotion-grounded conception of selfhood. In arguing for a closer link between selfhood and emotion than has been previously suggested, the author critically explores and integrates self research from diverse academic fields. This is a provocative book that should excite anyone interested in cutting-edge research on self issues and emotions that lies at the intersection of psychology, philosophy of mind, moral philosophy, and moral education.

Kristján Kristjánsson received his PhD in moral philosophy from the University of St. Andrews, Scotland. He has taught at the University of Akureyri, Iceland, and at the University of Iceland, where he is currently Professor of Philosophy of Education. He has been a Visiting Fellow at Cornell University, University of Konstanz, St. Edmund's College (Cambridge University), and Institute of Education (University of London). Kristjánsson has written four books in English and three in Icelandic. He has published numerous articles on topics in moral philosophy, emotion theory, and moral education in international journals. He is a member of the International Society for Research on Emotions and a member of the editorial board of the *Journal of Moral Education*.

For my beloved one, Nora (Chia-jung), who helps me sustain my selfhood.

STUDIES IN EMOTION AND SOCIAL INTERACTION
Second Series

Series Editors

Keith Oatley
University of Toronto

Antony S. R. Manstead
University of Cambridge

(Continued on page 273)

The Self and Its Emotions

Kristján Kristjánsson

University of Iceland, Reykjavík

CAMBRIDGE UNIVERSITY PRESS
Cambridge, New York, Melbourne, Madrid, Cape Town, Singapore,
São Paulo, Delhi, Dubai, Tokyo

Cambridge University Press
32 Avenue of the Americas, New York, NY 10013-2473, USA

www.cambridge.org
Information on this title: www.cambridge.org/9780521114783

First published 2010

Printed in the United States of America

A catalog record for this publication is available from the British Library.

Library of Congress Cataloging in Publication data

Kristjánsson, Kristján.
The self and its emotions / Kristjánsson, Kristján.
    p.   cm. – (Studies in emotion and social interaction)
Includes bibliographical references and index.
ISBN 978-0-521-11478-3 (hardback)
1. Self.   2. Self (Philosophy)   3. Self psychology.   I. Title.   II. Series.
BF697.K75   2010
126–dc22   2009038055

ISBN 978-0-521-11478-3 Hardback

Contents

List of Tables

Acknowledgments

I started working on this book when I was a Visiting Fellow at St. Edmund's College, University of Cambridge, in 2006, and completed it during my sabbatical semester as a Visiting Fellow at the Institute of Education, University of London, in 2009. I would like to express my gratitude for the friendship and support of Professor Terence McLaughlin who was my host at St. Edmund's College, but who sadly passed away while I was there; and Professor Paul Standish who invited me to the Institute of Education.

I thank Professor Keith Oatley, the editor of the series to which this study is a contribution, for his unfailing enthusiasm and encouragement from the first time I contacted him (and later for his incisive comments), and Simina Calin and her colleagues at Cambridge for their professionalism, positive approach, and attention to detail. Many friends and colleagues – too many to name here – as well as numerous journal referees have read earlier versions of different portions of the book and have made valuable comments. I am indebted to all of them, especially to Professor Sigurður J. Grétarsson, who read the final draft of a substantial part of the manuscript and helped me weed out some unfortunate errors, and Nina Lee Colwill who did her best, as always, to remove any remaining infelicities of language. Audiences at the University of Akureyri, University of Iceland, University of Edinburgh, University of Swansea, University of London Institute of Education, Philosophy of Education Society of Great Britain 2008 Conference, Hume Society 2008 Conference, and Association for Moral Education 2009 Conference provided helpful criticism. I gratefully acknowledge a grant from Hagþenkir: The Icelandic Society of Non-Fiction Writers. My heartiest thanks must, however, as always go to my wife, Nora, for her constant sustenance and care.

I am grateful for permission to reprint material from the following articles: 'Measuring Self-Respect', *Journal for the Theory of Social Behaviour*, 37, 2007; 'Justified Self-Esteem', *Journal of Philosophy of Education*, 41, 2007; 'Suicide Bombings and the Self', *Journal of Global Ethics*, 4, 2008; 'An Aristotelian Critique of Situationism', *Philosophy*, 83, 2008; 'Hiltonism, Hedonism, and the Self', *Ethics and Education*, 3, 2008; 'Education and Self-Change', *Cambridge Journal of Education*, 38, 2008; 'Self-Esteem, Self-Confidence and Individualised Education' in *International Perspectives on Education*, eds. Chau Meng Huat and Trevor Kerry (London: Continuum, 2008); 'Medicalised Pupils: The Case of ADD/ADHD', *Oxford Review of Education*, 35, 2009; 'Recent Social-Scientific Work on Interdependent, Independent, and Bicultural Selves: The Moral Implications', *American Philosophical Quarterly*, 46, 2009; 'Realist versus Anti-Realist Moral Selves – and the Irrelevance of Narrativism', *Journal for the Theory of Social Behaviour*, 39, 2009; 'Putting Emotion into the Self: A Response to the *JME* Special Issue on Moral Functioning', *Journal of Moral Education*, 38, 2009; 'Does Moral Psychology Need Moral Theory? The Case of Self-Research', *Theory & Psychology*, 19, 2009; 'Valuing the Self' in *International Handbook on Values Education and Student Wellbeing*, eds. T. Lovat and R. Toomey (Dordrecht: Springer, 2010); and 'Educating Moral Emotions or Moral Selves: A False Dichotomy?', *Educational Philosophy and Theory*, 42, 2010.

1. Introduction

1.1. The Age of the Self

On the Oprah Winfrey show, whenever something has not gone right for her guests (all of whom, by the way, seem to live in a world where it never rains, but pours), the hostess tells them they must be lacking in *self-esteem*. A much-read self-help manual asserts that *self-disesteem* lies at the bottom of all conceivable personal and social ills, ranging from excessive masturbation to serial killings. When the life of the socialite and 'it girl', Paris Hilton – famously famous for being famous – hit a moral low and media high with her probation violation in 2007, flaming debates raged on Weblogs addressing the kind of *self-concept* she projected. 'Hedonistic', with 95,000 entries, was a narrow winner over 'postmodern', with 85,700 entries, for the 'Hiltonistic' self-concept. In the wake of the decision of Mohammed Sidique Khan and his three friends to pack a rucksack full of explosives and destroy the lives of 52 innocent people on the London underground, whole conferences were devoted to the issue of the irreconcilable multicultural *self-images* that had torn asunder the rational selves of these four men. According to the analysis of eminent German Professor of Culture and Pedagogy, Thomas Ziehe (virtually unknown in the Anglo-Saxon world, unfortunately), subjectivisation of the self is the major characteristic of today's young in the West. 'That is how I see it' has become a dead end: a no-go area for educators. When the students' 'inner light', their incontrovertible *self-view*, is turned on, the once invincibly shining aura of the school fades into oblivion.

As can be seen from those examples – derived from diverse contexts, popular, semi-academic and academic, most of which I have occasion to revisit later – the potential range of illustrative examples is huge.

They all tell us the same story, however, about the age in which we live: the age of a self that has become apotheosised and some would say bloated beyond good sense. Indeed, if there is one value that seems beyond reproach in modernity, it is that of the self and the terms that cluster around it, such as self-esteem, self-love and self-confidence. It is not clear, however, that all those who invoke the self really know what they are talking about – or, even if they do, that they are all talking about the same concept. *What is this thing called 'self', then, and what is its actual philosophical, psychological and educational significance?* Moreover, if we know what the self is, will that change our view of morality, of ourselves as human beings or of how we would like to bring up our children? Those, simply put, are some of the basic questions that I raise and try to answer in this book.

I still remember the day when I started to think about the nature of selfhood. I was an undergraduate, and wanted to appear bright and clever to my professor by asking how one could measure one's own level of self-respect. He retorted without a pause: 'Make a list of the things you would never do for all the tea in China. The longer the list, the more self-respect you have.' Perhaps because I was reading Plato's *Symposium* at the time, my mind immediately turned to Socrates. Now, there was a man with a long list of will-not-dos! Consider the place where the intoxicated Alcibiades tries to describe the singularity of Socrates' character. He likens him to the popular Silenus statues: ugly on the outside, but once cracked open, found to contain images of gods. Even a feeble report of Socrates' words strikes one with awe and admiration, Alcibiades muses, and that is only a thin shadow of the experience of being in his presence. It is no wonder that thinkers as different in time and philosophical persuasion as Aristotle and Nietzsche have both described Socrates as the best and most blessedly happy human being one could ever aspire to be. Socrates' wisdom is, of course, one thing: his love of the examined life and the cultured mind. What intrigued me more as a young student – and still does – were his virtues of character: his warmth of feeling, his steadfastness of purpose, fortitude, temperance and prudence, as well as his modesty-mitigated pride, humour and equanimity. Socrates was a man at one with himself, yet one with hidden depths that he – in his ready admittance of his own ignorance – realised that he could scarcely fathom. I recall thinking at the time that any proper theory of selfhood and self-respect would have to account not only for our exteriors and self-beliefs, but also for the interiors and emotional depths that make someone like Socrates the person he really is. This is not a book about Socrates, but some of my disillusionment with what I describe below as the 'dominant self-paradigm' of late can be understood against the backdrop of my old revelation that any decent self-theory would have to satisfy this 'Socratic condition'.

Recent years have witnessed an unprecedented outpouring of writings about the self and its oscillations. These writings have been initiated by academics from various quarters – psychological, philosophical, sociological, educational and sub-camps within those quarters – and have been brought to bear on diverse issues. I engage with many of those writings in what follows for purposes of commendation or confrontation. In general, I believe that in order to reach out to the perplexities of the matter at hand, we need to provide as many windows as possible on existing *self research* (a term used in this book to denote research on the self rather than research on myself). To further that ambition, I proceed by forays into various areas of debate about the self, reaching out – as I explain later – across established disciplinary boundaries. Seeking convergence in an existing bedlam of divergence has its perils. The success of this study rests in large measure on how well it helps its readers to join all the sundry dots.

It may be difficult to pinpoint anything singular in the prodigious plurality of discursive traditions generated by recent self research. Academics from diverse domains tend to be more concerned with rushing off in their own homemade directions than with interacting constructively with one another. Nevertheless, if one tries to trace some general patterns of convergence, what seems to have been gradually evolving is a 'dominant' *cognitive, constructivist self-paradigm*. One must be careful about terminology: 'Cognitive' should be understood narrowly here to denote 'cold' self-processes that exclude the affective – as distinct, for example, from the use of 'cognitive' in such locutions as 'cognitive theories of emotion', in which the cognitive is also typically meant to embrace 'hot' sentiments. This narrow understanding of 'cognitive' explains, among other things, how some moral psychologists have come to debate whether it is the cognitive construction of moral selfhood *or* the availability of moral emotions that bridges the gap between moral knowledge and moral action. Similarly, by 'constructivist' I am referring not to a plausible if somewhat trite didactic constructivism (according to which education is most effective when it connects to the learner's existing knowledge structures), but rather to a form of anti-realist epistemological constructivism.

In this book, I try to offer an 'alternative' *self-paradigm* which, while remaining 'cognitive' on a broader understanding of the term, will essentially be *emotion-based* and *realist* (in a sense of 'realist' that unfolds in Chapter 2). For example, the true Socrates was not a mere self-construction of intellectualist beliefs, but a full-blooded person with strong and profound emotions. And his selfhood, in so far as it was accessible to him, was also accessible to others – perhaps, in some respects, even more so. On this 'alternative' paradigm, persons possess 'actual full selves' and emotions are central to those selves: their creation and sustenance. More specifically, what I hope to demonstrate is *how emotions are implicated in selfhood in all its manifestations and at all levels of engagement*. Each of the following chapters, with the exception of the methodological interlude in Chapter 3, constitutes a variation on this single theme. My aim is to let the contours of the 'alternative' paradigm emerge inductively in the course of my discussion, rather than presenting it fully at the outset and arguing for it deductively thereafter. I conclude in Section 10.5, however, by connecting the various strands of my argument. Notably, as I have on previous occasions aired similar suggestions under the banner of Aristotelianism (Kristjánsson, 2002, 2006, 2007), I might have been tempted to call the alternative paradigm 'Aristotelian'. I refrain for reasons of methodological parsimony, however, as I explain later. Nevertheless, the 'alternative' paradigm remains tantalisingly Aristotelian in spirit, if not in letter (see Section 1.3).

The ancients had an intense interest in the first-person 'Me' and its epistemological and ontological ramifications, but it was not until Enlightenment times that the modern notion of selfhood became prominent (see Seigel, 2005; Martin & Barresi, 2006; and Sorabji, 2006, for detailed histories of self-theories; cf. Reddy's useful meta-history, 2009). At the end of the nineteenth century, this interest rubbed off on the precursors of modern psychology, most notably William James (1890). Interest in the self, as in other 'internal constructs', fell on evil days in psychological circles during the heyday of behaviourism. In his 1953–54 Gifford Lectures, the astute Scottish philosopher John Macmurray rued the 'crisis of the personal': the then currently grave insensitiveness to the inner aspects of life (1958). Macmurray's worries were largely misplaced, however, as interest in the self was rekindled with redoubled force in the 1960s (though perhaps not entirely to Macmurray's liking), with the advent of humanistic psychology, which was all about 'finding' and 'actualising' one's true self. Since then, and spurred on even further by the tenets of contemporary 'positive psychology', the self has become the object of unremitting academic – and public – attention. The 'inward turn' (Taylor, 1989) shows no signs of abating: in academia, the media or in everyday dinner talk.

Before I proceed, some conceptual clarifications and caveats are in order. The term 'self' is ambiguous in a number of ways (see, e.g., Velleman, 2006, chap. 1), often run together promiscuously in the self-literature. When I talk about *self* in what follows, I shall, unless otherwise stated, be referring broadly to what I call the 'commonsense view of the self' (spelled out in Chapter 2) as *the set of a person's core commitments, traits, aspirations and ideals*: the characteristics that are most central to him or her. By *self-concept* I mean, in turn, *the set of a person's self-conceptions or beliefs about his or her self*. Not all reflexive uses of that ubiquitous prefix 'self-' identify features of the commonsense self. 'Self-mutilation', for instance, refers to the self as body; 'self-love' means love of one's own person as a whole, not merely of one's self as part of oneself (so, usually, does the term 'self-improvement'); 'self-fulfilment' points to the self as an ideal to be completed; and 'self-sameness' refers to the features (physical, mental or both) that sustain numerical identity. Even if the commonsense view succeeded in distinguishing all those uses systematically from its own use of 'self', current literature is teeming with various approaches to and perspectives on that very self: moral, empirical, phenomenological and transcendental. Perhaps there are many commonsense views of the self, or perhaps there are even multiple commonsense selves. Allow me to assume that such is not the case, however. As Jon Elster (1986) has argued convincingly, the notion of multiple selves is deeply problematic, barring rare pathological cases of so-called multiple personalities. We are better off by abiding – initially at least – to Owen Flanagan's 'one-self-to-a-customer' rule (1996, p. 65), anchored in James's notion of a 'self of selves' (1890) – although James had something more fundamental in mind there than the commonsense notion of selfhood, namely the active element in all self-consciousness.

What concerns me most as a moral philosopher is the 'moral self': the self as the subject of moral agency and the object of moral evaluation. I do not consider the discursive tradition on moral selves (see, e.g., Chazan, 1998) to be *sui generis*, but merely one of the avenues to approach what the commonsense view calls 'one's self': that self as seen from a particular (namely the moral) point of view. David Jopling's cleverly orchestrated metaphor of the self as a city is helpful here (1997, pp. 258–59). What matters is that the self constitutes but a single city, viewable from different perspectives. I take that assumption as my starting point. Unless otherwise noted, I also assume that the self-accounts canvassed in the following chapters are about the same self, this single 'city' – different conceptions of the same concept, if you like – and hence competing. Whether or not the self is more similar to a centrally organised modern city or a rambling medieval one is a question that remains to be answered. Another question is whether the city of the self is a mere cognitive construction or if it has an objectively existing self-city as its referent; in other words, if *self* is the same as *self-concept*. The first of those questions neatly evokes what is at issue between so-called moral dispositionists and situationists, a debate that I enter in Chapter 6. The second question, however, which forms the bone of contention between self-realists and anti-self-realists, is addressed in Chapter 2.

Limiting my focus to the commonsense view of the self and adhering to the rule of one *such* self per customer does not mean that I dismiss other possible uses and meanings of the word 'self' as misplaced. There are perfectly respectable discourses, for instance, among metaphysicians and neuroscientists about the composition of a person's numerical identity in time and space. A distinction made by Ricoeur (1992) between *idem* as personal identity or self-sameness in the metaphysical sense and *ipse* as identity in the psychological sense may aid us here. *Idem* is given in response to the question of *what I am* as a self; *ipse* is given in response to the question of *who I am*. I admit to having no doubt that *ipse* requires *idem*: that the type of selfhood under discussion in this book is parasitic upon one's selfhood as a fundamental entity in a metaphysical sense (see, e.g., Gunnarsson, 2002). This latter type of self-identity inevitably appears at some points in the following, but I try to eschew it as far as possible and remain – for reasons explained later – deliberately agnostic as to its nature. I take no stand here, for instance, on the question of mind–body dualism versus monism. I do share Charles Taylor's belief that to possess a self (in the everyday *ipse* sense), beings must possess enough 'depth and complexity' (1989, p. 32) to count as full-blown persons – a condition generally satisfied by human beings but not by (other) animals, not even perhaps by the Great Apes. Whether or not the possession of a self requires the possession of a 'soul' in the metaphysical sense is a question I am happy to be able to bypass here. I also circumvent discussions of what phenomenologists call 'the experiential core self of phenomenal consciousness' (see, e.g.,

Zahavi, 2007). I do accept that self-concept requires phenomenal awareness of self. But self-awareness is not only awareness of one's 'self' in
the everyday sense but also of various other aspects of oneself, such as
one's personality, outward appearance and bodily functions. It should
be stressed once again that it is the everyday 'moral' self and our conceptions of that self that are of interest to me in this study.

1.2. 'Bracketing' the Author

Textbooks on qualitative research methods, especially those inspired
by phenomenology, typically ask researchers to 'bracket' (set aside,
suspend or hold in abeyance) all their personal suppositions (knowledge, history, culture, experiences, values and orientations) concerning the research topic, in order to concentrate on the pure phenomena
at hand. Now, one only needs a modicum of Popperian philosophy
of science, Wittgensteinian-inspired linguistics or, for that matter, of
ordinary common sense to realise that such disengagement from one's
suppositions is neither advantageous nor possible. The idea of the completely detached research stance is a mere illusion. On the other hand,
if 'bracketing' is understood in a more restrictive sense to mean self-
consciously trying to identify and articulate one's suppositions at the
outset, such an endeavour may indeed be helpful for both researchers
and their readers. The readers can then decide to bracket those suppositions 'in' or 'out' as they like. I sometimes think of philosopher-writers
as qualitative researchers with only themselves as interlocutors, and in
this section I attempt to articulate some of the points of departure of the
'internal conversation' in which this study engages.

I have already noted that the perspective on the self that interests me
most is a moral perspective. This is not a mere idiosyncratic interest,
however. Given the wide-ranging socio-moral implications that both
philosophers and social scientists have been tempted to elicit from
their respective self-accounts, one could argue that the most natural
provinces of self research are in moral philosophy on the one hand and
moral psychology (broadly construed as the empirical study of moral
development, beliefs, emotions and behaviours) on the other. I have
more to say about that in Chapter 3. I never try to hide the fact that I am
a philosopher – that fact steers the focus of my inquiry in various places
throughout this book. As a philosopher, I am deeply curious about the
nature of the self, for instance: Is it an objectively identifiable entity or
'all in the mind'? It is no coincidence that following on the heels of this

introductory chapter is an extensive treatment of self-realism versus anti-self-realism. Some practically minded psychologists might not find such a chapter worthwhile. I could argue in turn that they *should* find it worthwhile, but I refrain from doing so. I am who I am, and Chapter 2 is simply there.

Let me elaborate a bit more on my presuppositions as a moral philosopher and how they influence my choice of topics. Throughout the history of moral philosophy, most of its best-known practitioners have occupied positions antithetical to moral relativism. With a number of significant exceptions and caveats which need not be rehearsed here, one could go as far as to say that the history of moral philosophy is the history of an ongoing battle against such relativism in its various forms and guises – ranging from the man-is-the-measure-of-all-things doctrine of the Sophists to early twentieth century anthropologically inspired cultural relativism, late twentieth century power-focused post-structuralist discourse and the ever-present moral subjectivism of first-year undergraduates. Nor is there an end in sight; this battle seems to be a never-to-be-completed Sysiphian task.

The majority of moral philosophers are against moral relativism, but it is more difficult to give a collective characterisation of what exactly they are for. Technical terms such as 'moral objectivism', 'moral absolutism' and 'moral realism' all contain historical-cum-theoretical baggage that some moral anti-relativists would not want to carry. The fact that a common denominator of anti-relativism is difficult to determine is not surprising, given that its advocates hail from otherwise divergent moral camps. In their midst are, for instance, Kantians, virtue ethicists, utilitarians, followers of various religious moral doctrines, moral conservatives and moral cosmopolitans of unspecified provenance. Nevertheless, for simplicity's sake I posit that the opposite of moral relativism can serviceably be termed *moral objectivism*, a position that requires me to provide the latter term with a somewhat permissive understanding. On such an understanding, moral objectivism incorporates four general beliefs which I share: the *ontological* belief that moral properties exist independent of any particular (non-interhuman) preferences, perspectives or points of view; the *epistemological* belief that human beings can become acquainted with and understand those properties in a way that is independent of any particular (non-interhuman) preferences, perspectives or points of view; the *psychological* belief that human beings are capable of forming intentions to honour those properties and, with time, that they will acquire stable and robust dispositions to do so; and the *moral* belief that the honouring of the relevant moral properties constitutes a necessary condition of the rightness of an action. This characterisation leaves ample room for conflict among the various camps of anti-relativistic thinkers. It is, after all, only meant to capture what unites them under one specific description.

Moral objectivism, as here defined, is not only the *modus operandi* of much of what goes by the name of moral philosophy, it has also informed modern moral psychology: the empirical study of moral beliefs, attitudes and behaviours. The undisputed high priest of twentieth-century moral psychology, Lawrence Kohlberg – himself an avowed Kantian – saw it as one of the fundamental duties of moral psychology to combat moral relativism. Kohlberg's well-known stages of moral development were constructed in such a way as to make progress in this area synonymous with a gradual retreat from relativism (Kohlberg, 1981). Part of moral psychology's Kohlbergian legacy is the gap to be found between moral cognition and moral behaviour. In fact, only modest correlations have ever been recorded between Kohlbergian stages of moral reasoning and people's actual behaviours. Looming large in contemporary personality psychology is the suggestion that the construction or nonconstruction of a 'moral self' constitutes the central explanatory concept in moral functioning: the missing link between cognition and action. I explore that powerful idea in Chapter 4.

Social psychologists are famously sceptical of the conceptual repertoire of personality psychologists, especially with respect to 'static' human traits. According to the situationism proposed by some social psychologists, psychological experiments, such as the famous Milgram (1974) experiment, show that people's actions are irredeemably situation dependent. This charge has percolated down to philosophers (see, e.g., Doris, 2002) who have used it to attack virtue ethics, character education and other schools of thought in moral philosophy and moral education that assume the existence of robust dispositional states of character. Situationism – in its extreme forms at least – poses a threat to moral objectivism by rendering it infeasible in practice: If such situationism is true, the psychological belief underlying moral objectivism – that human beings are capable of forming stable and robust dispositions to honour moral properties – is undermined. Relativity creeps in, at the practical if not the theoretical level. It is no coincidence, therefore, that moral philosophers have expended considerable energy in recent years in countering situationism. Without moral character, there is no moral self. Hence, my extensive critique of situationism in Chapter 6.

Social psychology presents another challenge to moral objectivism that arguably poses an even greater threat than does moral situation- ism, by eating away its epistemological core. You say, the social psycho- logist would begin, that selfhood underlies moral agency. In that case, people's conceptions of themselves as moral agents determine how they chart the moral terrain and how they act and react with regard to it. But repeated empirical findings recorded by social scientists have shown that there are two general self-concepts abroad in the world: that of an interdependent (traditional, 'Eastern') self-culture and that of an independent (liberal, 'Western') self-culture. These self-concepts are conceptually and practically irreconcilable; combining them res- ults in disorientation, rootlessness and anomie at best and complete self-loss or destructive violence at worst. Moral objectivism rests on the epistemological belief that human beings can become acquainted with and understand moral properties in a way that is independ- ent of any particular (non-interhuman) perspectives. Research into the two conflicting self-concepts undermines this belief in so far as it shows that human beings inhabit two mutually impenetrable moral worlds. Has the moral relativism that generations of philosophers – aided, certainly, by contemporary moral psychology – have tried to throw out the front door now crept back in through the back door via social-scientific research into an interdependent versus an inde- pendent self-concept? This is the question that explains my interest in 'multicultural selves' and underlies the ponderings of Chapter 8 and parts of 9.

Next, to education: Most of my working life, I have been employed as a philosopher in faculties of educational studies, first at the Uni- versity of Akureyri, then at the University of Iceland. This work has brought me into contact with a host of colleagues and students passion- ately interested in issues of young people's upbringing and schooling. I have been infected with their enthusiasm, a fact which explains my repeated references to the educational ramifications of self research in this study. They range from the role played by the construction of moral self-identity in Chapter 4, through the expected educational correlates of self-esteem in Chapter 5, to the culminating discussion of self-change and self-education in Chapter 10. I make this point here as an explan- ation rather than a justification. A justification would be superfluous because a considerable part of contemporary self research – especially research on self-esteem and self-confidence – has been animated by exactly the same concerns.

We live in the 'Age of the Self'. I do little in what follows to diagnose its appeal. Rather, without much ado, I jump into self research at the deep end. It behoves me to give at least a nod here to sociological-cum-historical accounts of the sources of the modern 'inward turn', graciously provided by such thinkers as Thomas Ziehe, Ulrich Beck, Antony Giddens and Charles Taylor. Although I allude only briefly to those accounts in following chapters, they serve as a historical back-drop to my study. Taylor traces the inward turn back to the Enlighten-ment. What motivated it were changes connected with a wide range of practices – religious, political, economic, familial, intellectual, artistic – that converged and reinforced each other:

> practices, for instance, of [...] self-scrutiny [...], of the politics of consent, of the family life of the companionate marriage, of the new child-rearing [...], of artistic creation under the demands of originality, of the demarc-ation and defence of privacy, of markets and contracts, of voluntary asso-ciations, of the cultivation and display of sentiment, of the pursuit of sci-entific knowledge (1989, p. 206).

Taylor is illuminating no less than the creation of a new intellectual cul-ture that was individualist and self-focused in at least three senses: by prizing individual autonomy, promoting personal moral and political commitment, and giving pride of place to self-exploration – including the exploration of feeling (1989, p. 305). This was also a culture that was radically secularised and had already, as some historians have wanted to put it, replaced 'God' with the 'self'.

Ziehe, Beck and Giddens pick up this thread in the twentieth century, describing the trajectory of the inward turn in the Western world in 'late modernity'. Among the refrains of their accounts are the continu-ing erosion of established cultural forms, the ensuing cultural release and the creation of a 'risk society' (Beck, 1992) with the confused indi-vidual at its epicentre. This is an individual whose basic condition and existential demand is that of self-reflexivity, inexorably reflecting on and 'reflexing in' new types of situations, an individual whose very self-identity has become a 'reflexively organised endeavour' (Giddens, 1991, p. 5). The role of the whole educational system subsequently becomes that of feeding the hungry, insatiable self – a self that, by the way, has always the last word on what it wants to consume (Ziehe, 2000). I shall not try to improve on those accounts *qua* historical explor-ations. In so far as they are normative rather than merely descript-ive, however – Taylor's philosophical dissection unflinchingly is, and

Giddens ventures circumspectly into the normative with his claim that late twentieth century individualisation has occurred 'under conditions of substantial moral deprivation' where the idea of individual self-mastery substitutes for morality (1991, p. 169) – they invite responses that are equally normative in nature (cf. also Hammershøj, 2009). And such responses I shall not hesitate to give, most notably in Chapters 9 and 10.

1.3. Aristotelian Presuppositions

Continuing to nail my colours to the mast, let me next come clean on my Aristotelian predilection. My latest book was on Aristotle, emotions and education (Kristjánsson, 2007). There I defended a broadly Aristotelian approach to a number of issues that are directly related to topics pursued in this study. Allow me to make a brief list of Aristotelian 'basics' in this section with which I concur in principle and which permeate subsequent chapters in various guises as overt presuppositions or 'background noises' (see further in Kristjánsson, 2007, chap. 2). If I did not list those presuppositions here as points of reference, I would have to articulate them at regular intervals in the following pages. So bear with me.

First, in the *Nicomachean Ethics*, Aristotle proposes a theory of 'happiness' (*eudaimonia*) – perhaps better translated as 'wellbeing' or 'flourishing' – as the ultimate good and unconditional end (*telos*) of human beings, for the sake of which they do all other things. An action or a reaction is morally right if and only if it is conducive to human flourishing.

Second, according to Aristotle, it is empirically true that the flourishing of human beings consists of the realisation of intellectual and moral virtues and in the fulfilment of their other specifically human physical and mental capabilities. The virtues are at once conducive to and constitutive of *eudaimonia*; each true virtue represents a stable character state (*hexis*) that is intrinsically related to flourishing as a human being. Importantly for present purposes, Aristotle's *eudaimonia* is an explicitly moral notion; it is impossible to achieve *eudaimonia* without being morally good – without actualising the moral virtues. Each moral virtue constitutes a specific medial character state, flanked by the extremes of deficiency and excess. There is only one way – the medial way – to be 'correct': to be inclined to act in the right way, towards the right people, at the right time. But there are a number of ways in which to be 'bad' (1985, p. 44 [1106b29–35]). One of the moral virtues occupies a special position: Great-mindedness (*megalopsychia*) is a higher-order virtue which incorporates the others and makes them greater; great-minded persons thus possess greatness in each virtue, while exhibiting some unique features that cannot be reduced to the other virtues (see further in Kristjánsson, 2002, chap. 3). The great-minded person 'thinks himself worthy of great things and is really worthy of them' because he truly exhibits all the moral virtues (1985, p. 97 [1123b2–5]). Aristotle clearly states that the greatest virtues are necessarily those most useful *to others*. Moreover, he goes out of his way to 'try to offer help' in solving moral quandaries, while admitting that 'is not easy to define [such] matters exactly' (1985, pp. 36, 241 [1104a10–11, 1164b26–30]). In stark contrast to contemporary virtue ethics, which share Aristotle's assumptions about the rightness of actions, nowhere does Aristotle suggest that the virtues are of equal or incommensurable standing, or that we must rely solely on particularist insights rather than generalist principles in moral problem solving. In addition to the moral virtues, the intellectual virtue of *phronesis* is essential to moral functioning. It serves the moral virtues; for, while the moral virtues make 'the goal correct', *phronesis* 'makes what promotes the goal [correct]' (1985, p. 168 [1144a7–9]). This intellectual virtue helps the moral virtues find their right ends and the suitable means to their ends. We cannot be 'fully good' without *phronesis*; nor can we possess *phronesis* without virtue of character (1985, p. 171 [1144b30–32]). Stripped of the virtue of character, *phronesis* degenerates into a mere cunning capacity that Aristotle calls 'cleverness'. *Phronesis* comes to the fore in my discussion of multicultural selves in Chapter 8.

Third, although nowhere does Aristotle produce a definitive list of all the character states that can count as moral virtues, it is crucial that not only proper actions but also proper reactions are conducive to and constitutive of *eudaimonia*. A distinctive feature of Aristotle's virtue theory is, therefore, the assumption that emotional reactions may constitute virtues. Emotions are central to who we are, and they can, no less than actions, have an 'intermediate and best condition' when they are felt 'at the right times, about the right things, towards the right people, for the right end and in the right way' (1985, p. 44 [1106b17–35]). If the relevant emotion is 'too intense or slack', we are badly off in relation to it, but if it is intermediate, we are 'well off' (1985, p. 41 [1105b26–8]). And persons can be fully virtuous only if they are disposed to experience emotions in this medial way on a regular basis.

Strictly speaking, however, specific episodic passions do not constitute virtues, any more than individual actions do. Rather, the virtues comprise settled character states. We are praised or blamed for our virtues and vices, but we 'do not blame the person who is simply angry' (1985, p. 41 [1105b20–1106a7]). So the issue here is about emotions *qua* general emotional traits that we *have*, not about the *experience* of individual episodic passions. The precise relationship between virtues of action and emotional virtues is not always entirely clear in Aristotle's texts. He often seems to suggest that there is a general emotional trait that corresponds to each moral virtue, yet he is inconsistent on this topic. Some virtues are simply such emotional traits in a mean (such as compassion). Other virtues regulate emotions (courage regulates fear, for example). Others are dispositions towards a lack of specific emotional traits; modesty, for instance, is a disposition not to feel vanity. Yet other emotional virtues dispose one to a range of emotions; justice, for instance, is an overarching emotional virtue that involves various justice-based emotions (Kristjánsson, 2006).

Fourth, Aristotle could not have implicated emotions in moral virtues if he had not presupposed that emotions have a cognitive component amenable to rational and moral evaluation – and, if necessary (if it turns out to be irrationally formed, morally unjustified or both), liable to criticism and change. Cognitive theories are no novelty in the present age, of course; indeed, they constitute one of the dominant research models of emotions in psychology (*qua* appraisal theories) and the predominant one in philosophy since the 1970s. In the well-known cognitive model of late, an emotion is typically considered to be comprising four main components: (1) a characteristic *cognition* (belief, judgement or construal) that gives the emotion its focus on a propositional object; (2) a characteristic *desire*, the satisfaction or frustration of which gives rise to (3) the emotion's typical *affect* (feeling); and (4) a common *behavioural pattern*. Of those components, the cognitive and the conative are the crucial ones, which set emotions apart, because many emotions differ little if at all in their 'feel' and can, in fact, result in a wide range of behavioural responses, or none at all. Contemporary cognitive theorists are often accused of being overly focused on the cognitive and conative components of emotion and of ignoring or underestimating the affective element. If we accept as a defining feature of a cognitive theory that it relegates to a side issue the way emotions *feel*, then Aristotle is not really a 'pure' cognitive theorist. He specifies all emotions as being necessarily accompanied by pain (*lupē*) or pleasure (*hēdonē*), which are sensations rather than beliefs or judgements. For Aristotle, the sensations of pleasure or pain provide the 'material conditions' or physiological substrates of emotions, whereas the relevant cognitions provide the formal conditions or 'formulable essences'. Because the sensations of pain accompanying different painful emotions are phenomenologically indistinguishable, however (and *mutatis mutandis* for the pleasant ones), the cognitive consorts (Aristotle's formal conditions) set them apart. Thus Aristotle specifies the emotions as those things on account of which 'people come to differ in regard to their judgments, and which are accompanied by pain and pleasure' (1991, p. 121 [1378a20–22]). Aristotle would be baffled by today's talk of 'basic' (cognition-independent) versus 'non-basic' (cognition-dependent) emotions – an issue to which I return in Chapter 4. He would admit, however, that some emotions may be *basic* relative to other emotions in such respects as developmental priority and moral significance. He would also question, I believe, the salience of the now commonly drawn distinction between 'negative' and 'positive' emotions, in which the former simply means negatively felt (painful) and the latter means positively felt (pleasant). He would do so because of the moral irrelevance of this distinction (according to which compassion becomes 'negative' and *Schadenfreude* 'positive', for example) and its psychological inaccuracy, as pain and pleasure are not mutually exclusive in a single emotion. Anger, for instance, includes both (cf. 1985, p. 37 [1104b13–16]).

Fifth, the claim that cognitive factors set emotions apart invites a problem of emotion individuation: How can we distinguish those cognitive elements that can form the basis of an emotion from those cognitive elements which cannot? And how we can distinguish clearly between different emotions if what matters is not mere difference in felt quality or physical expression? The Aristotelian response to this problem is to acknowledge that a proper analysis of emotions cannot avoid being normative. Moulding badly moulded meanings necessarily involves normative regimentation. This does not mean that the conceptual specifications of particular emotions that result from such regimentations are merely stipulative; they should be supported by arguments that have not been arbitrarily chosen and are derived in various ways from our theory of human nature and the world in which we live. But the arguments will necessarily invoke normative criteria – not merely non-evaluative criteria. More specifically, Aristotle seems to suggest that there are normative reasons for individuating emotions in such a way that each general emotional trait corresponds to an essential universal human sphere of experience, and that there is one proper way to feel (as well as many improper ways to feel) in any such sphere (see Kristjánsson, 2007, chap. 4).

Sixth, educational concerns enter Aristotle's discussion of virtues as actions and emotions at all levels of engagement. We progress towards moral excellence only if we are educated from an early age – indeed from birth – to do so. Such education involves at the outset the sensitisation to and instillation of the correct habits in the young: teaching them how to act and how to feel. A study of (moral) selfhood, such as this study, would by Aristotle's lights be an entirely fruitless and otiose enterprise if it did not gauge the educational implications of its findings. In this supposition, as in so many others, I side with Aristotle (see Chapter 10).

There is one important juncture at which I shall refrain, however, from adopting Aristotelian insights. In Chapter 2, I avoid going as far in the direction of strong self-realism as required by the position that one could reasonably ascribe to Aristotle. It would take me too far afield to delve into the matter in detail here, except to note that, generally speaking, I consider it reasonable to follow a principle of *methodological parsimony*: not scratching where it does not itch. The 'alternative' self-paradigm that I try to develop in this book does not require me to follow Aristotle the whole way in his pursuit of 'hard' realism, and it would be logically counter-productive and inimical to the persuasiveness of what I have to say to try to do so.

1.4. Interdisciplinary Focus

The final background supposition that I want to bring to the table in this chapter is my concern for giving this study an interdisciplinary focus. Despite the recent burst of research on the self, there has been little rapprochement between self-theorists from diverse academic backgrounds. Philosophers theorising about the self have historically and with rare exception turned a blind eye to empirical evidence about self-beliefs as gathered by social scientists. A corollary fault on the part of social scientists is their disregard for the conceptual work of philosophers. So while philosophers have tended to pursue the self at the level of uppercase abstractions, social scientists have commonly treated self-beliefs as if springing from an intellectual vacuum. This mutual lack of engagement forms part of a larger picture: the general reluctance of both philosophers and social scientists to consider the insights gleaned from each other's work. Social science bashing has even been a favourite sport of some philosophers, just as philosophy bashing has been a favourite sport of some social scientists – a practice that has led to a clash of two cultures. Instead of aiming at integrative work when examining the same or similar phenomena, the relationship of social scientists and philosophers has typically degenerated into grudging sidewise glances, reflecting mutual suspicion. I have argued elsewhere that this suspicion is for the most part unreasonable (Kristjánsson, 2006, chap. 1.2), and I consider the issue in more detail from the perspective of self research in Chapter 3.

In short, my underlying methodological stance is to question, as Gilbert Ryle once did, 'the native sagacity of philosophers when discussing technicalities which they have not learned to handle on the job' (1954, p. 12), and to nourish the belief that contemporary psychology can yield invaluable data, surpassing that which a philosopher can think of in an armchair (see, e.g., Flanagan, 1991). I fear that the lack of interest that philosophers display in empirical evidence leads, at worst, to conclusions that are irreducibly relative or hopelessly trivial, and that the lack of interest that social scientists exhibit in conceptual work fosters deceptions and logical errors. It is wise, therefore, to remain equally sceptical of philosophical armchair psychology and of a conceptually sloppy and morally barren 'moral' psychology. I hope my project can contribute to the development of a peacemaking, fence-crossing process, in which it is at once acknowledged that there cannot be a 'value-free' social-science theory of the self or of its constitutive elements, any more than there can be a reasonably developed philosophical theory of the self without a grounding in the empirical knowledge of the way people actually think and feel about the self.

To complicate and exacerbate matters, 'localisms' of research have also prevailed within psychology. Thus, fervent debates rage within the discipline, especially between social psychologists and personality psychologists, on the ontological-cum-epistemological status of the concepts of self and character. Furthermore, self research has been conducted primarily within the 'cognitive field', whereas researchers studying emotions have concentrated primarily on biologically driven affective processes (see Chapter 4). Tracy and Robins (2004), who have written at length on the so-called self-conscious emotions, understandably lament the way these methodological roadblocks and all the resulting diggings-in of theoretical heels have hurt research on self-relevant emotions. I aim at a paradigm which not only integrates philosophical and psychological self research, but also those two areas of research within psychology.

It is no coincidence that some of the best work on the self draws upon both philosophical and psychological sources. Perhaps Susan Wolf is right in that 'being a good moral philosopher makes one a better psychologist about moral matters, and being a good psychologist about moral matters makes one a better moral philosopher' (2007, p. 167). I would especially like to recommend the writings of philosophers Owen Flanagan (1991, 1996), a pioneer in interdisciplinary work, and David Jopling (1997, 2000), whose book on self and self-understanding (2000) is perhaps the most thought-provoking text ever written on the subject. This is not to say that when philosophers pursue academic ecumenism, their results will always coincide; witness for instance Jesse Prinz's book on the emotional construction of morals (2007), which uses psychological findings to argue for a form of ontological sentimentalism that goes far beyond my emotion-based view in Chapter 4, and for moral relativism that is at odds with my bicultural synergism in Chapter 8. (Arguing directly with Prinz would, however, be beyond the remit of this study, which addresses moral psychology rather than moral ontology.) From the psychological side, I am particularly impressed with Michael Chandler's integrative insights (1999, 2000) and with a recent contribution by Hart and Matsuba (2007). Last but not least, that tireless advocate of interdisciplinary work on the emotions, the late Robert C. Solomon, deserves mention here. He firmly believed that questions of self and personal identity 'now hold the key to peace in the world', and encouraged some 'sympathetic philosopher' to study the implications of psychological research on the subject (1999, pp. 191, 197). In assuming Solomon's challenge, my endeavour is facilitated immeasurably by his work and the work of other bridge-builders I have mentioned.

1.5. A Roadmap

This book challenges what I have called the 'dominant' self-paradigm, and gradually advances the case for an 'alternative' self-paradigm. I summarise some of the fundamental differences between those contrasting paradigms in Table 1.1.

Many readers have grown weary of writers who state beforehand what they are going to say and repeat afterwards what they have just said. Yet other readers still prefer to be primed about the general

Table 1.1. *The 'Dominant' Self-Paradigm versus the 'Alternative' Self-Paradigm*

	The Dominant Paradigm	The Alternative Paradigm
Ch. 2: What selves are	Anti-realism (selfhood as constructed identity)	Realism (actual selfhood as the cognitive object of constructed identity)
Ch. 3: Exploring selves	Psychologised morality	Moralised psychology
Ch. 4: The emotional self	Self as essentially cognitive; self-relevant emotions psychologically and morally peripheral	Self as cognitive and affective; self-relevant emotions psychologically and morally central
Ch. 5: Self-concept: self-esteem and self-confidence	Constituted essentially by self-relevant beliefs or satisfaction with perceived accomplishments	Constituted essentially by self-relevant background emotions
Ch. 6: The self as moral character	Constituted essentially by dispositional actions	Constituted essentially by dispositional emotions
Ch. 7: Self-respect	Cognitive and formalist (protected by a conception of dignity and rights)	Cognitive and affective (protected by pridefulness)
Ch. 8: Multicultural selves	Incorporate incommensurable beliefs and emotions	Incorporate incompatible but not incommensurable beliefs and emotions
Ch. 9: Self-pathologies	Caused by conflicting beliefs	Caused by conflicting emotional engagements
Ch. 10: Self-change and self-education	Enacted via cognitive reconstructions of identity	Enacted via emotion-driven search for objective truth

roadmap being followed in a scholarly book. In order to satisfy both types of reader, I recommend that the first group stop reading here and go straight on to Chapter 2. For the convenience of the second group, I offer some advance notice of how each of the following chapters makes a case against the 'dominant' self-paradigm and contributes to the development of the 'alternative' one.

Chapter 2: What selves are. According to the anti-realist stance pervading contemporary self research, there is no useful distinction between selfhood and identity/self-concept. My selfhood consists of my *conception* of the core attributes that make me what I am. The underlying assumption is that people tend to act in line with the attributes that they attribute to themselves or interpret themselves as having. Thinking that there is some objective basis of the self – some actual selfhood beneath the self-attributions – is dismissed as a pre-Enlightenment

anachronism. Realising that their notion of selfhood seems to undermine commonsense conceptions of self-understanding and self-
deception, today's anti-realists tend to invoke various coherence
criteria of 'narrative unity' or 'reflective equilibrium', to which our self-
beliefs must adhere. Others, at the postmodern fringes of anti-realism,
go further, and ask us to relinquish the notion of self-understanding
altogether. I discuss the lingering problem with all these manoeuvres
in Chapter 2. The realist alternative is to suppose that one's identity or
self-concept has actual selfhood – one's *de facto* states of character – as
its cognitive object, and that when it gets things right, one's identity
corresponds with one's selfhood. But self-realism has substantial problems of its own. Nevertheless, my aim in Chapter 2 is to get a modified
('Humean') version of it back on track. A subsidiary aim is to challenge
the view that recent 'narrative' conceptions of selfhood have made the
old self-realism versus anti-self-realism debate redundant by somehow
transcending it. 'Narrativism' about selves turns out to do little more
than recycle old arguments in fancy new packages, obscuring rather
than enlightening the underlying philosophical issues.

Chapter 3: Exploring selves. Much has been written lately about the
issue of fence-mending versus fence-crossing between moral philosophy and experimental social science. I focus on a specific manifestation of this issue, as instantiated in the recent debate between moral
psychologists and philosophers on how the psychologists should react
to the fall of Kohlbergianism. Is it advisable to react by focusing upon
'psychologised morality' rather than, as Kohlberg did, upon 'moralised
psychology'? That seems to be the emerging consensus in recent psychological ('dominant-paradigm') self research. I use that very research,
in fact, as a test case: Does moral psychology need moral theory to
account for the self, or can it assume the kind of academic sovereignty
that advocates of 'psychologised morality' suggest? Although the eventual answer runs counter to the idea of 'psychologised morality', I suggest that the idea of 'moralised psychology' must be modified by some
significant caveats.

Chapter 4: Emotional selves. As a genre that renounces the affective
and embraces the cognitive, the 'dominant' paradigm understands self-
creation in terms of an exploratory journey of 'selving', in which persons 'negotiate' their identities by trying out different life plans thorough interaction with others. Self-related emotions (more specifically
the so-called self-conscious emotions) do play a role in this journey,
but only a subsidiary role, as compared to the honing of the cognitive

faculties; and, after the construction of an identity, they remain psychologically and morally peripheral. The 'alternative' paradigm, in contrast, harks back to Aristotle's notion of emotions being implicated in all our states of character. For non-Aristotelians, it is salutary to recall that on Hume's account, the moral self is not only constituted, but also originally created, by emotion. According to the 'alternative' paradigm, various types of self-relevant emotions continue, after the initial self-creation process, to be psychologically and morally central in our engagements – all emotionally laden to a greater or lesser degree – with the world, other people and ourselves. I explore in detail the relationship between the self and its emotions, paying particular attention to the self-conscious emotions. I challenge the idea that the post-Kohlbergian 'moral gap' between moral cognition and moral action is to be bridged by *either* moral emotions or moral selves – a dichotomy that is both morally disabling and illusory – and criticise recent attempts at integrating the cognitive and affective for not being post-Kohlbergian enough.

Chapter 5: Self-concept (self-esteem and self-confidence). Since the 1980s, more has been written in psychological and educational circles about self-esteem and self-confidence than about almost any other subject. Yet the psychological status of both these psychological states remains clouded in mystery. Within the 'dominant' paradigm, self-esteem is understood in terms of either beliefs about the one's competences or satisfaction with the global ratio of one's achievements to aspirations, and self-confidence is understood in terms of beliefs in what one can achieve in the future. The 'alternative' paradigm focuses, in contrast, on the relationship between self-esteem and self-conscious background emotions, and between self-confidence and courage. I trace the rise and fall of the 'global self-esteem movement'. I argue for the value of self-confidence, and conclude that it is an aspect of self-concept that needs to be retrieved, along with domain-specific justified self-esteem, after the demise of global self-esteem. I also explore recent research on 'implicit self-esteem', which I claim is about one's actual full self rather than mere self-concept. At a more general level, I discuss the value of self-concept in human life.

Chapter 6: The self as moral character. Once our moral character has been 'constructed', the 'dominant' paradigm considers the morality of the self to be demonstrated essentially through intentional actions. Unfortunately, such actions have been shown, in Milgram-type experiments, to be seriously lacking in robustness and reliability, which

gives succour to the 'situationist' slogan that there is no such thing
as moral character. If that is true, not only Aristotelian virtue theory,
but folk psychology, contemporary virtue ethics and character education may all seen to have been seriously infirmed. Such experiments
do not hit at the 'alternative' paradigm, in which moral character is
understood in terms of dispositional emotional reactions rather than
actions. After all, people's reactive attitudes to what they have done
tend to be more stable than the actions themselves (especially actions
performed at the spur of the moment or under compulsion). The aim of
Chapter 6 is to offer a systematic classification of the existing objections
against situationism, to resuscitate a more powerful Aristotle-inspired
'alternative-paradigm' version of one of them than advanced by previous critics and to explore some of the implications of such resuscitation
for our understanding of the nature and salience of character.

Chapter 7: Self-respect. Self-respect – understood as the extent to
which one follows a moral code and is disposed to avoid behaving in
a manner unworthy of oneself – risks becoming conceptually impoverished and motivationally undernourished if understood along the
'dominant' cognitive lines as adherence to formal principles of human
rights and dignity. What is lacking is sensitivity to the affective dimension of self-respect and how it is protected by one's desire to avoid
shame and to experience pride in oneself as a moral agent. Can 'self-
respect' supplant the now much-maligned 'global self-esteem' in psychological research and therapy? The aim of Chapter 7 is to examine
this suggestion and develop it further. I argue that there are two distinct philosophical concepts of self-respect in the literature – Kantian
and Aristotelian – and that psychologists must choose between them.
The main components of Aristotelian self-respect are articulated at this
point, and, to a certain extent, operationalised.

Chapter 8: Multicultural selves. It does not do full justice to the vagaries of multicultural selfhoods to understand them (as the 'dominant'
paradigm would do) as battlefields of incommensurable beliefs – as the
belief that you should 'find yourself' independently through an inward
gaze and then express joyfully what you have found, for instance,
versus the belief that you should immerse yourself in culturally embedded interdependence and be willing to sacrifice your life for the welfare
of the group. What is missing there is an appreciation of the extent to
which emotional engagements steer the exploratory journey and help
adjudicate its outcome. More specifically, I explore empirical findings
showing there to be two conflicting self-concepts abroad in the world:

those of an interdependent (Eastern) self-culture and those of an independent (Western) self-culture. I subject the two-self-cultures view to scrutiny and bring recent conceptualisations from research into biculturalism to bear upon it, concluding that an alternative paradigm of 'synergic bicultural integration' may counteract the relativistic implications of the two-self-cultures view.

Chapter 9: Self-pathologies. Selves sometimes go astray and lose their footing. They become excessively medicalised, torn asunder by internal conflicts or taken in by extremist rhetoric that leads to their destruction. Those are some of the potential pathologies of modern selfhood. The 'dominant' paradigm typically explains such pathologies as resulting from cognitive dissonance. The defect in the 'dominant' paradigm and the advantage in the 'alternative' is, once again, that the latter does and the former does not shed light on the emotional iconographies that move the cognitive barometer – sometimes in the wrong direction. I explore three test cases: of suicide terrorism, excessive medicalisation and egoistical hedonism. I argue that suicide bombings are, first and foremost, acts of deluded self-enhancement, which must be understood against the backdrop of irrationally resolved emotional conflicts between the Western liberal and the traditional Eastern self-concepts. I then take issue with conservative, existentialist, liberalist and poststructuralist explanations of excessive medicalisation, all of which suggest that some sort of personal or social conspiracy is at work, serving the interests of specifiable social agents. I argue that the roots of excessive medicalisation are best sought in a certain culturally conditioned emotion-driven mindset, the Western liberal self-concept, for the existence of which no particular agents can be blamed (although some have more to gain from it than others). I analyse some of the ingredients of that mindset and the self-traps in which it catches us. Finally I explore the nature and implications of a hedonistic self-concept, by focusing on the 'Hiltonistic' (named after Paris Hilton) conceptions in current 'raunch culture'.

Chapter 10: Self-change and self-education. The 'dominant' self-paradigm understands self-change in terms of cognitive reconstructions of identity. This chapter explores three psychological self-theories – Gergen's theory of the crystallised self, Dweck's theory of the incremental self and Swann's theory of the homeostatic self – for their ability to account for radical self-change. Whereas all three theories provide important insights into self-change, none of them gives a fully satisfying account. By contrast, because the 'alternative' paradigm is also a realist self-account, it can explain the motive to self-change as an emotion-driven search for objective truth. I conclude the chapter and this book with an overview of the main facets of the 'alternative' self-paradigm and offer some practical lessons about the education of selves, drawn from preceding chapters.

I hope that the embryo ideas contained in this sketch of the 'alternative' paradigm will be seen to grow in form and outline as the book progresses. Let me simply end here with the reservation that although I am – perhaps ambitiously if not foolhardily – trying to turn the tide of current self research, my purpose is limited and my discussion selective: I do not aim at securing an understanding of selfhood in all its possible guises, but only selfhood in the everyday understanding broached in Section 1.1, and, in particular, that selfhood as seen from a moral perspective. Moreover, although I proceed on an extended – and even immodestly vast – interdisciplinary front, I can only hope to cover a fraction of all the research relating to the self and its emotions that has been conducted over the years. I need readers' cooperation, not only to connect the dots, but also to consider for themselves all the other directions into which such an inquiry could profitably trail.

2. What Selves Are

2.1. Personality, Character, and Self

What is this thing called 'self', and is it different from or the same as self-concept? Are we simply who we think we are – at least when we are being reasonably coherent – or are the stories we believe and tell about our lives and who we are essentially defeasible?

In this chapter I subject to critical analysis the tangled debate between realists and anti-realists about the status of the so-called self. The debate traverses various academic disciplines and discursive fields. What interests me here is the issue between *self-realists* and *anti-self-realists*, not between (scientific) realists and anti-realists, per se. To clarify, all self-realists are scientific realists. Standard scientific realism is the view that we ought to believe in the objective existence of the unobservable entities posited by our most successful scientific theories. The most common argument in favour of scientific realism is the 'no-miracles argument', according to which the success of science would be miraculous – straining credulity beyond its breaking point – if scientific theories were not at least approximately true descriptions of the world. There are, however, various forms of general scientific realism that make do without any notion of independent selfhood, simply because they do not consider the notion of 'self' to belong to any of our most successful scientific – here psychological – theories. Hence, not all scientific realists are self-realists, and it is only the latter type of realism that concerns me in this chapter.

Realism about selves has fallen on hard times of late; my aim is to get it back on track. Having made no bones in Chapter 1 about my Aristotelian orientation, I would have been tempted here to throw my support to an Aristotle-inspired conception of substantive selfhood. Three facts propel me to settle eventually for a more moderate, 'softer' kind of self-realism (see Section 2.5): (a) Aristotle did not work with our contemporary notion of selfhood (see Section 2.2); (b) substantive conceptions of the self contain ontological baggage that many moderns will be loath to carry; and (c) my 'alternative' self-paradigm sketched in Section 1.5 does not require substantive realism. It would therefore go against reasonable parsimony to insist on such realism here.

There are various overlapping debates about the self and its nature, as I have noted, and I enter those debates in several stages in the following sections. A natural place to initiate the discussion is with what I like to call the 'commonsense view' of what a self is. Such a view emerges as reflective agents ask themselves what they 'really are', deep down. The typical answers given to that question tend to assume common features, at least in Western societies. The self is thought to be some sort of a mental entity (notably in a loose sense of the word 'mental' which does not necessarily imply mind-body dualism) – the locus of moral agency (hence a 'moral self'), representing a conscious feeler, thinker and doer, with certain character traits that differentiate it from other selves (Strawson, 1997). Contemporary personality psychology has tried to operationalise this commonsense view with its now entrenched, if not uncontroversial, conceptual typology, which I broadly endorse.

According to the typology of personality psychology, 'the self' is located at the centre of a nexus of interrelated and partly overlapping concepts describing personhood (see, e.g., Goldie, 2004, pp. 31–33; Haslam, 2007, section I; Rorty & Wong, 1990). At the outer edges of this nexus lie the concepts of personality and character, personality being the wider of the two. *Personality* traits involve our temperaments, moods, habits, skills and dispositions, not all of which are reason-responsive or identity conferring. I may be too giggly or too gloomy, but such traits are probably not modifiable through mere acts of reason. They may not be modifiable at all, except through some type of behaviouristic conditioning. If the inevitable 'conditioning' exercised upon us by life's vicissitudes makes me less giggly as the years go by, my personality will have changed, but not necessarily my character, let alone my selfhood. Moreover, being a great dancer may be an essential part of the expression of my personality; losing a leg in an accident will change that, but may leave my character and selfhood untouched. Although certain personality traits, especially those comprising the Big Five Model of neuroticism, extraversion, openness, agreeableness and conscientiousness, have turned out to be relatively reliable predictors of reactions and actions across a range of situations, there is a certain superficiality and shallowness about many aspects of personality.

Character traits distinguish themselves from other personality traits in being potentially reason-responsive and having to do with a person's moral worth. The most prominent of character traits are virtues and vices, such as considerateness or callousness. A person who undergoes a moral conversion could end up as a truly 'different person' with a new vision of his or her selfhood. People can, however, undergo notable character changes and still retain their unaltered selfhood. An inconsiderate teenager may become slightly more considerate after experiencing some personal hardship, yet remain essentially the same old self: a spoiled brat. Character development is thus not automatically tantamount to self-change.

The notion of *self* penetrates even deeper into the core of personhood than does the notion of character; it encompasses those and only those character traits that are literally speaking self-shaping. On this understanding, the self denotes the set of a person's core commitments, traits, aspirations and ideals: the characteristics that are most central to him or to her. Character, then, represents a sub-class of personality, and the self, in turn, a sub-class of character. Self-traits persist over time and across different domains of life as salient patterns, taking precedence over other traits when competing in the psychological economy. If weakened or lost, the person is experienced as self-transformed (see further in Chapter 10). The self, on this understanding, is at stake in such everyday expressions as 'I was not really myself when I did that', 'He was not himself anymore after his wife passed away' and 'She changed herself by joining that religious sect'. This is precisely why I consider it a 'commonsense view' of selfhood.

These are exciting but challenging times for researchers of the self, as various complications threaten to undermine the commonsense-cum-personality-psychology conception and thereby defeat any prima facie presumptions that we may entertain in its favour. Notice, for instance, that the commonsense view has little to say about the ontological status of the self. For all we know, there may be nothing more to the self than self-concept. Simply because laypeople have a reasonably clear concept of their 'innermost core' and are able, with the generous help of personality psychologists, to peel away other concepts describing the 'outer' layers of their personhood, there is no guarantee that this concept corresponds to any objective reality. The commonsense view, as I have sketched it, may seem to presuppose the objective reality of selves, but it is, in fact, easy to reformulate it as a view of mere self-concept (the set of beliefs we have about the self). The commonsense view thus remains essentially ambiguous with regard to the realism versus anti-realism self-debate to be probed in this chapter.

2.2. Realism and Its Discontents

Aristotle is often presented as the quintessential substantive realist about selves. A realist he was, and an essentialist to boot, but the fact remains that Aristotle did not operate with a distinct concept of self – at least not the same concept that exists in contemporary discussions. He was interested in the metaphysical self *qua* soul (the form of the body), part of which survives death, and the self *qua* moral character: a set of substantive character states (*hexeis*) that are 'more enduring even than our knowledge of the sciences' (Aristotle, 1985, p. 25 [1100b12–14]). Neither of these concepts coincides with the 'self' of today's personality psychology, for instance – a self that has little to do with an imperishable soul and is supposed to penetrate even deeper to the core of a person's psyche than does moral character, as noted in the previous section. Yet, if we are ready to substitute what Aristotle says about moral character with today's jargon about moral selves, an historically important realist theme emerges from his writings: Some people are (morally) worthy of great things, and others are not; and some people know to which of those two categories they belong, and others do not. The possible combinations of those two criteria (objective worthiness of self and self-knowledge) then create four possible character types that Aristotle analyses, and he concludes that the *megalopsychoi* – those who are objectively worthy and know it – form the ideal type (Aristotle, 1985, pp. 97–104 [1123a33–1125a35]; see further in Kristjánsson, 2002, chap. 3).

In Aristotle, the mind has a faculty, whether well or badly honed, of attending in a secondary way to its primary operations, as it would to any other objective processes. Another textbook icon of self-realism, Descartes, took this faculty to an un-Aristotelian extreme by making all knowledge dependent upon self-knowledge. Also contrary to Aristotle, Descartes considered the self to be a simple, single, permanent, non-material entity, immediately accessible to introspection at any moment, the experience of which undergirds the only certainties we can ever have in life. Locke, the third alleged 'founding father' of self-realism, considered the unity and reality of the self to comprise a certain type of self-consciousness over time: consciousness appropriated by the self to the self through memory. Although the received wisdom of characterising these three historical philosophers as self-realists is not wrong, one should note how strikingly different are their conceptions of the essence of the self (settled character states; self-transparency; self-conscious memory). Locke and most subsequent realists rejected the Cartesian picture as epistemologically naive, although this fact seems to have escaped the notice of many current critics of self-realism. Since Locke's time, of course, numerous other realist variants have appeared on the scene, some of which I mention at later junctures. All this divergence notwithstanding, it is salutary to try to elicit the commonalities of the realist positions, past (minus Cartesian self-transparency) and present.

The first and most obvious realist tenet is that the self is one thing and self-concept another. Self-concept, or identity, when it gets things right, has an actual self as its cognitive object: the referent to which it corresponds (see, e.g., Flanagan, 1996, p. 69; cf. Funder's personality-realism, 1999). Flanagan (1991) couches the difference between self and self-concept in terms of the distinction between actual *full identity* (only to be known comprehensively from an ideally objective perspective) and necessarily simplified, subjectively known *represented identity*. To avoid conceptual confusion, full identity would perhaps more felicitously be termed 'actual full selfhood'. Rather than equating self and identity, we should therefore speak of the self *and* its identity – in the same way that James (1890) famously spoke of the I-self that constructs and the Me-Self that is constructed. Whereas identity is a construction, self is not. As Moshman puts it, identity is 'not generated ex nihilo but rather is constructed via reflection on a preexisting self' (2004, p. 87). Although the constructed self-concept or identity (terms used interchangeably hereafter) never represents the self with complete accuracy (see Jopling, 2000, pp. 46–47) – or we would end up in a surreal Borgesian world where the map of a territory *is* the territory – we should, as rational agents, aspire to representations that are as accurate as possible. And the construction is not accurate simply because we believe, choose or want it to be accurate, but because – and only in so far as – it represents what we truly are, in line with a correspondence theory of truth.

This first realist tenet trails off naturally into the second, which concerns the meanings of the terms *self-knowledge* and *self-deception*.

Self-knowledge denotes, for the realist, harmony between one's self and self-concept; self-deception denotes disharmony or discrepancy. For instance, I may consider myself strong willed and really be strong willed, or I may consider myself weak willed and really be weak willed. In either case, I could be said to possess self-knowledge. Alternatively, I may consider myself strong willed but really be weak willed, or consider myself weak willed and really be strong willed. In either case, I would be self-deceived. Or to take examples from Aristotle's classic discussion of great-mindedness, the vain and the pusillanimous both fail as *megalopsychoi* – the former because, while objectively worthy of little, they think themselves worthy of much; the latter because, while objectively worthy of much, they think themselves worthy of little (1985, pp. 97–104 [1123a33–1125a35]). And such self-deceptions are common because, unfortunately, self-concepts 'have the bad habit of being taken for the reality they represent' (Jopling, 1997, p. 251). Notice that for self-concept to harmonise with self, it is not necessary that one is able to articulate one's self-knowledge fluently. Although the relevant beliefs will, like other beliefs, be articulable in principle, they may, at any given time, be well or poorly articulated. There is no reason to believe, for instance, that because Icelandic children are less adept than US children at explaining their self-conceptions to others, they possess less self-knowledge (discussed in Hart & Fegley, 1997). It is more likely that, coming from a relatively homogenous culture, they have had fewer opportunities to defend their self-conceptions from criticism, and hence to learn to express them in words.

The third realist tenet – and here standard self-realism departs from the Cartesian picture – is that the self is able to reflect upon itself as an object, rather than simply being there as an immediately given subject. In doing so, it will routinely avail itself of introspection, but that method will be subject to the same evidentiary criteria as will any other method of inquiry. Introspection can easily get things wrong, and there is something to be said for the idea that other people (parents, siblings, children, friends, peers) may know 'our selves' better than we do ourselves. Knowing 'our selves' means here to have insight into the nature of – and the causal factors determining – one's core commitments, traits, aspirations and ideals (see Jopling, 2000, p. 12). Although first-person reports will be the normal first route of inquiry, they do not entitle the subject to any essential epistemic privileges. I return to this issue at the end of the chapter.

These three realist tenets (about the selfhood–identity distinction, the meaning of 'self-knowledge' and the epistemic nature of self) do not mean that self-concept simply describes the self without influencing it. Just as noticing a blemish on your face in a photograph may induce you to remove the blemish from your face rather than merely airbrushing it from the photo, so the projection of one's self-concept may prompt one, consciously or unconsciously, to recast any of one's core traits, beliefs or commitments. Some traits will be relatively malleable to such description-driven alterations; others are more resistant and even unchangeable. This situation presents no mystery; some things happen because we think they should happen; other things happen irrespective of such expectations (see Flanagan, 1996, p. 69; Neisser, 1997; Jopling, 1997).

Jopling's book (2000) contains the most careful and balanced analysis that I have seen of the subtle relationship between self and self-concept. He repeatedly reminds us that there is two-way traffic between them, and that whereas all good realists will focus more on self than on self-concept, to ignore self-concept would render them guilty of what he calls 'naive realism'. Recall here that even the realist par excellence, Aristotle, refused to grant people the status of *megalopsychoi* unless both their objective moral characteristics and their conceptions of those characteristics were up to scratch. Citing the philosopher Stuart Hampshire, Jopling notes that intentional states of mind are not independent objects which remain unchanged by the subject's changing views of their nature; rather, watching and trying (successfully or not) to know oneself – and the conclusions of that watching – become, in part, constitutive elements of selfhood (2000, p. 65). To take a parallel example, an anthropologist's theory about the culture in which he or she lives is part of that culture and may influence it in various ways. Moshman makes an even stronger point when he maintains that 'there is a deep sense in which my theory of self is not merely about myself but becomes myself', as I transform myself to a certain extent into the person I theorise myself to be (2004, p. 88). Jopling uses these considerations to criticise Flanagan's strict distinction between actual selfhood and represented identity. While agreeing fully with the realist claim that veridical self-accounts must go beyond experientially based claims of the first-person perspective, Jopling faults Flanagan for his insensitivity to the fact that the self cannot be analysed adequately by blissfully disregarding whose self it is and how one identifies with oneself (2000, pp. 32–37). In Chapter 5, we shall see empirical examples of how, for instance, one's domain-specific self-concept as a maths student (well-founded or not) may influence one's actual score in maths tests.

One way to make this point about the relationship between self and self-concept is to say that one's self-concept forms part of one's self, if perhaps not – the circumspect realist would add – its most significant part. Yet, just as in Milan Kundera's (1987) novel, *Life is Elsewhere*, there appeared a woman who could only be herself by being insincere, so we can think of a case in which people are so thoroughly deceived about their 'selves' that their self-deceptions have become central to who they are – and that, contrary to the typical realist description of self-knowledge as knowledge of who one really is, they can acquire self-knowledge only at the expense of who they are. All these concessions may seem to lead realists into a logical blind alley where they will stumble upon a version of Plato's Third Man Paradox. If the full self includes its own mirror (self-concept) as part of itself, does that not require another mirror to reflect the two, and so on, ad infinitum? The stumbling block for Plato was, however, the assumption that copies of his original 'forms' must be distinct from the originals. Self-realists need make no such concession. They can maintain that just as a mirror can both reflect the furniture in the room in which it is placed and be itself part of that furniture, so self-concept can both represent selfhood and be part of selfhood. The buck simply stops there – with the essentially self-reflexive nature of much of human experience. Ryle famously rejected such a mirror model, or, more specifically, the image of a torch which 'illuminates itself by beams of its own light reflected from a mirror in its own insides' (1949, p. 39). He understood self-knowledge, however, as a specific kind of activity or behaviour. My exploration of self-creation and the self-conscious emotions in Section 2.5 and Chapter 4 suggest that both Ryle's view and the one he was arguing against may, in fact, be true.

Recent self-literature is replete with more straightforward objections to self-realism. As well known as these objections are, they require only the briefest of rehearsals here: According to the *metaphysical* objection, realism about selves invokes a mysterious substance, be it a soul or some other active and enduring entity that is supposed to reside at the core of one's personhood. But there is no reason to suppose that such an entity exists. The *epistemological* objection buttresses this point by noting that although contemporary realists shy away from their Cartesian inheritance, self-knowledge, on the realist account, is basically knowledge of the self by that same self gained through introspection. To be sure, introspection is said to be corrigible; in complete default of it, however, there would be no self-knowledge in the realist sense. Contemporary personality testing is a case in point. Despite all its standardised structure and alleged scientific rigour, it is self-reports that matter in the end for measures of, say, self-esteem. Yet self-reports are a notoriously unreliable source of knowledge. We make enduring mistakes not only about our supposed ongoing feelings and cognitions, but even about conscious events as apparently simple as auditory experiences and visual imagery (Schwitzgebel, 2008). The *anthropological* objection, then, deals the alleged final blow to self-realism by noting that the realist conception of a unified, knowable self is a peculiar Western notion, unique to that part of the world and essentially tied to one historical period: the Enlightenment (see, e.g., Rose, 1996). A mountain of so-called postmodern literature now exists depicting self-realism as a noxious historical residue of a long-bankrupt 'Enlightenment project', and taking to task the 'Enlightenment conception' of selfhood (see, e.g., Kinsella, 2005). Cast in the role of a villain is the typical 'Enlightenment thinker' with sunny optimism about the stability, transparency and potential authenticity of transcultural human selves. With the post-Enlightenment sea-change, in which humanism, essentialism and universalism were thrown overboard, the Enlightenment self-conception fell by the wayside, too.

The 'Enlightenment conception' of the self may serve as a good foil for postmodernists, but the problem is that it never existed. As we have already seen, there were various, and only partly overlapping, realist conceptions in Enlightenment (and pre-Enlightenment) times. The so-called 'Enlightenment conception' seems to be an eclectic mixture of the Cartesian *cogito* and Locke's unifying idea of self-consciousness (although postmodern writings tend to contain disturbingly little reference to any specific Enlightenment thinkers). Furthermore, the most vocal critic of the substantive realist conception of selfhood was no other than the Enlightenment thinker par excellence, David Hume. Introspection reveals, according to Hume, no singular, substantive unity in the plurality of impressions that comprises consciousness. The alleged 'self' is nothing but 'a bundle or collection of different perceptions, which succeed each other with an inconceivable rapidity, and are in a perpetual flux and movement'. Our consciousness is like a theatre where various perceptions make their appearance simultaneously or in succession – but, alas, a moving theatre, without a fixed stage. However strong our natural propensity to imagine that flux of impressions as emanating from an underlying, unchanging unity, the idea is nevertheless fictitious – a figment of the imagination without intellectual basis. Mere feeling in this case is mere 'fancy'; merely feeling, as we do, that there is an identity-conferring unity between past, present and future impressions no more guarantees a substantive self than does our 'feeling of indifference' prove that the will is free. Substantive selfhood requires something 'invariable and uninterrupted', but there is simply no such substance beneath all the difference in what theorists call 'the self' (Hume, 1978, pp. 251–55). Equally famous and memorable, however, is Hume's eventual dissatisfaction with his treatment of selfhood, expressed in the Appendix to the *Treatise*, in which he confesses to find himself 'involv'd in such a labyrinth' that 'I neither know how to correct my former opinions, nor how to render them consistent' (1978, p. 633). What Hume is referring to there is the apparent contradiction between his deconstruction of substantive selfhood in Book I and his retrieval of an everyday notion of moral selfhood in Book II. I return to the latter in the final section of this chapter, but what matters at this juncture is the Book I deconstruction.

It is fair to say that most contemporary versions of anti-self-realism – to which I now turn – trace their origins back to Hume. A faithful modern follower of the Humean position is Daniel Dennett (1992). He thinks of the self as a convenient fairy tale: an 'abstract center of narrative gravity', in which all types of self-illusions intersect. Although motivated by different philosophical concerns than Dennett is, contemporary postmodernists would happily concur with this characterisation (see, e.g., Rose, 1996, p. 37). They, too, have been influenced by Hume, although Humean scepticism seems to have typically filtered down to them through Nietzsche (who hated Hume, but replicated most of his anti-realist arguments).

It is important to distinguish clearly between postmodernism as an historical condition (the current period in time after the demise of high modernism, especially in art and culture), and as a philosophical position. Certain current self-conceptions often termed 'postmodern' – conceptions characterised by carnivalisation, irony, pastiche, excess and camp; explicitly represented by such current media cult figures as Paris Hilton – turn out on closer inspection to be inspired by old-fashioned hedonism which is anything but philosophically postmodern (see Section 9.5). What need concern us here is the philosophical version – or versions – of postmodernism, based on ontological anti-realism and epistemological perspectivism, according to which there is no objective reality for us to apprehend. People see and conceptualise things from different discourse-dependent perspectives, and no transperspectivist evaluations are possible. Terms such as 'sham', 'pretense', 'fictional self' and 'self-alienation' belong to an outdated modernist canon and should be laid to rest (Rose, 1996, p. 55; Gergen, 1991, pp. 13, 187).

Postmodern psychologist Kenneth Gergen gives us a revealing historical account of the alleged erasure of the Enlightenment/modernist self and the creation of a new postmodern self-construct. In late modernism, he maintains, the prevailing self-conceptions began to be undermined by 'technologies of social saturation': exposure to a wide range of pluralistic values, unique opportunities and special intensities. Life became a candy store of potentialities, and selves became pastiches, 'imitative assemblages of each other'. This led to the 'populating of the self': the acquisition of multiple and disparate potentials for being, the splitting of the individual into a multiplicity of self-investments and the infusion of 'partial identities'. This early 'restless-nomad' stage of playful, uncritical postmodernism was not the closing moment in the trajectory of the self, however. The phase that we have now entered – critical postmodernism or critical regionalism – is that of the 'relational self', in which fragmentation has given way to a 'reality of immersed interdependence' (1991, pp. 49–156).

Gergen contends that it is not until the beginning of this critical stage that the 'positive potentials' of the postmodern self begin to unfold: namely, its potential to be crystallised: cleaved and transformed. Crystallisation is a positively valenced term, although one may wonder how progress is to be judged on this theory. Understanding ourselves as scattered terminals of networks of human interaction, rather than as agents of conscious and intentional human action, is, in any case, considered more appropriate (perhaps closer to the spirit of the times), if not 'truer to facts' in the ordinary 'outdated' sense. People who understand the nature of the relational self will learn to 'complicate themselves' – to experiment with a multiplicity of self-understandings and self-commitments – but avoid an endorsement of any of those accounts as standing for the 'truth of self'. Because there is no coherent self to start with, one is free to express a delimited aspect of oneself to others without responsibility to the remainder of the self. No single expression is 'telling' of oneself, because there is no self about which to be told. There are, so to speak, only masks, no faces. Individuals do not 'mean anything'; their intentions and actions are nonsensical unless coordinated with those of others. The temporary joining of tribes, therefore, is the only way to construct self-coherence and validity – albeit internal coherence and local validity (Gergen, 1991, pp. 173–254).

Attributionism – a powerful approach in contemporary psychology (Heider, 1958) – does not import all the ontological relativism and florid polemics of postmodernism, but like postmodernism, it assumes that selves are invented rather than discovered. According to attributionism, people tend to act in accordance with the explanations they like to give for their own behaviour and with the attributes they believe they possess, whether or not they actually possess them. How well or how badly a person does in life, then, depends primarily on the subjective 'self-theory' that the person possesses (see, e.g., Dweck, 1999). The process of adopting such a theory has a name: *selving*. Through an exploratory process of selving, the agent 'negotiates' various identities through interactions with other people until some sort of internal and external harmony is reached: a coherent identity that the agent stubbornly endeavours to maintain and reinforce (see, e.g., Swann & Bosson, 2008).

Although uncritical and critical postmodernism, attributionism and other current variants of anti-self-realism differ considerably in radicality, they have common refrains: Selfhood is constructed cognitively, like a theory is constructed, and amounts, in the end, to no more than self-concept. There is no independent target object 'out there' or 'in here', no 'self of selves' specifiable by a determinate body of empirical evidence. As Harré has said: 'Considered from this point of view, to be a self is not to be a certain kind of being but to be in possession of a certain kind of theory' (cited in Rose, 1996, p. 9). James's distinction between the 'I' (the constructing self-as-subject) and the 'Me' (the constructed self-as-object) collapses because, for the anti-self-realists, there is no such thing as 'I' independent of the 'Me', antecedent to how I understand and interpret myself. And this idea has gained such a strong foothold in contemporary psychology that as eminent a researcher of the self as Susan Harter ventures to claim that 'most scholars' now 'conceptualize the self as a *theory* that must be cognitively constructed' (1999, p. 7). Greer (2003a) agrees with that assessment of the current consensus, although he is more critical of it. It is precisely in light of this prevailing opinion among psychologists that I consider anti-self-realism part and parcel of today's 'dominant self-paradigm'.

What about self-knowledge versus self-deception, then, if these terms do not denote correspondence versus lack of correspondence between self-concept and actual self? An important distinction needs to be made here between what we could call 'hard' and 'soft' anti-self-realism. For uncritical postmodernists and other hard anti-realists, 'self-deception' is a redundant term, because human beings have no hidden inner depths that can be captured or missed. Self-knowledge, on the other hand, is the same as self-choice: People decide at will at any given moment what they are and who they are, and what we call 'self-knowledge' is nothing but their avowal of this choice (ideally mixed with a generous portion of ironic detachment). There are, in other words, no specific warranty conditions that one's identity – one's 'self-weavings' – must satisfy in order to count as true or appropriate. The underlying theory of truth is an anything-goes – or at best a pragmatist – one. Critical postmodernists, attributionists and other soft anti-self-realists refuse to go that far. In line with a coherence theory of truth, they claim that in order for one's identity to count as appropriate, the beliefs underlying that identity must be coherent – internally and with regard to the group of people with whom one identifies. Soft anti-realists try, therefore, to have what they consider to be the best of both worlds: combining an agreeably hip (true to the spirit of our times) conception of a socially constructed and context-dependent self with the acceptance of a logical-cum-psychological connective tissue (coherence) that makes some self-conceptions rationally and morally warranted and others not.

2.3. Problems with Anti-Realism and Some Realist Alternatives

Anti-realism about selves is not without its problems. To start with the 'hard' postmodern variant, it must be said that the typical accounts of it (e.g., those of Gergen, 1991, and Rose, 1996) sound pretentious but academically lightweight. One is left to wonder if, stripped of its linguistic decorum and its apocalyptic musings about the failure of the 'Enlightenment project', such postmodernisms produce anything more than rhetorical gas. Take Rose's explication of the common 'error' of ascribing to ourselves a nonconstructed self: The human being, he says, is 'like a latitude or a longitude at which different vectors of different speeds intersect. The "interiority" which so many feel compelled to diagnose is not that of a psychological system, but of a discontinuous surface, a kind of infolding of exteriority' (1996, p. 37). This reads like a parody of willful obfuscation. One is tempted to retort, along with Strawson, that 'people are not that stupid' (1997, p. 405). All the stylistic hoopla aside, the self-construct of uncritical postmodernism bears little resemblance to actual human psychology and actual moral experience (Jopling, 2000, p. 20). At fault is perhaps not so much that lack of resemblance. I am, indeed, more sanguine than Jopling (2000, p. 8) about the possibility of revising the psychological vocabulary of everyday discourse *as a whole*, if certain unexpected truths emerged from scientific research – truths about either the essential malleability or complete predictability of all human actions, for instance. The problem is rather – to apply a version of the 'no-miracles argument' introduced in Section 2.1 – that postmodernists have launched no well-argued attack on entrenched tenets of folk and academic psychology: about the relative stability of people's emotional self-traits and the intractability of radical self-change, for instance. They simply assume that those tenets are misconceived. Without the notion of a persisting intrapsychic sameness over time, however, such mundane everyday notions as personal moral responsibility disappear (Frimer & Walker, 2008; cf. Chandler, 2000; Jopling, 2000, p. 123). The self of hard anti-realism is no longer a moral self. There must be something amiss in a theory that accepts such a possibility without pause. So although there is something to be said for the view that Hume's scepticism about self-realism does not get the better of him – given his later concessions about the existence of a moral self – there is, I submit, nothing to be said for the view that the postmodernists' version of anti-self-realism does not get the better of them.

Both the hard and soft variants of postmodernism, along with attributionism and most current forms of anti-self-realism, share a common allegiance to radical constructivism about knowledge, and take potshots at the notion of truth as correspondence with reality. There is a basic difficulty with rejecting this notion: Almost all human actions, communications, interactions and investigations seem to presuppose its truth (Fox, 2001). Of course, it may still turn out be false. But in order to demonstrate its falsehood, it is incumbent upon anti-self-realists to give us a more plausible description of, say, a brutal wife-batterer who takes himself to be loving husband than simply saying, as the self-realist would, that the husband in question suffers from disharmony between identity and actual self. From the postmodern camp, at least, no such alternative description has been forthcoming. Generally speaking, constructivists want to replace the very idea of truth with that of adaptability or viability. Paradoxically, however, because no academic or lay theory of truth has turned out to have as much adaptability as the theory of truth as correspondence, there seem to be good constructivist reasons for adopting it.

As for the soft anti-realist coherence accounts of self-concept and self-knowledge, they do have some clear epistemic advantages over their anything-goes counterparts. Yet it is difficult to shake the suspicion that a person may possess a completely coherent self-identity that is nevertheless false. In his challenging paper, Moshman (2004) notes that false identities can easily be maintained through self-serving manipulations. He even claims that we may all have false moral identities. Recall that anti-self-realism is not about an actual self that we possess (because we do not possess any such self); rather, it is about our theory of what that self is. Identity, then, is a self-theory, and identity formation is theory formation. But as Moshman correctly notes, theories (and thus identities) can be evaluated with respect to truth and may turn out to be false. Is the debunking of such falsehoods not precisely the stuff of much of the world's best literature (see examples in Jopling, 2000, p. 17)? At this point we are confronted a problem, the full brunt of which is felt in cases of serious, pathological self-deceptions. Sidestepping the question of whether or not self-knowledge is always good (cf. Flanagan, 1996), it strains credulity to hold that pathological self-deceptions can be 'cured' simply by bringing the patient's self-conceptions into internal harmony. It seems prima facie more plausible to maintain that even after all the necessary coherence adjustments have been made, the patient may still be utterly deceived about who he or she really is. If natural scientists were to find a correlation between natural phenomenon x and a theory about natural phenomenon y, they would normally hypothesise that a correlation obtained not between x and the theory about y, but between x and y themselves. This option (where x would be action or reaction and y identity *qua* theory about one's self) is not open to the anti-self-realists, however, because they do not assume that there is any self apart from the theory: 'You are simply what you think you are, at least when your ruminations about what you think you are have been brought into some sort of a reflective equilibrium'. Such considerations make it easy to understand why critics of general psychological anti-realism, such as Crispin Wright (2002), conclude that there simply is no coherent anti-realism of that kind, and that we have no alternative but to acquiesce in ordinary psychological discourse about selves and other posits, under a face-value construal, as providing the resources for objectively true accounts of our natures and the causal springs of our actions.

What options are there among current theorists to the now-dominant anti-realism about selves? I have cited philosophers Flanagan and

Jopling repeatedly here. Both have taken up arms against anti-self-realism in general and its postmodern variants in particular. Flanagan is the author of the previously adopted 'one-self-to-a-customer' rule. Although he rejects the notion of multiple constructed selves, he thinks that selves are 'multiplex': We show different facets of our selves to different audiences, and rarely does our self-concept have the whole of our self as its cognitive object – merely certain aspects. Nevertheless, the various facets of a multiplex self permeate each other and can be comprehended – if not by agents themselves as parts of grand auto-biographical narratives, then at least by an objective, ideally realised scientific inquiry (1996, pp. 67–71). Jopling, although more guarded in his epistemic optimism, picks up the thread from Flanagan and weaves it further, connecting it, inter alia, to the naturalist observation that because of their common biological heritage and natural environment, human beings in different societies and in different periods are capable of deep and profound understandings of each other's selfhoods (1997; 2000, chap. 2). I happen to agree substantially with both these authors; and as whistle-blowers on the inadequacies of anti-self-realism they are second to none. Their contribution lies more in articulating the state of play in mainstream self-realism, however, rather than in advancing it further. Neither Flanagan nor Jopling provides new arguments that will persuade the uninitiated.

Psychologist Ulric Neisser has been a tireless advocate of the existence of a nonconstructed realist self. He concedes to anti-realist self-pluralists, however, that people possess multiple selves. Every person has an ecological self, an interpersonal self, an extended self, a private self and a conceptual self (self-concept) – and each of these selves is amenable to its own specific kind of self-knowledge (Neisser, 1988). But some selves are positioned prior to others in the psychological and historical order, particularly the ecological self and the interpersonal self. And of those two, the ecological self – the self as perceiver of the physical environment – is the pillar of all the others. Neisser, like Jopling, stresses the extent to which all forms of selfhood are responses to 'the basic human predicament' (1997, p. 12); hence the ecological selves of all human beings will, for example, have a great deal in common. The ecological self seems to correspond substantially to James's 'I': the basic self of self-awareness that engages with the world and its own workings. But at issue there is precisely the substantive self – or an attribute of such a self – the existence of which Hume so fervently questioned. Neisser does not seem to have any specific answers to Humean scepticism; he simply ignores it. Unfortunately also, it is unclear where we are supposed to locate the moral self in Neisser's self-pluralism. Is it one of the selves he mentions or a combination of more than one self? The relevance of everyday self-talk hinges in great measure on the identification or non-identification of core elements in a person's character that can be called to account and appraised as the locus of moral agency. To be sure, the realism–anti-realism debate is psychologically and metaphysically salient as such. Yet the reason for so many academics from disparate disciplines having entered it is, no doubt, its moral ramifications. A self-realism such as Neisser's, which fails to engage with the moral dimension of selfhood, leaves too much to be desired.

Psychologist Michael Chandler is perhaps the most eloquent current critic of hard anti-self-realism. It helps that in addition to having the gift of the gab, he has, with his colleagues, conducted extensive research into the self-conceptions of people in various cultures and subcultures (Chandler, Lalonde, Sokol & Hallett, 2003). Chandler starkly repudiates the view that the notion of a permanent self is simply an artefact of some cultures. In contrast, he takes it to be both logically and psychologically true that permanence over time, or 'sameness-in-change', is a 'necessary and constitutive feature of what it could possibly mean to have or be a self' (2000, p. 210). Otherwise, not only would the possibility of moral evaluations (including those of just or unjust deserts) be undermined, but so would the possibility of an ecological self in Neisser's sense. Self-concepts do assume different forms relative to time and culture (as we shall see in Chapter 8), but they share certain common characteristics, substantial enough to say that they are 'about' one and the same thing. Chandler seems to think that the transcultural designs of selfhood provide sufficient proof that self-continuity is an ineradicable feature not only of constructed self-concepts, but also of unconstructed selves. He cites Aristotle, Locke and various other realist philosophers to make good his claim. That is fine with me, but for convinced anti-realists, it will sound like a mere *argumentum ad verecundiam*. In fact, trying to resuscitate the realist accounts described in Section 2.2 would be next to impossible in today's academic climate. The snag in Chandler's empirical research is that it does not demonstrate that the permanence of selfhood necessarily signals anything beyond the conceptual coherence of soft anti-realism. True, the self-continuity assumption that Chandler and his colleagues have found wherever they go is a further punch in the nose of hard anti-self-realists. But in order to show that permanent self-concepts really track permanent, objectively identifiable target selves, more philosophical groundwork and psychological spadework is needed.

2.4. Interlude: A Narrativist *deus ex machina*?

It has become increasingly common of late to contend that the traditional realism versus anti-realism debate about selves is obsolete; what matters instead is the 'storied' nature of selfhood. This challenge has a rallying cry: narrativism. According to narrativism, people preserve and communicate their identities in storied form that makes self-knowledge meaningful and organises it into a coherent whole. Selves are embodiments of lived stories; *homo sapiens* is *homo narrans*. Narrativism is not only a psychological thesis, but a methodological one as well. Narrative research has thus gained currency in the last two decades as an overarching category for a variety of qualitative research methods (life-story analyses, auto-ethnographies and narrative interviews, for example) aimed at understanding what really makes people tick (Casey, 1995).

In its contemporary form at least, narrativism seems to have been systematically explicated for the first time in a book by an obscure German judge called Wilhelm Schapp (1953), who claimed that one's life is caught up in stories, and is nothing apart from the stories that confer identity upon it. This view received powerful backing in Alasdair MacIntyre's *After Virtue* (1981). In MacIntyre's view, personal identities inevitably possess a narrative structure. We dream, think, plan, love and hate in narratives. More specifically, the unity of an individual's life – the link between birth and death, beginning and end – is nothing more than the unity of a narrative embodied in that life; and the quest of an individual's life is to live out that unity successfully and to bring it to completion. MacIntyre considers the idea of a narrative self to be the natural opposite of both the idea of an emotivist self and the Enlightenment ideal of reductionism or atomism. Similar points about the inescapable narrativity of selfhood recur in Charles Taylor's work on the moral culture of the self (1989). He specifically foregrounds the normativity of narrative selfhood: the moral need and demand to make sense of our lives in terms of an unfolding story – a reflexive project – within moral space. For him, the narrative self is essentially a moral self. Paul Ricoeur (1992) claims with no less vigour that a necessary feature of selfhood on the commonsense understanding (as distinct from mere numerical identity) is that we can relate to ourselves as actors in a story upon which we can reflect. Our aim in life, he contends, is for meaningfulness through the narrative wholeness of a successful life plot. All these philosophical narrativisms are thought provoking for different reasons and have ramifications – some truly enlightening – in areas that cannot be pursued here. My sole concern in this section is, however, with narrativism as a putative solution to the realism versus anti-realism debate about selves.

Its overall popularity notwithstanding, narrativism has provoked an eruption of criticism from various quarters: (a) Logically, narrativism may turn out to be suspect in its equation of chronology with causality, and in its potential mixing up of the researching self as a knower of narrative structures, on the one hand, and a product of such structures, on the other. (b) Theorists of a phenomenological bent accuse narrativists of ignoring the experiential core self of phenomenal consciousness, which 'must be regarded as a pre-linguistic presupposition for any narrative practice', and of confusing core selfhood with extended and embodied narrative personhood (Zahavi, 2007, p. 191). (c) Galen Strawson (2004) has initiated an original challenge by holding that narrativism is empirically false. Some people – 'Episodics' like himself, as opposed to 'Diachronics' – simply do not understand their lives in terms of an unfolding narrative. Narrative theorists happen to be Diachronics, and for them narrativism is doubtless true both as a descriptive thesis about their psychology and as a normative thesis about their good life. But they are 'just talking about themselves' (2004, p. 437). Episodics, in contrast, only live for the moment, and for them the good life is the happy-go-lucky, see-what-comes-along life. Whether or not Strawson's radical thesis succeeds, it is at least true that there are significant cultural differences in the extent to which people describe their selfhood narratively (Chandler et al., 2003).

(d) Most relevant to present concerns are epistemic worries urged against narrativism: We can be – and often are – mistaken in our stories about who we are and why we act and feel the way we do. However dazzlingly plausible and grippingly coherent narrative accounts can appear to others, and even to the person who produces them, they can still be false. Is not every telling of the story at least a partial prevarication? Are we not all, to a certain extent, self-evaders, self-duplicators and self-fabulists? Do we not all have a knack for making duplicity look profound? Even if we accept the controversial thesis that experience is narratively constructed and needs to be explored narratively, we cannot assume that any old story will do. Aesthetic demands of continuity, closure, finality and conviction may suffice in the realm of fiction, but they lack epistemic relevance in real life. If narrative comes to be understood as a knowledge-bearing and explanation-giving genre, we need other criteria of validity, which have to do with truth in the most basic sense. Narratives as such, then, are of no intrinsic epistemic interest (see Phillips, 1994; Lamarque, 2004).

It will not have escaped readers' notice that what has emerged here as objection (d) is the same corrigibility objection urged in Section 2.3 against soft anti-self-realism: Coherence of self-concept – be it narratively structured or not – does not guarantee truth. One may wonder, then, if narrativism has really progressed any further than soft anti-self-realism has. It seems to be susceptible to correlative objections, and rather than removing any of the old problems, it imports a new one: what to say to those who, like Strawson, claim to be tone-deaf to the siren song of stories. Some narrative theorists such as Schechtman (1996) dig in their heels by placing epistemic constraints upon the kinds of narratives that can constitute persons' identities, positing, for instance, that they be intelligibly articulable to others and cohere with an 'objective account' – roughly the story that those around the persons would tell. But then old-fashioned correspondence-realism seems simply to have replaced coherentism. This observation does not reflect positively on the narrativist project in so far as it is supposed to have made the realist–anti-self-realist debate redundant. But the issue may be considerably more complicated than it appears at first sight.

I have proceeded as if there were only one type of narrative account of the self – the indication being now that it parallels that of soft anti-self-realism. On closer inspection, however, there are at least three narrative accounts of the self in the literature, mirroring the insights of hard anti-self-realism, soft anti-self-realism and self-realism, and making the strangest of bedfellows.

First, narrative accounts have found themselves to be the darlings of postmodern hard anti-realists, who use them to explain (or rather to explain away, as an evasive strategy) the illusion of a coherent self. By telling stories about themselves with a beginning, middle and end, people think they have stumbled upon something unified outside those narrations. Yet, in reality, it is simply the old, comforting – but entirely fictitious – realist self that is being superimposed upon human experience by people who refuse to acknowledge the 'death of the subject', and who confuse the masks with the face (Rose, 1996, p. 177). So, for hard anti-realists, narrativism has come to identify the fictional, socially conditioned reconstructions of the self that postmodernism exposes. Second, also manning the barricades of narrativism are soft anti-realists – ridiculed by their 'hard' counterparts – who claim that the possibility of storied selfhood proves the existence of coherent, constructed self-concepts, occupying conceptual space between unitary essentialist selves (which do not exist) and the decentred fragmented selves of uncritical postmodernism (which hardly exist either, except in pathological cases). Upholding this version of narrativism are, for instance, Jerome Bruner (2004) and Donald Polkinghorne (1988), who have elevated the narrative approach to the status of a respectable, widely used research method in education. For them, internally referential narrative coherence is the only viable recipe for constructing method out of the madness of human experience – with the plausibility of a plot ('verisimilitude' *qua* believability or even imaginativeness) having replaced truth as the basic epistemic warranty condition (for a trenchant critique, see Phillips, 1994). As Rudd (2009), who also supports this version, puts it: 'Of course there are bad, out-dated, self-deceived, or just plain inaccurate narratives; but the only conclusion we should draw from that is that we need to tell better ones. There is no possibility of getting away from the narrative form altogether.'

The third and perhaps most novel category of narrativist thinkers are those who try to combine the narrative thesis with a realist account of the self (cf. Jopling, 2000, pp. 48–51). That is, for example, the aspiration of philosopher of history David Carr (1986; not to be confused with his namesake, David Carr the philosopher of education, who will be one of the protagonists of the following chapter). Carr's claim is that narrativity resides not only in stories about the self; but rather, antecedently, in the very self about which the stories are told. Just as a story is constituted, so is life itself – and the self that lives. Stories describe the self; they do not construct it. A self-narrative is therefore true to the extent that it corresponds to the essential narrative elements of the underlying self. Self-narration is not a coherent imposition upon human experience (as it is for soft anti-realist narrativists), much less a fictional distortion of such experience (as it is for hard anti-realist narrativists), but rather an extension of its primary features. Like Carr, Flanagan is a notable representative of this version, bringing his good old iron-fisted self-realism to the table inside the velvet glove of narrativist naturalism (1996, pp. 65–69).

Why has narrativism come to be presented as a serious 'rival' to realist and anti-realist conceptions of the self (see, e.g., Vollmer, 2005), when it simply reproduces all the well-established anti-realist and realist positions in new packages? The blame may lie with certain (arguably skewed) readings of Alasdair MacIntyre (1981), the talismanic progenitor of most contemporary narrative accounts. His brand of narrative self-theory is seen by some to be enveloped in a fog of ambiguity. MacIntyre's main emphasis is on the 'naturalness' of thinking of oneself in storied terms. It seems reasonably clear to me that, for MacIntyre, the root of this naturalness lies in nonconstructed selves rather than constructed identities. This is evident both from MacIntyre's extensive elaboration of the social conditions that need to be in place in order to validate self-ascriptions and his unambiguous claim that the concept of narrative presupposes the concept of personal identity, rather than vice versa (1981, p. 203). When postmodernists cite MacIntyre's work, however, they systematically overlook such passages and focus on places where he stresses that it is only *our* narratives – and even the narratives *others* tell about us – that give unity to our lives. These MacIntyrean 'ambiguities' recur in many subsequent narrativist statements, giving the erroneous impression that narrativism straddles old distinctions and stands above the fray. Nothing could be further from the truth, however. I see no escape from the conclusion that the invocation of a narrative self exacerbates rather than palliates the problem of adjudicating between self-realism and anti-self-realism. Not only must we now determine whether selfhood is constructed or unconstructed – that is still the unsolved mystery – but, additionally, how it is unconstructed or constructed in a 'storied' way. Could we turn this argument on its head by saying that if we can at least establish that the self is storied, such a minimal starting point will go some distance toward solving the thornier problem of the self's constructed or unconstructed nature? I am afraid that the gaping gulfs among the three versions of self-narrativism described in this section do more than enough to vitiate that suggestion.

2.5. Out of the Impasse: Humean Soft Self-Realism

The realism versus anti-realism debate about selves seems to be stuck in an impasse – and the idea that narrativism offers a reprieve turns out to be illusory. To recapitulate, hard anti-self-realism makes travesty of everyday moral experience; soft anti-self-realism, whether of the narrative kind or not, fails to distinguish satisfactorily between self-knowledge and self-deception; Aristotelian or Lockean realism (not to mention the Cartesian kind) imports ontological baggage that most contemporary thinkers resist. There seems to be something rotten in the state of self research.

All may not be lost, however. The realism that I described in Section 2.2 was realism about a substantive, metaphysical self. Let us call it 'hard' realism. Just as there are hard and soft varieties of anti-realism, so are there 'softer' kinds of realism. In the remainder of this chapter, I explore the option of Humean soft self-realism and explain why it may possess the philosophical edge needed to forge our way out of the impasse.

Given his blatant rejection of a substantive, metaphysical self in Book I of his *Treatise* (1978), Hume's conception of *everyday, emotion-grounded selfhood* in Book II can serve as a minimalist jumping-off place for establishing the objective reality – if any – of a moral self. Hume's most significant statement is the one in which he claims that 'we must distinguish betwixt personal identity, as it regards our thought or imagination [described in Book I], and as it regards our passions or the concern we take in ourselves [described in Book II]' (1978, p. 253). In Hume's view, this latter type of selfhood is 'produced' through an association process involving the self-conscious emotions of pride and humility – a process that Hume describes as 'the double relation of ideas and impressions' (1978, p. 286). Hume seems to be arguing that, whereas the self as a succession of related ideas and impressions cannot be a direct object for the understanding, the self of whose moral actions each of us is intimately conscious can be a direct object for our emotions. (There is admittedly no consensus on how to interpret Hume here, but I rely broadly on the exegeses of Purviance, 1997; Chazan, 1998; and Ainslie, 1999; I explain Hume's emotion theory in more detail in Chapter 4.)

How can we make sense of the facticity of this emotion-grounded 'practical' or 'moral' self? (I use the latter designation.) Hume distances himself from the viewpoint of Aristotelian realists who may want to claim that the understanding infers the existence of a moral self from evidence produced by the emotions. He sees the moral self as constituted by emotional activity rather than intuited or inferred from evidence. This activity-constitution renders the self immune to the scepticism that hits at metaphysical accounts of the self. Although the moral self is not a substantive self, it can still be real enough to serve as the basis for practical self-understanding and self-criticism, and as the object of moral evaluation. One of Hume's main concerns is with the putative objectivity of this moral self: how, given its grounding in individual emotion, it can be considered an objective feature of persons. He emphasises the social nature of the moral self, pointing out that the need for 'seconding' renders absurd the possibility of successfully maintaining a wholly idiosyncratic self-concept (1978, p. 332). More specifically, a social dimension is built into the very mechanism for forming self-conceptions; how others understand me is central to how I do and should understand myself. Alien beings transported to this world would not know when to feel pride or humility until custom and practice had settled the issue for them, as they have for us (1978, p. 294). One's self-concept is thus *essentially corrigible*; it is constantly being polished though human interaction and comes to have an objective status in so much as it is decided not only by our own attitudes, but also by the extent to which its various features have been fixed by society's general rules about rational and appropriate emotions. This assumption is fully consistent with Aristotle's insights, for whom only those at the highest level of moral development have become one with their inner life – and yet even these are prone to occasional errors of judgement that stand in need of external rectification (see Kristjánsson, 2007, chap. 2).

Both the Humean and Aristotelian self-concepts are derived from and essentially sustained through social recognition, and to that extent they are 'heteronomous', as opposed to 'autonomous', in the standard Kantian sense. To have a self-concept, we need to have grasped the idea of things being esteemed and chosen by us. But to grasp that idea, we must first have grasped the idea of things being esteemed and chosen by others: primarily of ourselves as being valued and chosen, or disvalued and rejected, by them. In other words, the idea of our own self as distinct from, but still essentially of the same kind as, those of others must derive from the very possibility of evaluating our self and its existential connections as equal, superior or inferior to theirs, and such an evaluation is dependent upon external criteria for both its formation and its sustenance. It is through taking the role of the other, therefore, that the self originally acquires its reflexive quality: its capacity to reflect upon itself and obtain self-knowledge (see, e.g., Jopling, 2000, chap. 6, on the social conditions of self-knowledge; cf. Taylor, 1989, p. 36). Moreover, there is every reason to acknowledge the social nature not only of self-concept, but also of self. Given the nature of human beings, it is impossible to imagine that a newborn's personhood could acquire enough depth and complexity to constitute selfhood, in the commonsense understanding of the term, outside of a community of other human beings. Any developmental concessions to 'social constructivism', if you like, still stop well short of the symbolic interactionist 'looking-glass view' of the self, let alone the idea that selves are social constructions all the way down, 'negotiated' (Swann & Bosson, 2008) – much like executives broker a business deal – in interactions with others. Such radical social constructivism fails to account for both the genetic underpinnings of many of the personality traits that constitute selves, and of the autonomy that originally heteronomous beings gradually acquire, enabling them to develop and nourish self-traits wholly independent, or even in total defiance, of social expectations.

There are a number of reasons why Humean soft realism could recommend itself to people on both sides of the realism–anti-realism divide, not so much by blunting the force of that distinction as by ironing out some of the irritating problems attached to both hard self-realism and soft anti-self-realism. *First*, it preserves the commonsense notion of the self as a unique entity: the locus of human agency (see Section 2.1). It simultaneously explains how the human self is first and foremost a moral self. We are interested in the self as moral beings. *Second*, the appropriateness of our self-concept as moral beings will – along realist lines (see Section 2.2) – depend on correspondence with objective reality. Our self-concept is thus essentially fallible and other-dependent; mere internal coherence does not guarantee its truthfulness (see Section 2.3), and the nature of the self may always remain richer than our knowledge of it (cf. Jopling, 1997, p. 256). *Third*, all this is achieved without any strong ontological commitments (see Section 2.2). The choice turns out to be not only between mere identity, on the one hand, and an Aristotelian full-blown, hard realist self, on the other, as has been the received wisdom. There is no mention here of human essences, absolute realities, indivisible (let alone imperishable) substances or metaphysical entities. The self is simply seen as an everyday psychological unit, targeted by emotions. The question of the reality of the self is not conflated, therefore, with that of the substantiality of the self. The Humean moral self is no mysterious mini-Me. It is simply on a par with 'the voter', 'the citizen', 'the tax-payer' and 'the consumer': oneself as seen from a certain perspective (here: emotion-driven and moral). Yet, this self is, like Aristotelian 'character', a 'full-blooded self – a self outfitted with its qualities, possessions, relations, likes and dislikes' (Schmitter, 2009). *Fourth*, the Humean self-hypothesis explains the intimate link between moral selfhood and emotions – a link not well accommodated or even positively resisted in much of the recent literature. We even glimpse the makings of an explanation for the tendency of emotional traits to be more robust and morally salient than other character traits. I shall have much more to say about this fourth consideration in subsequent chapters, as it lays the basis for my 'alternative' emotion-based self-paradigm.

There is no denying, however, that various vexing questions concerning Humean soft self-realism remain unanswered. Leaving aside the interpretative question of whether or not this was really Hume's considered view, one may ask, for example, how self-conscious emotions such as pride can be simultaneously 'about' the self and 'produce' the self (as Hume puts it), and who is the subject of the emotional experiences in the first place if not that very ecological or phenomenological self which Hume renounces. Has Hume done anything more than to push the problem back one stage? Clearly, for this type of soft self-realism to work, Hume's emotion theory must be brought up to date, as I attempt to do so in Chapter 4. Suffice to say here that Hume does not need to deny the claim that *people* experience self-conscious emotions; what he denies is simply that *selves* do so, as long as one understands 'selves' to be entities that can be understood prior to and independent of the emotions.

Another troubling question concerns the more general claim that entities such as the self are somehow (non-intellectually) constituted by activity rather than (intellectually) inferred from evidence. The activities in question are then presumably either *constitutive of* the self (but activities are by their nature transient and unstable, and where does that leave the persistence of the self?) or they *create* the self (in which case an ontological account of the entity thereby created is still pending). Those concerns challenge not only Humean self-theory, but also any soft realist programme that aims to somehow pry moral facticity loose from the metaphysical pretensions of hard realism. This is not the place to enter those murky waters, except to point out that Purviance (1997) has worked out a Humean account of soft self-realism that is at least internally coherent and (in my view) reasonably faithful to Hume's own text. On Purviance's account, Hume tries to defend two realist tenets regarding the self – that (1) moral evaluations of the self require self-objectivity, and (2) practical activity is grounded in moral facts about a self (a) emotionally concerned with itself and (b) possessing enduring character traits – without seeking refuge in a speculative metaphysics about the existence of a substantial self in the context of a unified reductionist ontology. Nature has made the self a fact of moral experience by means of the self-conscious emotions that cement perceptions into that of moral selfhood – and reason alone would vainly try to support or dispute this fact (cf. Hume, 1978, p. 286).

I leave it to readers to judge the general merits of such a fact-of-agency ontology, and simply point out here that Humean soft self-realism bears a certain resemblance to the *structural realism* that has recently been gaining ground as a modification of traditional scientific realism (see, e.g., Ladyman, Ross, Spurrett & Collier, 2007). Structural realism is characterised as the view that scientific theories tell us only about the form or structure of the unobservable world and not about its nature. This leaves open the question as to whether the nature of things is posited to be unknowable for some reason, eliminated altogether or simply left out of the equation for reasons of methodological parsimony, as I have suggested here. Nevertheless, the 'troubling questions' above indicate that the invocation of the Humean moral self will not signal an eureka moment for all researchers of the self. For those who, like me, are deeply concerned about the present deadlock of the realist–anti-realist self-debate, it may, however, offer a fresh way forward: a working hypothesis of the 'alternative' self-paradigm to be pursued in the remainder of this study.

Let me end this chapter with a few terse observations about the type of techniques that self-realists would recommend when exploring selves. Although more wary of self-reports than anti-self-realists are, self-realists would not shy away altogether from the use of such instruments. They would encourage psychologists, however, to use all the tricks of their trade to try to forestall bias (see, e.g., the ingenious instruments used to measure so-called 'implicit self-esteem', to be mentioned in Chapter 5; cf. also Funder's multicriterial probabilist-realist approach to measuring personality, 1999). Scheff (1997, chap. 1), for one, has described what he calls 'the morphological method', in the form of microanalysis of verbatim dialogue, to enhance the reliability and validity of self-reports. Through subsequent interviews with respondents, asking them to explain their answers to paper and pencil tests, Scheff suggests that one may be able to form an accurate idea of the specific meaning that these interviewees attach to their answers, and thereby weed out deceptions or self-deceptions. A related observation is that people can often be helped to learn to view themselves from the outside, as it were: to observe their own emotions and behaviour and make reasoned inferences about its sources, rather than trying to locate those sources through introspection (see Koole & DeHart, 2007, p. 32).

Refusing to equate self with self-concept, self-realists will reject the view that only the wearer knows where the shoe pinches. Other people often know who I am better than I do; therefore, peer reports and reports of significant others will be vital to self-knowledge. Moreover, as a person's self-traits reveal themselves gradually over an extended period and under varied circumstances, self-realists will prefer longitudinal studies to single-case studies. There is also the possibility of using physical evidence: Emotion-revealing hormones can be identified trough saliva tests (see Webber, 2006, pp. 209–211) and brain scans have opened up a new exciting area of investigation. The idea underlying all these techniques is that although the truth about selves does exist, there is no easy pathway to it. The accuracy of measurements will depend upon, among other things, the qualifications of the judge and the 'judgeability' of the person whose self is being gauged. Even at best, however, the accuracy of self-measurements remains a probabilistic matter (cf. Funder, 1999).

An ancient Chinese fable tells us of a simple-minded peasant from the State of Zheng who wanted to buy himself a pair of shoes. He measured his feet and then headed for the market. Upon arriving there, he realised that he had forgotten his measurements, and went back to get them. But when he returned, it was too late; the market had closed. 'Why didn't you try the shoes on?' someone asked him. 'I'd rather believe in my measurements than my own feet', he replied. For self-realists, although the measurements one takes of one's self through self-concept can be revealing, there are often more accurate ways to identify one's actual full self. By denying that, the anti-self-realist league, so dominant in today's intellectual atmosphere, risks the same mistake as the Chinese peasant made.

3. Exploring Selves

3.1. Fence Crossing or Fence Mending?

I mentioned in the Introduction that I favoured an interdisciplinary approach to exploring selves – more as an articulation of faith than a reasoned conclusion. I want to make amends in this chapter by *arguing* for crossover engagement of a certain kind in self research. There are those who find methodological ruminations recherché or even pointless. They believe that the proof of the pudding lies solely in the eating, not in any justification of cooking methods. I recommend that those readers skip this methodological interlude and go straight to Chapter 4. For those who want to persevere, however, let me note that my discussion will be set in the context of a certain current discourse about the relationship between moral philosophy and moral psychology. There we have recently witnessed burgeoning literature on the need for more integrative work – a fence-crossing, peacemaking process – between these two research cultures. Rather than confining themselves to their previously preferred armchair psychology, some moral philosophers have begun to realise that they may be putting themselves at a competitive advantage by utilising evidence extracted by social scientists on people's actual moral beliefs. Similarly, the idea of availing oneself of conceptual insights delivered by philosophers evidently now meets with less hostility in some social science circles than it has in the past.

Entering this renegotiation-of-boundaries discourse as a moral philosopher, I find it easy to understand why many of my colleagues have succumbed to Owen Flanagan's suggestion: Given that the 'scientific study of the mind is now officially over one hundred years old [...] one would think that it might have begun to yield some reliable, surprising, useful, and fine-grained findings about persons to complement, confirm, or unseat those discovered from the armchair' (1991, p. 16). The recent upsurge of virtue ethics and other forms of *moral naturalism* have rendered Flanagan's suggestion appealing. All such naturalisms are based on the assumption that we live in a single unified world of human experience where so-called moral properties are exclusively natural properties and hence, in principle at least, are empirically defeasible. Another related reason for the acceptance of Flanagan's stance is precisely the rising philosophical interest in the notion of moral selfhood – to which I for one have succumbed – an interest shared also by many academics from the other side of the fence. It seems far fetched to believe that considerations about moral selfhood as an ethical metaconstruct or a normative ideal can be developed in isolation from empirical evidence on the lives of concrete people. Those are examples of the pull towards fence crossing. The recent demise of Kohlbergian moral psychology has, however, pulled some scholars in the opposite direction. Moral psychology is still busy cleaning up the philosophical (Kantian) messiness imported by its founding father, Kohlberg. Is that not a classic case of the unhelpful mishmash that can occur when legitimate fences are crossed rather than mended?

Much that needs to be said about the general issue of fence crossing versus fence mending between moral philosophy and experimental social science has already been said (see, e.g., Flanagan, 1991; Doris & Stich, 2003; cf. Kristjánsson, 2006, chap. 1.2). I shall concentrate instead on a specific manifestation of this issue, as instantiated in the recent debate between psychologists and philosophers on the appropriate reaction of moral psychologists to the Kohlbergian paradigm's fall from grace. Would it be reasonable to react by focusing on 'psychologised morality' rather than, as Kohlberg did, 'moralised psychology' (see Section 3.3), and what repercussions would such a change of focus have for future cooperative work between the two 'cultures'? In what follows, I explore the views of Daniel Lapsley and Darcia Narvaez, the most vocal proponents of the call for 'psychologised morality' as a new research paradigm in moral psychology. Subsequently, I unpack some arguments – given by philosophers Bruce Maxwell and David Carr – against that suggestion, while considering Carr's alternative perspective, which unabashedly 'moralises' the field of moral psychology. Yet advocates of both those conflicting perspectives recommend further cooperation between moral philosophers and moral psychologists. They do differ on a crucial question, however: Is it psychology or philosophy that should 'assume the leading or defining role' in such cooperation (Carr, 2007, p. 389)? Put plainly: Who is to call the shots in the cooperative ventures? Who controls the fence-crossing or fence-mending process?

Whereas the discussion in Sections 3.2 and 3.3 is conducted at a relatively general level, it is fully in the spirit of attention to natural and contextual nuances, extolled by both parties to the debate, to look for answers in an actual discursive tradition. In Section 3.4, I return to current self research, therefore, and use that as a test case: a peg upon which to hang my analysis. This research has been conducted, as shown in Chapter 2, by philosophers of various stripes, as well as psychologists. It is salutary, therefore, to ask: Does moral psychology need moral theory to account for the self, or can it assume the kind of academic sovereignty that Lapsley and Narvaez suggest via their idea of 'psychologised morality'? Although my eventual answer to this question runs counter to the idea of 'psychologised morality', my adherence to 'moralised psychology' is modified by more caveats that Carr, for one, would want to enter (see Section 3.5).

Notice that I use the term 'moralised psychology' (as well as its sister term 'psychologised morality') in quotation marks throughout. This terminology is borrowed from the current literature, but I am not sure that it is a felicitous one. For most psychologists, the word 'moralised' has, I take it, relatively negative connotations. In ordinary language, to 'moralise' typically means to preach or sermonise, and in academic parlance, the descriptive term 'moralising' tends to be connected to something overweening and inappropriate – something foreign to scientific inquiry. But 'moralised psychology' in the discourse under scrutiny here simply means psychology informed by moral theory. Choosing a negatively loaded term should not give critics of such psychology an unfair starting point.

3.2. Four Types of Naturalism

In order to finesse the problem under discussion, it is helpful to invoke and elaborate upon the distinction that Maxwell makes among three approaches to the value of empirical evidence for moral theorising, suggested by the various kinds of naturalism that have been gathering speed in recent years (Maxwell, 2008a, 2008b, 2009). The first approach is what Maxwell calls 'neo-Aristotelian naturalism', but could better be termed 'virtue ethical naturalism' given that most of its proponents are modern-day virtue ethicists with a considerably more self-focused and particularist view of morality than Aristotle had (see Kristjánsson, 2007, chap. 11). According to this approach, moral notions cannot be comprehended in abstraction from human ethology and the natural environment in which we live. This approach tends, however, to be short on specific empirical considerations about what makes people flourish, as distinct from broad-ranging reminders about 'the virtues' being conducive to human wellbeing. The harbingers of modern virtue ethics, such as Philippa Foot and Rosalind Hursthouse, have not produced their own brand of armchair psychology so much as they have indulged in armchair zoology and botany. Examples of what makes people tick thus typically assume the form of parallels drawn from the lives of animals and plants: We need the virtues just as bees need wings (for a continuation of this trend, see McKinnon, 2005).

The second approach is that of 'naturalised normative ethics'. It draws on Flanagan's principle of 'minimal psychological realism', which asserts that theorists must ensure, when constructing a moral theory or ideal, that the character, decision processing and behaviour prescribed are 'possible, or are perceived to be possible, for creatures like us' (Flanagan, 1991, p. 32). Although Flanagan pays more attention to actual psychological evidence than do traditional virtue ethicists, he may be accused of a restrictive view of the role of moral exemplars in moral theorising. Can Mother Teresa not serve as a helpful moral *ideal* although the standard of living she maintained during most of her life is probably not fully attainable for the rest of humankind?

The third approach is that of 'evidential ethical naturalism', according to which moral theorising should, in part, be an *a posteriori* inquiry, richly informed by relevant empirical findings of people's actual moral beliefs, values and behaviours. Moral philosophers must 'court empirical danger by making empirical claims with enough substance to be seriously tested by empirical evidence from psychology' (Doris & Stich, 2003, pp. 115 and 122). Although this would probably be the most widely agreed upon approach in the current academic climate, it is also the most ambiguous one, as evidenced, for instance, by the fact that both defenders and critics of the idea of 'psychologised morality' have found occasion to commend it (see Lapsley & Narvaez, 2008; Maxwell, 2008a, section 1.4). To be sure, moral philosophers need to be informed about and consider existing empirical knowledge; but precisely how and to what extent should they do this?

Maxwell has graciously granted me authorship of a fourth approach: a sub-variety of the third approach, entitled 'neo-Millian evidential ethical naturalism' (Maxwell, 2008b, 2009). Although not claiming originality, I see this approach as an attempt to flesh out and, to a certain extent, operationalise the tenets of evidential ethical naturalism (Kristjánsson, 2006, pp. 13–15). Taking my cue from Aristotle's advice that we need to heed the counsel of the many and the wise, and John Stuart Mill's advice that what matters most in moral inquiry is the verdict of experienced and competent judges (with the best reason for something to be deemed morally desirable being that it is actually desired by such judges), I point out that whatever moral experience and expertise there exists is out there in society. The actuality of a large number of people having converged upon the same moral view does not in and of itself provide a reason for giving that view a constitutive role in the justification of moral principles, for one cannot assume that those 'we' (sadly, more often than not in current psychological research comprising only a subgroup of *homo psychologicus*: first-year psychology students) constitute wise and experienced judges. Nevertheless, one should reject the imperial outlook that philosophers can discover truth by means that are, in principle, unavailable to lay people. In that case, the actuality of a large number of people having converged upon the same moral view, *combined* with the fact that the research into their opinions is conducted in accordance with the best available standards (such as sufficient formal and substantive determination of research design and measure procedures, careful choice of respondents) provides good reason for giving this evidence a justificatory role in moral theorising. Their view may still be wrong, as shown after further scrutiny by philosophers or lay people; but then again, the possible fallibility of all theories (moral, political or otherwise) is no novelty in post-Popperian times. I contend, therefore, that well-designed research into the moral views of ordinary people provides important *triangulating evidence* of the appropriateness of moral theories – evidence that can be overridden only by dint of convincing arguments showing that those views are somehow incoherent or misguided. Conversely, I argue that the requirement of sufficient formal and substantive determination of research design requires psychologists to take account of prior conceptual considerations – more often than not produced by philosophers (Kristjánsson, 2006, chap. 4).

The existence of these four different approaches shows that even for those of broadly naturalist sympathies – be they moral psychologists or philosophers – a host of questions remains. How is empirical evidence to be translated into moral theories, and to what extent should moral precepts inform the design of empirical research in moral psychology? Simply claiming allegiance to 'ethical naturalism' does not alleviate the need of renegotiating the philosophy–psychology boundary. The debate to which I now turn – a debate between proponents of 'psychologised morality' and 'moralised psychology' (all of them proclaimed naturalists) – is a case in point.

3.3. 'Psychologised Morality' versus 'Moralised Psychology'

In a classic display of academic parricide – given Lawrence Kohlberg's paternal standing within the field of moral psychology – Lapsley and Narvaez (2005, 2008) argue that Kohlberg saddled this field with disabling presuppositions: that he unduly 'moralised' psychology instead of 'psychologising' (research into) morality. (Recall my earlier misgivings about the label 'moralised', but let us take it here at face value.) Moral psychologists still carry Kohlbergian millstones around their necks that must now be discarded. More specifically, Lapsley and Narvaez fault Kohlberg for having given moral psychology the *a priori* task of refuting moral relativism, and for what they call his 'phenomenalism': the view that only decisions resulting from cognitive, conscious and rational processes count as moral. 'Phenomenalism' is a strange term to use in this context; the idea they criticise is simply the Kantian-inspired one that for an action to have moral worth (positive or negative), the agent performing it must have done it for a reason available to the agent at that time. The prototype of a *moral* action in the Kantian/Kohlbergian understanding is thus an *intentional* action, which excludes actions derived from subconscious processes, unreflective habituation or 'mere feelings'. (As shown in Chapter 4, such 'phenomenalism' still holds strong appeal for self researchers.)

What Lapsley and Narvaez object to most strenuously is not those particular Kohlbergian aberrations, however, but his general 'moralising' approach to doing psychology, in which all the academic relevance led in one direction: from moral philosophy to moral psychology. First, defining the terms of reference in this philosophical way isolated the new sub-discipline of moral psychology from other domains of psychology and suggested an absurdly narrow delineation of its field of research; second, it made moral psychologists vulnerable to guilt by association ('Your grounding philosophy is wrong, so your empirical research must be faulty'); third, it distorted the mission of psychological inquiry, which should be a scientific enterprise aimed at objective truth.

What Lapsley and Narvaez propose instead is 'psychologised morality', in which *a priori* philosophical constraints have been jettisoned and moral psychology has asserted its autonomy. It thereby realigns itself with and can avail itself of the full range of considerations (tools, theories, methods, findings) from other sub-branches of the science of psychology, including personality and cognitive psychology, evolutionary psychology and the neurosciences.

Lapsley and Narvaez (2008) frequently express their sympathies with the rise of (virtue-ethical) naturalism at the expense of (Kantian) rationalism within moral philosophy, and they claim that proponents of 'psychologised morality' and evidential naturalisms have a great deal to learn from each other. In that case, the authors need to be careful not to fall into the very trap from which they have allegedly tried to spring. Their claim must not be understood to mean that 'psychologised morality' is theoretically dependent upon virtue ethics or other contemporary forms of moral naturalism. Otherwise, it becomes susceptible to a new example of 'guilt by association', in which possible reservations about the underlying philosophy begin to transfer into the psychology. This is not a mere pedantic observation about the need to comply with one's own rhetoric; Augusto Blasi, an earlier critic of Kohlberg's 'moralised psychology' (1990), had barely finished his chastisement of moral psychologists voluntarily handcuffing themselves to philosophy when he began to utilise the ideas of a particular philosopher, Harry Frankfurt, as the very foundation of his own construct of 'moral selfhood' (see, e.g., Blasi, 2005 – I return to Blasi's concerns in Chapter 4).

Faced with the task of showing precisely how 'psychologised morality' renegotiates the boundary between moral psychology and moral philosophy, Lapsley and Narvaez (2008) wax poetical. They attempt a literary reinterpretation of Robert Frost's poem *The Mending Wall*, showing that mending a wall can be a cooperative enterprise in so far as it brings together and thus creates a sense of partnership between people on opposite sides of the fence. Maxwell (2008b) remains unimpressed, and describes Lapsley and Narvaez's intention as simply that of re-erecting the fence that Kohlberg had lowered between the two research cultures. What does Lapsley and Narvaez's depiction of moral psychologists and moral philosophers as fellow fence-menders really mean? As far as the psychologists are concerned, it seems to mean little more than that they are engaged in the same problematic as the philosophers. As for the philosophers, they are strongly advised to assume the same moral position as Lapsley and Narvaez occupy (or would occupy if they did moral philosophy) – namely that of ethical naturalism.

It seems, then, that moral philosophers have more to learn from moral psychologists than vice versa. Indeed, one may wonder if moral psychologists have anything to learn from moral philosophers, as distinct from taking well-earned inspiration from them (namely from those of a naturalist bent). Lapsley and Narvaez (2008) give examples of two philosophical notions – the 'unity of the virtues' and Aristotle's conception of an ideal person – that would run counter to the findings of 'psychologised morality' and had better be abolished. It is not clear in the first example where the potshots are being aimed. If it is at Kohlberg's conception of a single moral virtue, namely justice, then many moral philosophers would agree, although it is difficult to comprehend how pure empirical findings could refute that conception. If, however, by 'the unity of the virtues', Lapsley and Narvaez are referring to Aristotle's well-known thesis, according to which each virtue implies all the others (one cannot have one without having all), then I do not think the charge sticks. It may be possible to understand Aristotle's thesis as implying, unrealistically, that because all their virtues will be in complete mutual harmony, fully virtuous persons will never be caught up in virtue-conflicts or moral dilemmas. But there is a much more charitable understanding of that thesis, according to which it simply means that a person who has acquired *phronesis* (practical moral wisdom) has the wisdom to adjudicate the relative weight of different virtues in conflict situations and to reach a measured verdict – an understanding to which I return in Chapter 8. After all, what Aristotle actually says, when arguing for the inseparability of the virtues, is simply that when one has got *phronesis*, which is a single state, one has 'all the [moral] virtues as well' (1985, p. 171 [1145a1–3]; cf. Kristjánsson, 2007a, chap. 2; Wolf, 2007; cf. my earlier introduction of *phronesis* in Section 1.3). I have yet to see any empirical findings refuting that thesis.

As for Aristotle's notion of an ideally virtuous person, it is far from clear to what extent it is meant as an idealisation, defined with reference to its most fully realisable instance – although perhaps not wholly realised by anyone yet – and to what extent it is a description of actual paragons of moral virtue around us. If it is meant as the former, I wonder why that should bother moral psychologists or moral educators; the fact that the rarified concepts of pure mathematics do not exist in the real world does not seem to bother applied mathematicians. Even if it is meant as the latter, Aristotle describes various ways in which persons of full virtue may act wrongly on occasion (succumbing to overwhelming pressures, acting temporarily out of character, having tiny glitches in their virtues), while still remaining virtuous overall (see Curzer, 2005). So if Lapsley and Narvaez's complaint is that Aristotle's description of the ideally virtuous person falls afoul of Flanagan's principle of 'minimal psychological realism', that complaint most likely misfires. Without becoming unduly mired in Aristotelian exegesis, the counterarguments offered here suffice to show that one must be careful when asserting that philosophical theses have been undermined by empirical evidence – which is not to say that they can never be undermined in that way.

Turning next to two critics of the idea of 'psychologised morality', it is noteworthy that neither of them recommends a return to Kohlbergianism. In so far as Maxwell embraces 'moralised psychology' obliquely and Carr straightforwardly, it is not exactly the same kind of 'moralised psychology' that constitutes the *bête noire* of Lapsley and Narvaez. Maxwell initially puts a damper on the idea of 'psychologised morality' rather than positively renouncing it. Lapsley and Narvaez do not appreciate the full variety of naturalisms that are abroad in contemporary moral theorising, he argues, thereby creating ambiguity with their suggestion of future collaboration between 'psychologised' moral psychologists and moral philosophers of a naturalist orientation (Maxwell, 2008b). Lapsley and Narvaez have recently made it clear (2008) that of the options presented by Maxwell, strong 'evidential ethical naturalism', which reduces moral theory to more fundamental naturalised theories, is closest to their view. How much their answer satisfied Maxwell is a moot point, given the variety of outlooks that exist even within that specific form of naturalism. After all, Lapsley and Narvaez do not flesh out in any detail their vision of the desired collaboration – in particular, what the moral psychologists could possibly gain from it. More critically still, Maxwell wonders if moral psychologists do not do their own discipline disservice by insisting on the mending, rather than the crossing, of fences. 'Complementarity' – the assumption that social science must cut its coat from the theoretical cloth provided by philosophy – is namely, in Maxwell's view, not Kohlberg's original invention, but rather an ineluctable fact of all social science (Maxwell, 2008b). By that contention, Maxwell moves explicitly in the direction of Carr's radically 'moralised' view of social science.

Carr attacks 'psychologised morality' head on by insisting that the most apparent feature of so-called empirically grounded theorising in social science is that it is no less beset by conflict than is philosophical reflection when addressing the same issues. Indeed, it reproduces more or less the same divisions that characterise philosophical treatments, thus providing a (lean) counterpart of, rather than an alternative to, those treatments. In moral psychology, the reason for this state of affairs is obvious: What 'we regard as a matter for moral empirical investigation must [...] depend on what we count (conceptually or normatively or both) as morally significant rather than vice versa'. And because moral philosophers disagree on questions of moral significance, moral psychologists will differ too. Moral naturalism – the claim that moral inquiry should start from empirical facts about human beings – is not an empirical fact, for instance. It is the background claim of a specific normative theory. In that light, the project of naturalising or 'psychologising' morality 'rests on a reductive mistake concerning the relation of ethical theory to moral practice' (Carr, 2007, pp. 391, 398–99, 402). Carr has argued elsewhere that the notions of moral development and moral education are normative (prescriptive) all the way down (2002). His radically 'moralised' view of social science not only 'moralises' moral psychology, therefore, it also reduces pedagogy to a sub-branch of value theory and elevates moral teaching from a chosen educational profession to an ineluctable educational condition. If this makes social scientists the 'under-labourers' (Maxwell, 2009) of moral philosophers – in Carr's view – so be it. They could not possibly avoid that predicament except by becoming full-blown moral philosophers pursuing good old normative inquiry – rather than fooling themselves into thinking that they are engaged in a non-normative enterprise and, consequently, producing at best hollow-ringing platitudes or at worst profusions of confusion on matters of the utmost importance for human wellbeing.

3.4. Self Research as a Test Case

Does moral psychology need moral theory, as Carr's notion of 'moralised psychology' implies, or is Lapsley and Narvaez's description of an academically autonomous 'psychologised morality' a more appropriate characterisation of the desirable subject matter and research orientation of this discipline? Given the subject of this book, I find it reasonable to choose the abundant latter-day research on the self as a test case to adjudicate this question.

At first blush, that choice may seem odd for two reasons. First, most of the psychological self research has been conducted by personality psychologists (narrowly understood) rather than moral psychologists. It does well to remember, however, that once the strict Kohlbergian conception of morality as having to do exclusively with prescriptive 'ought' judgements has been relinquished, the subject matter of moral psychology widens considerably to include, inter alia, assessments of selfhood, character and 'the good life' (see, e.g., Flanagan, 1991, pp. 17–18). This is, indeed, the virtue ethical understanding of morality, with which Lapsley and Narvaez sympathise. It is no coincidence, therefore, that one of the research topics with which Lapsley and Narvaez and many other prominent moral psychologists are currently most concerned is that of the 'moral self'. Although the term 'moral' is used there as (a) an antonym of 'amoral' or 'immoral' rather than (b) an antonym of 'non-moral', it stands to reason that selves cannot count as 'moral' in sense (a) unless they are 'moral' in the general sense (b) – unless they qualify as relevant issues of morality (and hence moral psychology), as opposed to being merely 'non-moral' psychological issues. Although personality psychologists rarely talk about 'self' or 'self-concept' as 'moral' concepts, the preponderance of relevant research has been conducted – as we see in Chapter 5 – with the declared aim of locating correlations to (morally) significant personal, social and educational factors, which clearly brings self research within the province of moral psychology. The second reason for the apparent oddness of choosing self research as a test case is the potential for it to slant the evidence in favour of the empirically oriented proponents of 'psychologised morality' (given that the vast majority of that research is social scientific). Much self research has also been conducted by theoretically oriented philosophers, however – and I am obviously exploring both avenues in this book.

If self research is to provide a window on the problematic of this chapter, the crucial question to explore is this: Does psychological self research possess the kind of academic autonomy from moral philosophy that Lapsley and Narvaez envisage as the ideal for moral psychology, or is this research essentially dependent upon moral theory? The first hurdle to overcome is that term 'moral theory' does not refer to a single literature dealing with the same set subject matter from the same set research perspective. There are moral theories that are (a) theories of *moral genealogy*, critically exploring why certain moral beliefs come about and how they influence or motivate other beliefs; (b) historical theories of *moral beliefs*, mapping logical commonalities and differences between prevailing moral views at different times and places; (c) theories of *moral ontology*, accounting for the existence and nature of moral properties; (d) theories of *moral evaluation* (value theories); and finally for present purposes – this list is by no means exhaustive – (e) theories of *moral 'oughts'* (prescriptive theories). Although most of the historical greats in moral philosophy from Plato and Aristotle onwards have advanced multi-faceted theories encompassing most and sometimes all of these five characteristics (apart from (b), which has been left primarily to historians of ideas), one could say, for instance, that Nietzsche was particularly interested in (a), Hume in (c), Mill in (d) and Kant in (e). Considering these moral theories in turn, I now address the level of autonomy of self research with respect to each of them.

Can psychological self research be understood without recourse to (a) theories of *moral genealogy*? As I mentioned in Chapter 1, psychological self research as we know it today flourished with the advent of humanistic psychology in the 1960s and has blossomed yet further under the aegis of modern-day positive psychology. This is no historical happenstance. The humanistic and later the positive psychological understanding of the self and its trajectory seem to constitute no less than the practical consummation of the Western liberal self-concept (to be analysed further in Chapter 8), which has its origins in Enlightenment times but culminated in the individualisation ideology of late modernity. There is no doubt that Western liberal conceptions of the self and its trajectory has entered the texture of public thought, feeling and conduct. There is no doubt either that they have influenced psychological research into the self. I would go even further and contend that current psychological research into the self is almost exclusively research into the self as understood from this particular historically situated moral perspective. In a series of articles, psychologist Scott Greer has traced the historicity of the self-concept at work in current psychological research and the advent of what he calls 'esteem culture' (Greer 2003a, 2003b, 2007; cf. Martin, 2006; Kristjánsson, 2007, chap. 6; Christopher & Hickinbottom, 2008). Greer argues persuasively in general terms, for the mapping of moral culture as a necessary 'prolegomena' for empirical psychology; and more specifically, for the Zeitgeist history of the self-concept that he delineates. The overemphasis on self-esteem – which has at times even overtaken the whole of self-concept – cannot be understood independent of a moral culture that sees subjective wellbeing as the ultimate goal in life and understands it in terms of 'loving' and 'esteeming' oneself. Hence, also, the scant interest in self-respect, focusing on objective wellbeing (Roland & Foxx, 2003). Psychological measurements of self-esteem are not 'amoral-theoretical' or 'basic-science' constructs, but applications of a particular ethnocentric understanding of what the self is and what it should aim to be.

Further evidence for the moral-genealogy hypothesis about the origin and nature of the notion of 'self-concept' can be extracted from the abundant literature on subjective wellbeing (*SWB*). Christopher (1999) freely acknowledges that *SWB* is based on a particular 'moral vision': that of political liberalism and liberal individualism. Individuals must aim at being 'independent and autonomous beings', and in order to achieve that aim they must be self-contained and find support and emotional resources from within rather than from others. As happiness is equated with *SWB*, the person with the highest self-esteem and the highest proportion of pleasant versus painful emotions is also the happiest person. No wonder, then, that this measure of personal happiness shows the average *SWB* of a nation to be strongly correlated with its degree of individualism. Some psychologists consider the finding that self-esteem is highly correlated with *SWB* in Western liberal democracies to indicate a significant empirical connection (see, e.g., Diener & Diener, 1995). To the average philosopher, this would seem to be an obvious logical connection, however, as the self-report instruments typically used to measure self-esteem on the one hand and *SWB* on the other pinpoint precisely the same personal characteristics.

The answer to (b) – whether self research relies on historical moral theorising about logical connections and disconnections between different *moral beliefs* at different times and places – is contained within the answer to the first question. Yes, it does. Self research in the West relies typically, as already explained, on logical connections between various representations of the prevailing Western liberal self-concept. The term 'self-esteem' was rarely used in the popular media before the 1990s (Furedi, 2004, p. 3). As Charles Taylor correctly notes, the current Western self-discourse is 'a function of a historically limited mode of self-interpretation [...] which has a beginning in time and space and may have an end' (1989, p. 111). In Chapter 8, I compare the Western self-concept to that of Eastern countries (or, for that matter, Western countries today to Western countries before the Enlightenment). People with a more 'collectivist' self-concept do not score as high on *SWB* tests and do not present the same correlation between happiness and self-esteem as do contemporary Westerners. Are we really entitled to interpret those findings to mean, for instance, that Asians are, in general, less happy than Americans? In Eastern countries, happiness tends to be defined more in terms of interpersonal connectedness, and the important goal for the self is to learn to respect, rather than esteem, itself. Emotional harmony is understood as the correct balance of pleasant and painful emotions, not as the uninterrupted flow of pleasant emotions (Uchida, Norasakkunkit & Kitayama, 2004).

The provisional conclusion, which we have now reached – that self research is unavoidably (genealogically and historically) tailored by culture – may not raise too many eyebrows. Philosophers will be quick to point out that such culture specificity does not necessarily imply moral relativism (I do so, for instance, in Chapter 8). Moreover, it has been decades since social scientists realised that their research cannot in any strict sense be value free, in so much as cultural forces and ideological commitments inevitably influence the choice of topics, hypotheses to be tested and the way in which they are tested. 'Hard facts' do not lie unproblematically before our gaze; our interests and values steer the process of discovery. But this does not change the fact that once a research field has been demarcated, the investigation *can* proceed in a value-free manner. Charles Taylor has called this position the 'mitigated positivist view' (1967, p. 27). Its interpretation here could be that although psychological self research has been focused primarily on the Western liberal self and its contours – and hence relies, in an almost trivial sense, in its choice of measurements on genealogical or historical 'moral theories' about what that self is – this is not tantamount to saying that moral psychology is dependent upon moral theory in a more substantive sense.

To proceed further, let us now consider (c): Is moral psychology dependent upon theories of *moral ontology*? Does psychological research on the Western liberal self, for instance, take a stand on controversial ontological issues *within* the Western tradition about what that self is? In Chapter 2, I noted that philosophers as distinct as Aristotle and Hume were realists about the self – either 'hard' or 'soft' – understanding the term to denote the set of actual characteristics that truly make us what we are, whether we are aware of it or not. Most modern-day psychologists exploring selves – as well as some philosophers – turn out not to be interested in this targeted true self, however; most of them do not even believe that such a self exists. This ontological commitment (or rather, perhaps, lack of one) is in no way necessitated by empirical findings. It precedes the findings in the construction of research measurements. That is clearly taking a stand on an ontological question, and a crucial one at that.

Question (d) is whether or not self research relies on theories of *moral evaluation* and is, hence, normative. Does self research merely describe the world of evaluation or does it evaluate the world of description? It should be evident from the preceding considerations that psychologists see self-esteem as a moral aspiration. That is in fact – as becomes pellucid in Chapter 5 – the basis of their interest in the topic. Indeed, the entire literature on self-concept in general and self-esteem in particular is driven by a moral concern. Although shying away from the words 'moral' and 'values', psychologists will admit that high self-esteem is 'positively valenced' and low self-esteem is 'negatively valenced'. There is something *prima facie* 'maladaptive' (here a euphemism for 'morally wrong') with the person whose self-concept is not in order. The finding that someone has low or high self-esteem is thus not essentially a value-free empirical finding. It is a value judgement. It is not even an isolated value judgement, but a judgement that makes sense only against the background of an entire moral theory of individualistic liberalism.

Ending with (e), the question of whether or not moral psychology relies on theories of *moral 'oughts'*, the answer in this case must be more guarded. The self research that I canvass in this book does not normally presuppose any of the prototypical prescriptive moral theories, such as Kantianism or utilitarianism – not even virtue ethics (in so far as it is prescriptive in addition to being evaluative). Psychologists may find a person to have high or low self-esteem without committing themselves or the subject to any particular reaction. It is, after all, according to liberalist ideas, up to individuals what they want to make of their lives. In the Kohlbergian days, when 'moral' was equated with 'prescriptive', this conclusion would have amounted to a rejection of the claim that moral psychology needs moral theory. Nowadays, on the other hand, moral psychologists such as Lapsley and Narvaez subscribe to a much broader specification of the moral. Unfortunately for them, however, that approach makes it more difficult to swallow their claim that moral psychology should focus on 'psychologised morality' rather than 'moralised psychology', and, if the argumentation of the present section holds water, is simply wrong.

I have argued that self research *has* depended upon moral theory, and promise that we shall see ample evidence of that in subsequent chapters. But *must* it so depend? As far as I can see, there would be no *historical or logical point* to self research if not in virtue of 'moral theory' in senses (a) *qua* theory of moral genealogy and (b) *qua* theory of moral beliefs. Moreover, such research could not *get off the ground methodologically* if not for the support of 'moral theory' in senses (c) *qua* theory of moral ontology and (d) *qua* theory of moral evaluation. Far be it from me to be saying that in order to damn the entire field of psychological self research or detract from its scientific value. I am simply saying that, for better or for worse, this is the situation in which self researchers find themselves.

3.5. Moving Forward in Unison

It needs to be acknowledged, I submit, that there cannot be a 'philosophically neutral' or 'value-free' social-science account of the self or of its constitutive elements, any more than there can be a reasonably developed philosophical theory of the self without grounding in the empirical knowledge of the self 'in practice'. Although this book is about the self and, therefore, uses self research as a test case, my previous arguments apply, *mutatis mutandis*, to other research topics that fall broadly within the purview of moral psychology. The stereotypical philosophers' 'pure-theory' fetishism and smug attitudinising ignorance of empirical findings is to be deplored, but so is the stock naivety of some psychologists who seem to think that by looking after the molehills, the mountains will somehow look after themselves. Moral theorising does not hold social science back or undermine its scientific project; rather, it enables it to move forward.

On balance, this conclusion brings me considerably closer to Carr's notion of 'moralised psychology' than to Lapsley and Narvaez's conception of 'psychologised morality'. Moral psychological research does sit atop more fundamental theorising; Kohlberg was right in that moral psychological explanations must be grounded in *philosophical* studies about morality (although not necessarily studies conducted by *philosophers*). Mitigating Carr's radical thought that moral psychology simply *is* moral philosophy, however, are two considerations or caveats. The first is that whereas most of the 'big' theories in moral philosophy involve a prescriptive element, moral psychology is not, and need not be, prescriptive. I think Carr goes too far in his insistence that the 'idea of moral development' is inherently normative in the sense of being *prescriptive*, although it is surely normative in the sense of being *evaluative* (Carr, 2002, p. 17). These two senses of normativity often run together in the literature. Carr, however, is well aware of the difference, as can be seen from his writings, which makes it more difficult to understand why he insists on the stronger claim in the case of moral development.

The second caveat is that psychologists have managed something that should be basically impossible according to Carr's understanding: namely, to self-correct, to deconstruct their own constructs through mere empirical findings. The latest example is the demolition of the notion of 'global self-esteem' as a useful psychological category via meta-analyses of the empirical literature (to be discussed in Chapter 5). In general, I am more sanguine than Carr about the usefulness of a division of labour between those doing the theoretical groundwork and those doing the empirical spadework, and that the spade workers can learn to correct themselves as well as the ground workers, rather than merely taking instructions from them or trying to emulate them. Notice that nothing in what has been said in this chapter revives the particular Kohlbergian ideas about the 'phenomenalism' underlying moral judgement that Lapsley and Narvaez resent, or about the *a priori* task of moral psychology to undermine moral relativism. We do not need the sledgehammer of 'psychologised morality', however, to crack those nuts.

Ludwig Wittgenstein famously talked about the lamentable state of affairs in modern psychology which has 'experimental methods and conceptual confusion': where the practitioners think they have the technical means of solving the problems at hand, but where 'problem and method pass one another by' (1958, p. 232 [II, xiv]). While the advocates of 'psychologised morality' focus on the 'method', the most avid defenders of 'moralised psychology' concentrate on the 'problem'. I have suggested in this chapter that we may be well advised to try to bring the two into line. And that is precisely what I try to achieve in this book.

4. The Emotional Self

4.1. Emotions and Selfhood

Recall the 'Socratic condition' (Section 1.1) that I, as a young under-graduate, decided to place on any decent theory of selfhood: Such a theory must be able to account for the emotional depth and complexity of Socrates' character. According to the 'dominant' self-paradigm that I take to task in this book, emotions are peripheral rather than essential to selfhood. Such an assumption does violate the 'Socratic condition'. Yet it would be premature to reject it out of hand; before advancing my view of the self-relevance of emotions in Section 4.2, I want, at any rate, to consider how this assumption came about.

From the Enlightenment onwards, much of the learned world star-ted to celebrate the 'modern individual' – a secular, scientific, rational, self-interested but self-controlled social actor whose selfhood had been freed of emotion (Reddy, 2009). Nevertheless, at the turn of the twen-tieth century, the pioneers of psychological self research such as James (1890) and Cooley (1902) included self-feelings as salient facets of the self. James made it abundantly clear that the self is not 'cognized only in an intellectual way', but rather that when 'it is found, it is felt' (1890, p. 299). As explained in Chapter 2, however, psychologists have recen-tly tended to equate self with identity and to understand it exclusively as a cognitive construct. That would not necessarily have created a rift between self research and emotion research, except that most psycholo-gists have simultaneously embraced a biological or natural-kind, 'non-cognition-dependent' approach to emotions, or at least to the 'basic' emotions that 'matter most' for our everyday moral life: emotions such as anger, fear, disgust, sadness, happiness and surprise (cf. Bosma & Kunnen, 2001; Tracy & Robins, 2004). According to such an approach, each of the 'basic' emotion concepts 'carves nature at its joints' (to use a Platonic phrase), and manifests itself uniformly across cultures. These emotions constitute natural kinds because each one allegedly has a distinctive pattern of inter-correlated outputs: autonomic nervous system arousal caused by a homeostatic mechanism within the brain, facial expressions and behaviour. As natural kinds, these emotions are believed to form categories with firm boundaries, scientifically discovered but not cognitively constructed by us. Among the popular refrains of current natural-kind theories is that the 'basic' emotions on which the theories focus are 'modular' and 'informationally encapsulated' – that they are controlled by information processing that is rapid, strictly feed-forward, largely unconscious, most likely innate and unsusceptible to direct modification by any higher cognitive processes. Hence, the gaping gulf between emotion and the self.

The natural-kind approach is susceptible to a number of well-known objections, and what follows here is merely a starter kit of problems (see further in Kristjánsson, 2007, chap. 4). (a) *The problem of basicness*: The long tradition in emotion research of trying to identify a group of 'basic' emotions has yielded no unanimous results, probably due in part to the disparate search criteria that relate to such diverse domains as evolutionary history, developmental priority, universality, prevalence, forcefulness and moral significance. The number of 'basic' emotions listed by leading researchers ranges from two to eleven, and a comparison of a number of such lists does not locate a single emotion that figures on all of them (see further in Solomon, 2002). Moreover, strong correlations among the various biologically driven outputs (e.g., neural, facial, behavioural) of the supposedly 'basic' emotions have failed to materialise (b) *The problem of the irrelevance of language:* If emotions are hardwired into our brains at birth, there is no intrinsic role for language in the emergence of 'basic' emotional responses. Language simply creates semantic typologies that may have little relevance to the functioning of the nervous system. Because the 'basic' emotional appraisals are preconscious, linguistic awareness no longer presents, on this account, a vital step in differentiating emotions. These contentions, however, rub up against a whole mountain of philosophical and anthropological research. (c) *The problem of involuntariness:* If the 'basic' emotions are modular, they are, in a strict sense, involuntary, which means that emotion management is a much more restrictive enterprise than recent theories of emotional literacy and schooling suggest.

Some psychologists have been partly won over by objections to a comprehensive natural-kind approach. It has thus become fashionable to assume that there are two types of emotion in human psychology. On the one hand are the pan-cultural 'basic', 'non-cognition-dependent' or 'affect-programme' emotions; and on the other, the cognition-dependent complex emotions, intimately related to people's linguistic repertoires. Among the cognition-dependent emotions – which make up the numbers on the peripheries of current emotion research – are, for instance, the 'self-conscious' emotions such as pride and shame that I discuss in Section 4.3. Incidentally, this distinction bears striking similarity to that made by Hume between the 'direct' and 'indirect' emotions in Books I and II of his *Treatise* (1978), the invocation of which is now considered passé by most philosophers. It is somewhat unfortunate that Tracy and Robins (2004, 2007a, 2007b, 2007c) – the very theorists who have done the most in trying to bridge the gap between self and emotion – uncritically embrace the cognition-dependency versus cognition-independency dichotomy. They concede – unhesitatingly it seems – that the cognition-independency model 'provides an adequate account of basic emotions' (2004, p. 109). Their chief complaint, with which I whole-heartedly agree (cf. also Scheff, 1997, Introduction), that the rift between self research and emotion research has hurt both fields would have been much more powerful if they had not only tried to reinstate a small number of 'non-basic', 'cognition-dependent emotions' as self-relevant, but rather renounced the categorisation of some other emotions as essentially 'basic' and 'cognition-independent'.

Notably, the majority of philosophers reject the notion of fully cognition-independent emotions. The typical philosophical approach of late is to understand *all* emotions as including a cognitive core element (belief, judgement or construal) – or even to be exhausted by their cognitive content. Such a cognitive approach to emotion is not without problems of its own, however, the most widely discussed being the problem of 'emotional recalcitrance': Emotions such as fear (for instance, of spiders) are thus often felt in apparent default of the allegedly necessary cognition, in this case the cognition that spiders are harmful. Philosophers have advanced a number of solutions to this problem, which are outside our present purview (see Kristjánsson, 2002, chap. 1). Another problem, to be laid at the feet of some philosophers, is that of underestimating the affective element of emotions. In response, recall from Section 1.3 Aristotle's middle-ground proposal: that *all* emotions comprise *both* a cognitive and an affective element. It would take me too far afield here to argue for the superiority of this middle-ground approach over the natural-kind approach; I have done so elsewhere (Kristjánsson, 2002, 2006, 2007) and will simply assume as much for the remainder of this discussion (for a recent middle-ground approach, see Barrett, 2006). On the Aristotelian approach, emotions can be felt only by beings possessing at least minimal cognitive capacities (for belief/judgement formation), if not necessarily complex self-beliefs. Even if apes do not possess full-blown selves (see Chapter 1), they could experience the emotion of fear, which involves the belief that a danger is nigh. 'Fears' experienced by lower animals would, however, be understood as mere non-cognitive feelings, not emotions. Because what we are interested in here are self-relevant emotions, however, the focus will be on those emotions that are felt *by*, *in relation to* and *about* selves. In order to do that, we need first to consider when and how selves develop.

4.2. Self-Creation and Emotion

There is obviously no juncture in a child's development at which we can point and say that it is exactly there that the child transforms from a non-self into a self (in the realist understanding from Chapter 2). What developmental psychologists agree about, however, is that children's self-concept (identity or objectified 'Me-self') does not develop until the second half of the second year, when they can demonstrate self-referential behaviour such as seeking and touching dots on their own noses in response to mirror-images as a sign of self-recognition. Similarly, there are normally no autobiographical memories before the age of two. At that age children also seem to begin to have emotions about themselves, such as pride. It is not until much later, however – about the age of 9 or 10 – that they start to distinguish systematically and 'correctly' between pride about a personal achievement for which they consider themselves responsible, and mere joy at a personal achievement based on good luck. In order for an emotion such as pride to emerge, three cognitive processes must be in place: (1) self-awareness, (2) the recognition of external standards of achievement or failure and (3) the adoption of such standards (see Lewis, Sullivan, Stranger & Weiss, 1989; Harter, 1999; Lagattuta & Thompson, 2007).

We cannot have pride coming into being without the self having come into being. But let us now revisit Hume's radical suggestion, invoked at the end of Chapter 2, that we cannot have selfhood without pride, either: that each dynamically presupposes the other (see, e.g., Chazan, 1998, p. 20). This claim is set in the context of Hume's distinction between the substantive self of our 'thought or imagination' (which he dismisses as fictitious) and the moral self 'as it regards our passions or the concern we take in ourselves' (1978, p. 253). The latter cannot, in Hume's view, be fictitious, for – although intellectual understanding may convey little more to us – how can we think of our minds as mere undifferentiated masses of perceptions when we feel an emotion such as pride?

Moral selfhood comes about through an association process, involving the emotion of pride and the corollary of humility, a process that Hume describes as 'the double relation of ideas and impressions' (1978, p. 286). Consider pride in one's beautiful house: The original cause is (1) an idea of a fine house owned by me, which causes a pleasurable impression (2). Through a relation of resemblance (because the house is mine), (2) excites (3) the indirect 'secondary impression' (emotion) pride. Finally, by an 'original quality' of the mind, one's view then becomes fixed upon the object of the emotion, namely (4) the idea of myself (here as a homeowner; 1978, pp. 277–86). The 'double relation' refers to the relation of impression (2), the pleasure caused by something related to me, to impression (3), the pleasant feeling of pride, on the one hand, and the relation of idea (1), my fine house, to idea (4), myself, on the other. Through the mutual reinforcement of those two associations, the attention turns towards myself. Thus, the emotion of pride [(3)] is 'plac'd betwixt two ideas, of which the one produces it [(1)], and the other is produc'd by it [(4)]' (1978, p. 278).

Every modern commentator has some bones to pick with Hume's account. I shall mention three possible bones of contention. *First*, until recently, Hume tended to be depicted in the emotion literature as a pure 'sensory theorist' who identifies emotions solely on the basis of their characteristic 'feel', while remaining stubbornly insensitive to their intentionality and necessary logical conditions. Antony Kenny may be responsible for this interpretation of Hume; his book (1963), which used Hume as a foil, was one of the harbingers of the cognitive turn. Kenny's interpretation was replicated in the introduction to Calhoun and Solomon's widely used classic readings volume (1984, p. 9) and various other sources. Now, admittedly, Hume does think that emotions have characteristic 'feels', but his 'indirect emotions' (most notably pride and humility) have clear intentional objects, to which the elicited emotions direct our view. (For a debunking diagnosis of Kenny's interpretation, see Sutherland, 1976; for the opposite error of offering a purely cognitive interpretation of Hume's indirect emotions, see Davidson, 'Hume's cognitive theory of pride', in 1989.) Kenny's interpretation of Hume as a pure sensory theorist is as skewed as Nussbaum's equally famous and commonly repeated one of Aristotle as a pure cognitive theorist (1996; see Kristjánsson, 2007, p. 19). Nevertheless, it has succeeded in pushing Hume out of the limelight of recent emotion literature.

Second, although the simple-minded depiction of Hume as a sensory theorist is misguided, there is obviously some confusion in Hume's account of pride between its conceptual conditions and what he regarded as its mere causal conditions and consequences. Hume had no inkling of the modern notion of an emotion's 'propositional content' or 'formal object'. For our present purposes, however, this confusion can be ignored with impunity.

Third, we must bear in mind that Hume typically expands or contracts the usual meanings of terms, thus giving them special technical uses. For today's psychologists and philosophers of a practical bent, such uses are a turn-off. Take Hume's 'pride', which comprises any favourable evaluation of oneself, including what we would now call '(high) self-esteem' and 'self-confidence'. Eminent Hume scholar Páll Árdal suggests that even though Hume's account of pride throws some light upon what is commonly called pride, this was not his real purpose (1989, p. 387) – a fact which threatens to compromise its current market value. Something similar could be said for Hume's notion of 'humility', which refers to all unfavourable self-evaluations, and incorporates under its rubric terms as distinct as 'humility', 'shame' and 'low self-esteem'.

I aim to overlook these shortcomings as far as possible in Hume's account, in order to concentrate on its central message: *that emotions are essential to the creation and sustenance of selfhood*. Recently, some attempts have been made in psychological circles to rebrand the Humean idea of emotion-grounded self-creation, albeit in a watered-down form as a genealogical link between emotion and mere identity (self-concept) formation (see various articles in Bosma & Kunnen, 2001; Vleioras, 2005). My 'alternative' self-paradigm goes further, to stipulate that emotions are intimately related to selfhood in a realist sense (as actual full selfhood) via three distinct, if partly overlapping, categories of *self-relevant* emotions.

First in line are the *self-constituting* emotions: emotions that define who we are. In the commonsense view of the self (fleshed out in Chapter 2) any emotion can, in principle, be self-constituting for given individuals, as long as it represents or instantiates some of their core commitments, traits, aspirations or ideals. For Person X, compassion with the victims of world poverty may be such an emotion; for Person Y, begrudging spite: pain at other people's deserved good fortune. I take it to be an incontrovertible empirical fact, known from everyday experience, that all people possess a number of self-shaping emotions of this sort, and if they stop experiencing them, they will have undergone a radical self-change (see Chapter 10). But they also possess a number of emotions that are not self-constituting: I feel excited when I listen to a certain pop song today, but I may have grown tired of it tomorrow, and I possess the same self although my emotional reaction to the song has dwindled. There is a proper place for undemanding, if sometimes powerful, emotions of that kind in human psychology: shallow emotions of casual delights and idle diversions (see Pugmire, 2005, chap. 2). So although all emotions are in a platitudinous sense 'self-related', simply because they are *felt by* the self, not all are profound enough to be self-constituting. By acknowledging the existence of self-constituting emotions, one is not committed to the view that the self comprises nothing but emotions. Emotions are not the whole story of selfhood, but they constitute a significant aspect of that story (cf. Scheff, 1997).

Second, some emotions are *self-comparative*; they involve the self as an indirect object – a reference point. All emotions include a comparative element: comparison with a baseline of expectations. One cannot, for instance, feel begrudging spite towards a person without having an idea of the lot that similar persons could expect in similar circumstances. My begrudging spite need not include any comparisons with myself, however; I may simply grudge the fortune of other persons and would prefer that the fortune be taken away from them. If begrudging spite turns self-comparative, it typically develops into another emotion, namely envy. This is not to say that begrudging spite is not often elicited by envy or that the two do not frequently co-occur; what I am noting is simply that begrudging spite is not, whereas envy is, necessarily self-comparative. I have elsewhere identified and explored a number of such salient self-comparative emotions as reactions to one's own deserved or undeserved fortune or misfortune (Kristjánsson, 2006, chap. 3.3).

Third, and most intimately connected to the self, are the *self-conscious* emotions, first indentified by Hume as 'pride' and 'humility'. 'Self-conscious emotions' is not a felicitous label ('self-reflexive emotions' is another less commonly used term, and Keshen, 1996, prefers to talk about 'self-esteem feelings'), although I shall not break with tradition by coining a new one. Those emotions not only involve *consciousness of* the self; they are – to use the language of intentionality – *about* the self. The self is, in other words, their direct attentional and intentional object: The self is not only *the* stage; it is *on* stage. Yet those emotions are simultaneously 'in' the self 'about' which they are – a fact that helps dissolve the regress problem of self-knowledge (concerning the relationship between self-concept and self) that was raised in Section 2.2.

As an aside, when we say in ordinary language that 'Mary is too self-conscious', we do not necessarily mean that Mary is experiencing here and now many or excessively strong self-conscious emotions, but rather that she takes herself too seriously, is afraid of making mistakes and of letting herself go. Such a person could perhaps be described as one fearful of being hit by painful self-conscious emotions before she really experiences them. Another way of characterising this situation would be to say there really is a self-conscious emotion at work there (namely shame) in a dispositional rather than an episodic sense. We can assume that Mary possesses a strong disposition to experience shame, and then when she encounters a potentially shame-inducing situation, this disposition acts on her in a forward-looking way – rather than through the ordinary backward-looking 'post mortem' shame – as a deterrent to engage in shameful activities.

Now, there are discordant views as to precisely how many self-conscious emotions there are and how they should be individuated. Hume made do with his famous two; contemporary listings tend to include at least guilt, shame and embarrassment on the negative side and pride (commonly divided into 'hubristic' and 'achievement-oriented' pride) on the positive side. Although I take a stand in this debate later in this chapter, I would like to reiterate at the outset the Aristotelian point from Section 1.3 that all such conceptual regimentations will by necessity be normative, and subject to philosophical rather than pure empirical considerations.

4.3. The Self-Conscious Emotions

Tracy and Robins (2004, 2007a, 2007b, 2007c), along with a number of other contemporary theorists, have done well to alert self researchers to the role that self-conscious emotions play in the creation and maintenance of selfhood, thus counteracting the narrow cognitive focus of the 'dominant' self-paradigm. I believe that these theorists should have gone much further in 'emotionalising' the self, however, by considering the other categories of self-relevant emotions and by offering more radical alternatives – be they Aristotelian, Humean or of some other respectable theoretical provenance – to the assumptions behind current self research, on the one hand, and current emotion research, on the other. In a move that smacks of strategic retreat, Tracy and Robins (2007b, p. 199) even cite recent findings of transculturally recognised nonverbal expressions of some self-conscious emotions as crucial evidence that they should be seriously considered as universal emotions. The underlying concern seems to be that unless such 'hard facts' can be produced, the scientific value of emotion research is somehow compromised.

Regrettable as is the neglect of other self-relevant emotions in recent literature, the self-conscious ones are admittedly most intimately related to the self. They are not only constitutive of or comparative with respect to the self, but actually about it, and thus deserve the special attention that has been given to them by previous theorists and will continue to be given to them here. Self-conscious emotions are evoked when persons believe or judge themselves to have lived up to or failed to live up to some ideal self-goal (expected, desired or morally required). Pleasant self-conscious emotions indicate self-goal congruence; painful ones indicate self-goal incongruence. Tracy and Robins (2004) talk about identity-goals rather than self-goals, but for self-realists, the common existence of, for instance, repressed shame (see Scheff, 1997) indicates that incongruence often takes effect even when there is no apparent incongruence between one's achievements and one's explicit identity. As noted earlier, lists of self-conscious emotions do not concur. Some of them include emotions such as nostalgia and humiliation (see Tracy and Robbins, 2007b, p. 202, note 2), even self-anger – but I focus here on the paradigmatic emotions, most often covered in the literature. And where better to start than with Hume's favourite emotion: pride.

In its simplest form, *pride* involves our self-satisfaction from having achieved something that we consider worth achieving, with at least part of the responsibility for the achievement being deemed by us to be attributable to ourselves. It is also possible to feel pride vicariously because of the achievement of some significant other(s) as long as one considers oneself to have contributed to the achievement in some way. Strangely enough, we do not have a term in English for pride in its dispositional form – a word akin to 'compassionate', which describes a person who experiences the emotion of compassion frequently and intensely. 'Prideful' may seem to be a candidate here, but its scope is wider than that of a mere dispositional counterpart of simple pride. Prideful persons are not only regularly proud; they are in general concerned with their self-image; they also – like Aristotle's great-minded *megalopsychoi* – expect recognition of their achievements from others. They are prone to frequent experiences not only of pride, but also of shame, if they fail to live up to their own expectations (see Kristjánsson, 2002, chap. 3). When we say that someone is 'a proud person', we normally mean 'prideful' in this sense; 'proud' there does not denote merely the dispositional version of simple pride. (Another candidate for that version would, however, be 'high self-esteem'; but I am shelving that possibility until Chapter 5.) To complicate matters more, there is a common locution in everyday language in which 'pride' denotes neither simple pride nor pridefulness, but rather self-respect (see Chapter 7), such as in 'Pride prevented him from doing that vile thing'. In the Aristotelian schema, persons who are regularly proud of the right things at the right times (whatever we should call their condition in English) succeed in hitting the golden mean of the emotion: a medial state flanked by the excesses of vanity, conceit, arrogance or hubris on one side, and the deficiencies of pusillanimity or humility on the other.

A consensus has been emerging in the recent literature on self-conscious emotions to the effect that a distinction needs to be made between two emotions of simple pride: pride in one's behaviour ('achievement-oriented' pride) and pride in one's general personal characteristics ('hubristic pride') – mirroring a similar (if contestable) distinction between (specific) guilt and (general) shame. The former type of pride allegedly results from internal, unstable, controllable, specific attributions of the 'I-am-proud-of-what-I-*did*' kind, but the latter from internal, stable, uncontrollable, global attributions of 'I-am-proud-of-who-I-*am*'. The underlying assumption is that whereas achievement-oriented pride is 'authentic' and 'adaptive', hubristic pride is 'inauthentic', and leads to narcissistic self-aggrandisement (Lewis, 2000; Leary, 2007a; Tracy & Robins, 2004, 2007b, 2007c).

Tracy and Robins claim that this distinction has found 'empirical support' (2007c, p. 267). Nevertheless, I have a number of misgivings about it; indeed so many that it is difficult to know where to start. *First*, these authors are self-declaredly pursuing a cognitive inquiry into emotions. Although they retain – wrongly, in my view – their blissful confidence in the existence of cognition-independent 'basic' emotions, they do not consider the self-conscious emotions to belong to that category. Now, to individuate emotions cognitively is a tricky business. One runs the risk of ending up with an uncontrollable proliferation of emotions: 'angling indignation' (the indignation of an angler seeing inferior anglers around him catching all the fish) being cognitively distinct from 'lost-tennis-match indignation' and so forth. To stem this tide, it is best to start with the emotions acknowledged in ordinary language – which has, after all, had centuries to identify and polish relevant distinction – and to depart only from the ordinary-language categorisations if one has found overwhelmingly good reasons to do so: reasons having to do with, say, conceptual clarity or economy. More specifically, giving good reasons will mean demarcating a sphere of human experience that is prominent enough to count as independent from other spheres: a general sphere in or about which people characteristically feel certain things. We thus need nothing less than to establish normatively the relevant spheres of human experience. Furthermore, the Aristotelian advice here (recall Section 1.3) is to define emotion words such that no emotional disposition in its ideal actualisation, but only its extremes of excess or deficiency, is expendable from human life. Various empirical considerations about the nature of human life will guide us on this journey, but the project of emotion individuation is, in the end, irreducibly normative. No analyses of respondents' narratives or responses to questionnaires can adjudicate whether or not one is dealing with varieties of a single emotion or two distinct emotions. Conceptual inquiries are not exercises in practical linguistics, although they must take actual language use as their starting point.

At this point I give what I take to be 'good reasons' to question the conceptualisation of two emotions of simple pride ('achievement-oriented' versus 'hubristic'), a conceptualisation that does not have a home in ordinary language. It seems to me that the emotion researchers in question have hit upon two distinguishing criteria: *scope* and *moral worth*: Some instances of pride have more scope than others; they are about one's global achievements or characteristics rather than about specific attainments. Some self-attributions of pride are morally justified (or, as some like to put it, 'adaptive'); others are morally unjustified (or 'maladaptive'). It is reasonable to suppose that the two criteria are empirically connected, in that global achievement attributions are more likely, given the frailties of human nature, to be unjustified than specific ones. There is, however, no conceptual link between the two; a select group of people (say, Aristotle's *megalopsychoi*) can afford to make global attributions of achievement about themselves because they are, in fact, paragons of moral virtue and all around worthy of great things. For most of us, such attributions will, in contrast, count as hubristic. Specific achievement attributions can also be excessive and hubristic, however. I may indulge in hubristic vainglory about winning a talent show, forgetting entirely that I won mainly because all my mates turned up and voted for me. All in all, it seems to me that pride researchers have committed a version of what D'Arms and Jacobson (2000) have termed the 'moralistic fallacy': the fallacy of confusing the moral conditions of an emotion with its representational fittingness conditions. The difference between 'achievement-oriented' pride and 'hubristic' pride seems simply to be that between pride being morally and immorally felt, spiced up with the observation that the more globalised positive self-attributions are, the less likely they are to be morally well grounded.

Turning now to the painful self-conscious emotions, there used to be a time in anthropological quarters when much was made of a distinction between the emotions of shame and guilt, reflected in no less than two fundamental types of societies: *shame societies* and *guilt societies*. The former were supposedly characterised by heteronomy: avoidance of wrongful action for fear of being found out and ridiculed by others, the reaction of running or hiding away, if caught. The latter were characterised by autonomy: avoidance caused by one's own sense of guilt, the reaction of self-loathing and of wanting to compensate one's victims, should one have fallen into temptation. The idea seemed to be that in shame, one's assessment of failure is merely external; whereas in guilt, it is purely internal – concerned only with the subject's own norms and evaluations without regard for the verdict of a detached observer or the gaze of an external audience. It is initially tempting to consider guilt an independent emotion distinct from shame, and it is certainly possible to envisage people experiencing some sort of shame which does not involve guilt. The conceptual allure of the Kantian distinction between autonomy and heteronomy, reflected in the guilt–shame dichotomy, has recently been waning, however. Furthermore, a close empirical look at actual uses of the term 'shame', even in paradigmatic 'shame societies' such as those of ancient Greece or medieval Iceland, reveals that the emotion of shame is, indeed, taken to include guilt as a sub-class

(Williams, 1993; Kristjánsson, 1998). If there ever was one philosophical book that undermined an entire social scientific theory, it is surely Williams's deconstruction (1993) of the strict shame–guilt dichotomy in relation to ancient and 'heroic' societies.

The shame–guilt distinction has been resurrected in recent literature on self-conscious emotions. Replicating the (misguided) achievement-versus-hubris distinction in the case of pride, the assumption is that internal, stable, uncontrollable and global attributions, like '*I* am a dumb person', lead to shame; whereas unstable, controllable and specific behaviour-related attributions, like 'I *did* not try hard enough', lead to guilt (Tracy & Robins, 2007a, p. 13). In this account, shame is a more painful emotion because one's core selfhood, not only the self's specific behaviour, is at stake (see Tangney, Stuewig & Mashek, 2007, p. 26).

The first thing speaking against this distinction is that it violates ordinary language. It is common in everyday language, popular literature and soap operas to see people lamenting about the global guilt they feel for having spent their whole lives failing to appreciate the people who really love them, or to hear them saying how ashamed they are of some inappropriate gesture or remark which slipped through their defence barriers at an awkward moment. One can thus feel guilty about general aspects of one's emotional make-up and ashamed over specific behaviours. (I wonder why Teroni & Deonna, in their otherwise insightful critique of the current consensus, still insist that guilt has 'some behavior as particular object', 2008, p. 736.) It is plausible to suppose that a painful emotion is more painful when it challenges the totality of one's selfhood rather than one aspect of it, but I am at a loss to understand why this difference should correspond with the difference between shame and guilt, given how pervasive and all-embracing guilt can be. Moreover, as the standard description of guilt considers it less painful and general than shame, one would think that it formed less enduring affective states. The opposite seems to be true, however. Guilt, once triggered, weighs on one and becomes typically such an enduring affective state that some theorists have even questioned if it can rightly be termed an episodic emotion (see, e.g., Mulligan, 2009). If the focus is on mere specificity as distinct from generality, then ordinary language suggests the emotion of *embarrassment*, which is typically elicited by minor specific breaches of norms (attributed to either internal or external causes) that are thought to diminish temporarily my standing in the eyes of others or myself (see, e.g., Gasper & Robinson, 2004, p. 147).

Perhaps there are good reasons for departing from ordinary language here, but I have yet to see them. In the meantime, a more productive avenue may have been suggested by Higgins's (1987) taxonomy of cases of actual-self versus ideal-self incongruence, in which the ideal self can be an 'ought'-self or not. It is perfectly in line with ordinary language to understand guilt as the kind of shame elicited when moral standards have been violated (cf. Teroni & Deonna's distinction between shame as the violation of 'values' and guilt as the violation of 'norms', 2008). Indeed, Mulligan (2009) considers guilt to be the prototypical 'moral' emotion: an emotion which is essentially moral by virtue of its objects. If we understand guilt as a moral subclass of shame – corresponding to the fact that moral norms are a subclass of general values – a statement such as 'I felt more guilty than ashamed' should not be taken to mean that shame was not felt, but that its focus was more on those elements which accompany guilt (moral breach, reparation) than on other common elements of shame, in the same way as the statement 'it tasted more creamy than milky' is not to be understood as a rejection of the fact that cream is also a milk product. Nevertheless, there is an important distinction to be drawn between cream and other milk products (see further in Kristjánsson, 2002, chap. 3). Just as there are emotions which are compounds of other more 'basic' (in a generic sense) emotions – for instance jealousy a compound of envy, anger and indignation (Kristjánsson, 2002, chap. 5) – so one emotion (here guilt) can involve a cognitive sharpening of another (here shame). Incidentally, one may wonder why a similar subordination does not exist in the case of pride, with a special emotion term being designated for cases of internally attributed self-satisfaction with specific *moral* attainments. (The proper pride felt by Aristotle's *megalopsychoi* is, for instance, exclusively of that kind.) The explanation may simply be that we have, generally speaking, a more nuanced emotional vocabulary to describe painful emotions than pleasant ones – a fact that evolutionary psychologists describe as an obvious adaptive defence mechanism. There are, it seems, fifty ways to feel bad for every one to feel good!

It is easy to get bogged down in the minutiae of emotion individuation, much of which would be outside the remit of the present work. For reasons of conceptual economy, I think it is helpful to divide the self-conscious emotions first into feelings of self-enhancement and self-diminution (cf. Keshen, 1996), and then each of these two into emotions that do or do not attribute responsibility to the self. That would leave us with four main self-conscious episodic emotions, which all have reasonably firm grounding in ordinary language: *pride* (pleasurable self-enhancement feeling relating to a positive outcome for which I am responsible, such as passing a difficult exam), *self-satisfaction* (pleasurable self-enhancement feeling relating to a positive outcome for which I am not responsible, such as being born handsome), *shame* (painful self-diminution feeling relating to a negative outcome for which I am responsible, such as failing an exam), and *self-disappointment* (painful self-diminution feeling relating to an outcome for which I am not responsible, such as being born ugly). *Guilt* would then be understood as a specific type of shame in which the responsibility for the negative outcome concerns the breach of moral standards, and *embarrassment* as a relatively minor specific occurrence of either shame or self-disappointment.

Too much intellectual energy may have been spent recently in carving out the exact boundaries between vaguely different emotional manifestations of emotional self-diminution and self-enhancement. What matters more, for present purposes at least, is the relevance of self-relevant emotions in general and the self-conscious ones in particular for the 'alternative' self-paradigm that I have been proposing. I have already reviewed Hume's radical suggestion about how self-conscious emotions are not only constitutive of the (moral) self and about that self but are actually responsible for its creation in the first place. Hume's point is that the experience of pride leads us to 'think of our own qualities and circumstances' and gradually produces a self of 'merit and character' (1978, pp. 287 and 303). Some of the details of this causal history can be questioned, as can aspects of Hume's emotion theory in general (see earlier). Less questionable is the *moral role* that those emotions play in Hume's theory: The constant habit of surveying ourselves through the self-conscious emotions, 'begets', in Hume's words 'in noble creatures, a certain reverence for themselves, as well as others, which is the surest guardian of every virtue' (1972, p. 276). This view is echoed in current emotion theory through the claim that because of their self-reflective and self-evaluative functions, the self-conscious emotions 'play a central role in motivating and regulating almost all of people's thoughts, feelings, and behaviors' (Tracy & Robins, 2007a, p. 3). Selfhood as we know it without those emotions is simply inconceivable. It is not only, as Cooley once put it, that the human being has a self 'about which his passions cluster' (1902, p. 216), like planets around the sun; emotions are an integral part of that very self – that very sun.

In Aristotle's moral system, pride plays no less important a moral role than it does for Hume, although it enters there more as a moral consequent than an antecedent. The *megalopsychoi* are not fully mature morally unless they take due pride in their moral attainments. Moreover – and more controversially – Aristotle wants them to be prideful: acutely sensitive to the recognition accorded to them by others, and comporting themselves with an aura of aristocratic grace (for clarifications and a modified defence, see Kristjánsson, 2002, chap. 4). Aristotle also considers shamefulness (which for him includes what we would nowadays call 'moral guilt') a suitable virtue for young moral learners, one that restrains them when they go astray. He believes, however, that its educative value diminishes with age; and it is no longer a virtue for the *megalopsychoi* because (ideally) they are not prone to wrongdoings (Aristotle, 1985, p. 115 [1128b16–20]). Replicating Humean and Aristotelian points about the moral value of pride – and backing them up with recent empirical evidence – Hart and Matsuba (2007) argue convincingly that pride sustains commitment to long-term moral action, and that this emotion is intimately linked to selfhood and volition from childhood onwards. More sanguine than Aristotle about the lasting effect and value of shame, Thomas Scheff (1997) hypothesises that shame is a human 'master emotion', one that is anticipated in virtually all human contact, albeit often repressed or hidden from the subject's own view. Shame is, in Scheff's view, crucial in social interaction because it ties together the individual and social aspects of human activity. As an emotion within individuals, it plays a central role in moral consciousness. But it also functions as signal of distance between persons, allowing us to regulate how close or far we are from others. Although Scheff concentrates on shame, it seems that most of his argument could be applied, *mutatis mutandis*, to the other self-conscious emotions as well.

When discussing the moral role of the self-conscious emotions, one must not forget that some emotions incorporate promptings towards a change of self: self-improvement, whether radical (as in psychotherapy) or moderate. Shame, and especially its moral sub-emotion, guilt, is surely among those improvement-directed emotions. What we see there is a comparison of actual with an ideal self, and hence a prompting for change towards this ideal. Pride may not encourage self-change, but at least it guards the self that we have through the 'reverence for ourselves' that in inspires in us. I discuss self-change and self-education in Chapter 10, and there we see how self-improvement can be motivated and achieved only by and through emotion.

When contemporary emotion researchers focus on what they call 'moral emotions', they typically restrict their attention to empathy or sympathy (and do not even deem those emotions fully moral unless somehow bonded to and guided by justice; witness Section 4.4). As Hart and Matsuba have clearly shown – by drawing on classical philosophers and contemporary psychological research, thin as it may yet be – this focus must be expanded substantially to include self-conscious emotions (and, I would add, all self-relevant emotions). People who are able to feel pride when performing moral actions and to feel shame/guilt when acting/reacting immorally are appropriately attuned to moral standards, and likely to be committed to them in the future (Hart & Matsuba, 2007, p. 130). Those emotions therefore represent fertile territory for future research: philosophical, psychological and, I venture to hope, interdisciplinary.

4.4. The 'Gappiness Problem'

What are the practical implications of the 'alternative' paradigm's view of selves as imbued with emotion? In this section and the following one, I show how the idea of an emotional self, an idea derived from the philosophical and psychological sources reviewed in the previous section, helps shed light on – and perhaps even resolves – recurring problems in two current discourses within moral psychology. One is the so-called 'gappiness problem'; the other concerns recent attempts at a post-Kohlbergian 'integrative model' of moral selfhood.

To start with the 'gappiness problem', a brief historical context setting is in order: The avowed goal of moral education has, from earliest times, been to provide students with motivation to act morally. From the days of Plato and Aristotle, the dominant consensus was that this goal would best be attained through the cultivation of moral virtues either gleaned from a conception of human nature or given by divine command. Despite the setback that these two sources of moral inspiration suffered during Enlightenment times (vividly portrayed in MacIntyre, 1981), moral education as practised in school settings seems to have remained essentially virtue-based until the middle of the twentieth century, when it took its notorious Kohlbergian turn. Sparked by his Kantian formalism and reliance on methodologically contentious empirical tests from the 1920s, which seemed to indicate that children's 'moral virtues' were inherently malleable and situation-dependent (discussed further in Chapter 6), Kohlberg initiated an ambitious research project with far-reaching psychological and educational implications. The latter pointed to the honing of students' critical reasoning faculties – especially through engagement with moral dilemmas – as the ideal method for moral education.

The Kohlbergian project was undone partly by its methodology, which equated an individual's moral maturity with the ability to offer solutions to far-fetched dilemmas, and partly by its ambition of supposing, *à la* Socrates, that people would act morally as a simple consequence of knowing how to act morally or merely of knowing how to articulate convincing moral judgements. Enter Augusto Blasi, who in 1980 published his much-cited meta-analysis of empirical studies that gauged the relationship between moral reasoning and moral behaviour. What Blasi found was that moral reasoning plays at best a modest role in motivating moral action (Blasi, 1980; cf. Walker, 2004). To take a classic example, Germans were not suddenly and miraculously relegated to a low stage of moral reasoning during the period surrounding World War II; yet a large portion of people from this highly developed and well-educated nation acted in ways that in retrospect appear to be the very paradigm of immorality. Thus, a 'moral gap' had been identified between cognition and action that theorists – including Blasi himself – have been trying to bridge ever since. The two most common intermediaries suggested to bridge young people's 'moral gappiness' and motivate them to 'act well' are the construction of *moral selfhood*, on the one hand (see, e.g., Blasi, 1993), and the cultivation of *moral emotions*, on the other (see, e.g., Montada, 1993; Hoffman, 2000). Philosophically minded readers should not confuse this psychological 'moral gap' with the gap commonly identified by moral externalists in their critique of moral internalism. The debate canvassed below thus does not coincide with the debate on whether or not moral judgement is necessarily motivating (*à la* moral internalism) or not (*à la* moral externalism). Although both parties to the debate explicitly reject radical internalism of the Socratic or Kantian types, it is not clear from the discussion whether they support moral externalism (that moral cognitions do not motivate without the addition of an extra factor) or some weaker form of internalism (that moral cognitions are intrinsically motivating but that, without the addition of an extra factor, those motivations are typically overridden by other considerations).

As fervent debates rage in moral psychology between moral-selfhood theorists and moral-emotion theorists, moral educators in the classroom or the home have every reason to feel bewildered. Should they emphasise moral virtues, moral reasoning skills, moral self-formation or moral emotions? Leo Montada (1993) advocates the *moral-emotions* solution to the gappiness problem. He notes that even when no gap seems to exist – when people score high in Kohlbergian tests on issue x and do happen to follow moral norms in handling x – a gap may still exist, for the norm-abiding behaviour may be motivated by technical or tactical, as opposed to moral, reasons. More salient are the agent's emotional reactions to norm-deviations: reactions such as guilt, shame or *Schadenfreude*. Montada understands emotions cognitively as 'predictable and understandable evaluative responses' (1993, p. 295) and claims that, by focusing on the presence or absence of such responses, researchers can inductively identify a person's operative moral rules. Montada's approach is – from my own perspective – agreeably Aristotelian (see Chapter 6), and contains various promising suggestions for future research. None of those suggestions, however, is worked out in much detail in Montada's article; nor does he take time to consider the educational repercussions of his approach.

Martin L. Hoffman (2000) offers a more detailed account of the role of emotions in (developmental) moral psychology. His work is also rife with practical tips for moral educators on how to stimulate emotional growth in children from an early age. Hoffman focuses on a single emotion – sympathy (originally growing out of a child's propensity for empathy and, somewhat confusedly in Hoffman's writings, termed 'empathy') – as the source of moral motivation. Children gradually accommodate as well the cool abstract principle of justice, however, which is needed for society's successful workings. The resulting concurrence of hot affect and cool principle 'creates a bond between them', a bond that, if all goes well, is strengthened by future concurrences. Thus, the sympathy-justice bond transforms justice into an emotionally charged 'hot cognition' with motivational force (Hoffman, 2000, pp. 14–15; chap. 9). Strangely enough, Hoffman fails to notice that the 'hotness' of justice may not derive from its bond with sympathy, but rather from specific justice-based emotions. Thus, Hoffman's rationalist view of justice blinds him to the fact that what is most plausibly set in motion when sympathy begins to interact with justice is a process of balances and trade-offs among different emotions, not the process of an emotion giving motivational force to an abstract principle (see my critique of Hoffman in Kristjánsson, 2006, chap. 4). Although Hoffman does not, in the end, trust 'pure' emotions to do the complete motivational job for him, he still counts as a notable representative of the idea that moral emotions bridge the gap between moral cognition and moral action.

More widely discussed in recent years than the moral-emotion solution to the gappiness problem is the *moral-self* solution, in particular Blasi's version of it. Blasi criticises the moral-emotion solution on a number of scores. A moral action must, in Blasi's view, be one for which the agent can be held responsible; in accordance with everyday intuitions this means that it must be intentional and conscious and must incorporate moral reasons. This fact is nothing less than the very objective foundation on which morality stands. He concedes that emotions do tend to elicit, direct and sustain behaviour. He refuses to acknowledge, however, that they can power a specifically *moral* engine. Emotions produce actions unintentionally (always) and unconsciously (often) and they presuppose (at best) rather than incorporate moral reasons. The reason is that emotions – which Blasi understands as psychological processes connected to bodily events – arise spontaneously and unintentionally and produce an 'automatic' readiness to act or to refrain from acting. Cognitive accounts of emotion that reject the essential involuntariness of emotions are 'ultimately unconvincing' because they 'contradict the most basic common understanding and experience' of what emotions are (1999, pp. 8–13).

Instead of moral emotions, Blasi suggests the construction of a moral self as the central explanatory concept in moral functioning: the missing link between cognition and action. He assumes that people have both a moral system and an identity system that initially develop independently, but which may or may not become integrated later (see Hardy & Carlo, 2005, p. 238). People with an integrated moral self-system have moral concerns rooted at the very core of their identity, a core to which all other concerns are subordinated. Philosophers who concentrate exclusively on the interpersonal aspects of morality often miss this intrapsychic fact (Blasi, 1993; cf. Walker, 2004). Although Blasi chastises philosophers for their damaging influence on moral psychology, he has no compunctions about enlisting the aid of a particular philosopher, Harry Frankfurt. When couched in Frankfurt's terms, Blasi's 'moral self-identity' signals the presence of a strong second-order volition for moral first-order desires to be operative (Blasi, 1999, p. 11; 2004, p. 342). Real integration between moral cognition and moral action is achieved only when one's moral understandings and concerns have become part of one's sense of selfhood: a selfhood thereby constructed under the influence of moral reasons. Acting against such a self-identity would represent unacceptable self-betrayal or even self-loss. At the same time, some people – the Paris Hiltons, not to mention the Hannibal Lecters, of this world – allow different concerns to define the central features of their self-conceptions. How does one know if a person possesses moral selfhood? One knows by gauging it through self-reports of the subject's core commitments in life, and by finding correlations between those reports and the individual's moral behaviour.

To the obvious Aristotelian-cum-Humean point that moral agency cannot be considered a contingent part of a person's selfhood – that everyone has necessarily, if you like, some sort of permeating moral selfhood – Blasi would respond that his term 'moral' is meant as an antonym of 'amoral' or 'immoral' rather than 'non-moral'. The idea is not that some people possess morally irrelevant selves, but rather that some individuals decide, while others do not, to let moral concerns represent a fulfilment of something central to them: their mainstay or ballast in life. For present purposes, it should be noted that such existential decisions do not take place until adolescence at the earliest, which firmly moves the spotlight of moral education from Aristotelian early-childhood emotion education to a later, more reflective, developmental stage.

Blasi is not the only advocate of the moral-self solution, although he has done more than anyone else to popularise it. Colby and Damon's (1992) case studies of morally exemplary adults from various walks of life also indicate that what distinguishes such persons from others is not so much their level of moral cognition as it is their willingness to place moral concerns at the core of their selfhood and to pursue these concerns with feverish but apparently effortless persistence. Those individuals see no inherent contradiction between their own interests and their moral goals because they have made the two synonymous (1992, p. 300).

As Roger Bergman puts it, Colby and Damon are on the same wavelength as Blasi: 'The integration of morality and personality is the key' (2004, p. 33) – the key not to an *aspect* of selfhood but to the *essence* of selfhood. Damon has since become involved in a longitudinal study aimed at providing answers to questions of how a 'sense of purpose' contributes to young people's lives. To ascertain, then, if those contributions are moral or immoral, the psychologist is forced to make blatantly normative distinctions between 'noble' and 'ignoble' purposes (Stanford Center on Adolescence, 2003). Another study of exemplary youths – inner-city adolescents involved in voluntarily chosen community service – yields results similar to those of the Colby and Damon study: The youths turn out to be 'exemplary' not in terms of a Kohlbergian moral-cognition framework, but rather to the extent that their self-conceptions and self-attributions incorporate moral concerns more prominently than those of comparison teens (Hart & Fegley, 1995).

These qualitative case studies draw on small samples. More generally, results of empirical studies of moral selfhood and moral action have tended to record small to moderate effect sizes, and not to allow for the establishment of direct causality from selfhood to action – rather, for example, than vice versa: that moral activity stimulates moral self-identity development (see Hardy & Carlo, 2005). Hardy's (2006) recent study tries to make amends for some of the limitations of previous research. His sample included ninety-one university students, and was designed to gauge their pro-social behaviour, pro-social self-identities, pro-social moral reasoning and pro-social emotions (empathy/sympathy). This study was the first to explore simultaneously the relative roles of the three contested factors in the motivation of moral behaviour. Indeed, moral self-constructs turned out to be positively associated with moral behaviour, but so did, interestingly enough, moral emotions (although Hardy decided for some reason to study only a single pair of them). Only moral reasoning fell by the wayside as irrelevant.

What are we to make of all of this? I have a number of difficulties with the moral-self solution in general and with Blasi's version of it in particular. The first is Blasi's anxious following of the natural-kind approach to emotion, which he calls 'the psychological view of emotion' (1999, p. 5), and to which I took exception in the opening section of this chapter. To be sure, many psychologists adopt such an approach, at least regarding the purportedly 'basic' emotions. Yet, natural-kind theories of emotion are susceptible to myriad serious objections, summarised in Section 4.1, which Blasi quietly ignores. Some psychologists and most philosophers currently adhere to a cognitive approach of emotion or to an Aristotelian middle-ground approach. It beggars belief to read in Blasi's article that 'there practically is unanimity among philosophers' concerning the involuntariness of emotions: that 'we cannot speak of responsibility in this context' (1999, pp. 8 and 10). On the most favourable reading of Blasi's proclamation, he is referring to emotions *qua* episodic experiences. It was noticed by Aristotle, after all, that we do not blame or praise persons for their immediately occurring emotional states; rather, we blame or praise people for their emotions *qua* settled dispositional states. But Blasi does not make this distinction between 'emotion' in an episodic and dispositional sense; were he to do so, he would have to acknowledge that we typically hold people morally responsible for having allowed certain emotional dispositions to take root and grow inside them. So the problem with the moral-emotion solution to the gappiness problem cannot simply be that emotions are – lock, stock and barrel – outside the purview of moral evaluation.

More generally, Blasi is saddled with an overly restrictive and disabling view of moral value. To be an object of moral evaluation, an action must be intentional and the result of moral reasons, Blasi claims, citing the 'overwhelming acceptance' of theorists and laypeople in favour of his claim (1999, p. 12). What about moral responsibility for negligence and unintentional omissions? Is such responsibility, then, merely a chimera? That is, at any rate, not the overwhelming majority view. And is the attitude of the person who gloats over other people's undeserved misfortune not the very paradigm of immorality – although the attitude is not intentional? (One does not intend to gloat; one simply gloats!) Moreover, what about people whose care and compassion come naturally to them, without the mediation of moral reasons or intentions? In his latest piece, Blasi goes even further, stating that 'according to common sense an action is morally praiseworthy only if it is aimed at the good *for its own sake*' (2004, p. 34; italics mine). Such a narrow view would elicit only acceptance from devout Kantians.

In post-Kohlbergian times, it seems strangely anachronistic and reactionary to hold that genuine sources of moral motivation do not emerge until adolescence or early adulthood. But this is, as I have already noted, one of the implications of Blasi's moral-self solution. Moral education needs, then, to backtrack on its current (Aristotle-inspired) early-childhood emphasis. What motivates pre-adolescents morally becomes a mystery (unless they are simply seen as non-moral creatures). As it turns out, Blasi has not so much slain the Kohlbergian rationalist dragon as repackaged it; the focus is still on 'genuine reasoning and rationality'. The proper construction of a moral self has simply replaced Kohlberg's later stages of moral reasoning. It is almost as if Blasi believes that he is resisting Kohlberg merely by asserting his rationalist demands with sufficient reluctance; Blasi's solution is still a cognitive one in a narrow sense of 'cognitive'. As Bill Puka ironically remarks in this context, Blasi is 'undaunted by the prospect of rehabilitating outdated ideas' (2004, p. 181).

Blasi constantly feeds the concern that if we yield an inch to the idea that emotions can have moral worth, we 'shed' morality of its objective foundation, of 'all traces of genuine reasoning and rationality' (2004, p. 338). What is anathema to Blasi are emotivism and the subjectivism that it elicits, as the opposite of rationalism. But emotivism is a radical version of epistemological-cum-ontological sentimentalism about emotions, a thesis to which Hume subscribes but that Aristotle, for one, does not (nor do I for that matter). Blasi confuses moral epistemology and ontology with moral psychology; it could well be true that emotions have moral worth as an important, even the *most* important, psychological source of moral motivation, although they are, from an epistemological-cum-ontological perspective, not the sole creators – and not even independent creators *at all* – of moral value. I would argue, by the way, that the traditional sentimentalist–rationalist distinction has lost most of its bite in current philosophical discourse. There are few 'hard' rationalists or sentimentalists left among current philosophers (see Prinz, 2007, nevertheless, for a hard variety of sentimentalism that entails both subjectivism and relativism). The sophisticated neo-sentimentalists of today, such as Ronald de Sousa (2001), freely acknowledge the essential fallibility of particular emotional value judgements, and that in order to validate them, we need to bring to bear not only the judgements of other emotions but also our 'background' knowledge, reason and logic. I think there should be little left in such 'soft' sentimentalism to disturb Blasi (or if it still does, he should tell us why); and in any case, the psychological sentimentalism of my emotion-based self-paradigm does not presuppose epistemological/ontological sentimentalism.

I am not quite done yet, for there are other contentious issues lurking in the background. The most serious of these is the issue of the putative *corrigibility* of people's moral self-identities. Larry Nucci (2004) complains that the invocation of a moral self-construct comes close to adding a reified 'homunculus' onto the scene: a moral mini-Me who actually makes the decisions. But how does one have access to this mini-Me? Empirical studies of self-constructs rely on self-reports, but such reports are commonly criticised in related research areas for being unreliable and liable to intentional (deceptive) or non-intentional (self-deceptive) distortions. At fault is not only the fact that the moral-self theorists do not pay enough attention to possible discrepancies between avowed moral identity and moral self; they do not suppose that there is even any real moral self in the first place – underneath all the layers of self-attributions, self-conceptions and self-narrations – with which an identity could be compared. The moral-self solution must thus be understood against the backdrop of the distinctively modern anti-realism about the self that I took to task in Chapter 2. Or, to put it differently, the *moral-self* solution to the gappiness problem is really just a *moral-identity* solution. Although Blasi and his colleagues prefer, for some reason, to use the former term, they mean the latter. Blasi explicitly names the natural need for consistency within one's identity-system (that is, 'identity integration') as one of the founding blocks of his moral-self solution (2004, p. 342). He pays no attention to the possibility of a person possessing an immoral self but a moral self-identity (which I take to be common), or a moral self but an immoral identity (which is probably less common). In general, he completely ignores all the objections levelled at anti-self-realism, 'hard' and 'soft'.

On the interpretative approach taken to Hume's notion of moral self-hood in Section 2.5, we saw how he appeared to have succeeded in rescuing from oblivion the notion of an objective moral self. Nevertheless, the rescued notion contained minimal ontological baggage. If such a (soft) realist account of the nature of the moral self is accepted, it shows the moral-self versus moral-emotion dichotomy to be fully illusory. Far from being an involuntary response, extrinsic to the moral self, an emotional reaction indicates precisely that the subject has internalised and integrated a certain emotional disposition into his or her moral self (cf. Montada, 1993, p. 300). This insight lends considerable backbone to the 'alternative' self-paradigm's understanding of the moral self as constituted by robust states of character, including emotional states.

4.5. An 'Integrative Model' of Moral Selfhood?

Let me turn finally to the second discourse upon which my 'alternative' self-paradigm may throw light. I take here as my point of departure the recent special issue of the *Journal of Moral Education* (September 2008) on a new 'integrated model' of moral selfhood. Synthesising and attempting to advance the current state of play in post-Kohlbergian moral psychology and moral education, most of the authors in this special issue seem to agree that what is needed to progress beyond Kohlberg's one-dimensional rationalist model is a new paradigm of moral selfhood that combines rationalist and sentimentalist elements. I admit to having been exhilarated by the promise of this suggested enterprise, but at the same time slightly irritated by how little it delivered (or perhaps, more charitably, that it did not deliver quite as much as it promised). The following reflections explain the sources of my irritation.

Kohlberg was, of course, the leading moral psychologist in the modern era, as well as an enthusiastic moral educator, and the special issue is published in observance of the fiftieth anniversary of his PhD dissertation. Now, Kohlberg was obviously not a self-theorist in the literal sense, but if we translate his Kantian rationalism and his cognitive developmental approach into contemporary self-talk, it falls snugly into line with that of the 'dominant' self-paradigm: The moral self is a social construction; self-constituting interactions are mediated by cognitive schemata; and these schemata constitute structures of action (see Reed's helpful overview, 2008, pp. 360–62). The tenor of the special issue is post-Kohlbergian, providing the reader with a good sense of where the centre of gravity lies in current theories of moral psychology and moral education that are still 'between paradigms' (Frimer & Walker, 2008, p. 352). The crest of the Kohlbergian wave has been broken, but a new one is not yet fully in sight: a new comprehensive model of moral functioning.

Blasi (1999) had tried to solve the Kohlbergian 'gappiness problem' with his moral-self solution – more aptly termed 'moral-identity solution' – as previously mentioned. The idea underlying most of the contributions to the special issue, and animating the whole project towards a new 'integrated model', is our need to depart less faint-heartedly from Kohlberg, and to embrace the affective more explicitly than Blasi allows, while still maintaining a vigil against the perils of moral non-cognitivism. Is it possible to have the best of both worlds? My own view is that we can, but that the suggestions made in this special issue reveal a somewhat impoverished notion of the affective. To begin on a positive note, however, it is pleasantly surprising to see Frimer and Walker tackling the topic of the ontological status of the self, and underwriting a realist account of the non-shattered self as a persisting psychological unit (2008, pp. 344–46). It is also heartening to see them refer to the research of Michael Chandler and his colleagues mentioned in Chapter 2 of this book (see especially Chandler, Lalonde, Sokol & Hallett, 2003). They provide a veritable oasis in the psychological anti-realist desert.

From that note to a less conciliatory one: There have been some attempts made in recent moral psychology to repackage Humean *Treatise*-Book-I sentimentalism for modern consumption. Best known, perhaps, is Jonathan Haidt's version of Humean feeling theory with an evolutionary twist, in his piece on the 'emotional dog and its rational tail' (2001). Haidt's main contention is that moral reasoning does not cause moral judgement (nor, in turn, moral action), but rather that moral judgement is the result of quick, affective and automatic (mostly unconscious) intuitions, including emotions, followed by slow ex-post facto moral reasoning. This is meant to explain why moral action co-varies with moral emotion more than with moral reasoning. We naive humans erroneously believe, however, that the after-effect (reasoning) produces the cause (intuition/emotion). This whole process is then given an evolutionary gloss by Haidt, as an invaluable adaptive mechanism. If this account of the role of emotion in moral life is supposed to be Humean, it is obvious that Haidt has never progressed beyond Book I in Hume's *Treatise* (1978). For in Books II–III, Hume describes the 'indirect' emotions (pride, humility, love and hate), with distinct target objects (ourselves and other people) that form the basis of the moral sentiments. Nor does Haidt take any account of the findings of contemporary cognitive theories of emotion. Unwholesome as Haidt's sentimentalist mixture is on its own, in my view, it will cause no less than serious moral indigestion if the topmost froth of sentimentalism and the last dregs of Kohlbergianism are gulped down together. I am not saying that this is the necessary outcome of the special issue, but I feel that some of its authors come seriously close to endorsing Haidt's restrictive understanding of the affective realm.

The overarching idea of the special issue is that there are two systems underlying moral behaviour: a conscious, rule-based, explicit, analytical and rational system, on the one hand; and an implicit, intuitive, experiential, automatic and tacit system, on the other. The latter system includes emotions. The two systems already interact in various ways, but through successful moral education, they can be made to interact more harmoniously, in order to forge an integrated moral self or personhood (see especially Lapsley & Hill, 2008; cf. Narvaez & Vaydich, 2008; Frimer & Walker, 2008).

To be fair, the 'experiential system' is not necessarily equated with Haidt's evolutionary intuitionist model. In contrast to his model, Lapsley and Hill suggest, for instance, that automaticity may be located at the backend of development as the outcome of repeated experience and instruction (2008, p. 324). What worries me, however, is the image of emotion as steam rising automatically from internal kettles and of the moral self as the battleground of two systems in which the desired end-product is some sort of armistice or dialectical harmony between two essentially opposing elements. This 'internal-kettles' view emerges clearly in Narvaez and Vaydich's paper when they discuss the 'affectively-rooted moral orientations' emerging from 'human evolution' (p. 305). Lapsley and Hill's two-systems view seems to be somewhat subtler with regard to the nature of emotions, and they clearly state that it is a 'model of moral cognition that articulates both the deliberative and automatic processes that underlie moral behaviour' (p. 315). Nevertheless – and despite their repeated emphasis on integration and complementarity – they subscribe to a separation between rational and affective systems. In contrast, the upshot of the 'alternative' paradigm of the self that I am proposing in this book is that of a unified moral self of rationally grounded emotion.

To mention briefly two other contributions to the special issue of the *Journal of Moral Education*, Haste and Abrahams (2008) do well to emphasise how the moral self can engage or 'do' culture, rather than simply being moulded by culture (I return to that issue in Chapter 8). But when they start to describe in detail how individuals 'reconstruct' their identities, the proposed triangular model (individual sense-making, society, interpersonal dialogue) seems to leave little space for affective engagement. Admittedly, Haste and Abrahams mention other perspectives on morality that could also be subjected to cultural analysis, but that they leave out of reckoning here – one of them being Humean, with an emphasis on moral emotions (pp. 377–78). They seem to think, however, that this Humean perspective has been credibly revived in moral psychology by Haidt's sentimentalism. As I noted earlier, Haidt is not Hume (or if he is, then he is Hume on steroids). Finally, the re-evaluation of Kohlberg's Just Community approach (Oser, Althof & Higgins-D'Alessandro, 2008) shows scant sensitivity to the emotional roots of justice: namely to the fact that children's sense of justice does not have its origin in lofty political insights but arises, rather, from the promptings of deep-seated emotions about deserved and undeserved outcomes (Kristjánsson, 2006).

My complaint about the special issue, in a nutshell, is this: Although explicitly post-Kohlbergian, the authors do not depart far enough from Kohlberg's impoverished notion of the role of the affective in moral life. Most of the contributors either cling to the cognitive (narrowly construed) remnants of Kohlbergianism, with only a marginal role for emotions; or, when departing from Kohlbergianism, try to incorporate emotions as intuitive thrusts in an essentially polarised two-systems moral self. A step is taken away from the 'dominant' self-paradigm – and that is surely to be applauded – but not towards the 'alternative' paradigm for which I have been advocating. All in all, the 'integrated model' is not integrated enough, in that it still marginalises emotion within the moral self, or, at best, understands emotion as distinct from – if complementary to – reason. I do hope that the special issue of the *Journal of Moral Education* will act as a bellwether for a paradigm change in moral psychology and moral education. Nevertheless, as they stand, I doubt that the ideas it represents constitute the next big leap forward in the field.

5. Self-Concept: Self-Esteem and Self-Confidence

5.1. The Self-Esteem Industry

As I am about to start writing this chapter, I can hear the background noise of a TV news commentator reassuring British viewers after the knockout of Andy Murray from the early stages of the Australian Open Tennis Championship. Although Murray's dream of Grand Slam glory may have faded away this time, he is bound to bounce back because of his positive mindset. Or as the commentator puts it: 'Those who believe can achieve'.

I sometimes wonder if media pundits are all born anti-self-realists. Or perhaps they are systematically exploiting a view that has lately been deeply ingrained in the public consciousness: You are what you think you are; you are as good as you esteem yourself to be. Recall that an essential part of the ideological 'inward turn' of modernity has been the exaltation of the self from a mere subject of value (a value-recorder, if you like) to an object of value: an object to be prized and valued independently, esteemed, respected and nourished. Without first valuing oneself or one's 'self', as the theory goes, one cannot learn to value other things. This assumption may not seem novel; even Aristotle posited that other-love presupposes an ability to love oneself (1985, pp. 252–56 [1168a5–1169b2]). In the last few decades, however, the idea of self-valuing has assumed a life of its own, taking on new forms and dimensions. Until recently, the bulk of experimental studies on selfhood and self-valuing has revolved around one facet of self-concept, originally made famous by William James in his 1890 classic, a facet most felicitously called 'global self-esteem': the level of one's satisfaction with the perceived global ratio of one's achievements to one's aspirations. 'Self-esteem is arguably psychology's most popular construct', state

Brown and Marshall unhesitatingly (2001, p. 580). Some psychologists have even failed to distinguish between 'global self-esteem' and 'self-concept'. Yet it is obvious that if we understand 'self-concept' – as I have done in this book – to refer to the totality of a person's beliefs in relation to the self-shaping core of his or her personality, global self-esteem forms only part of the total mosaic.

In this chapter, I review recent debates about the notion of *self-esteem*, and cast a glance at some of the neighbouring conceptual terrain, which includes, importantly, *self-confidence* as part of self-concept. I explore inter alia what has been considered to be the role that the cultivation of self-esteem and self-confidence play in the educational arena. But why should an avowed self-realist devote an entire chapter to addressing those issues? Is actual selfhood not more important than one's beliefs about that selfhood? To be sure, for self-realists it is. As I explained in Chapter 2, however, they cannot neglect self-concept with impunity. Not only is it conducive to people's flourishing to 'know themselves', self-concept also typically forms part of selfhood – or, as I illustrated earlier, the mirror in one's living room not only mirrors the furniture, but is part of that furniture. To paraphrase Charles Taylor's dictum, if 'we are going to live by the modern identity, it better be by the examined version of it' (1989, p. 504), we could say that if self-realists are to grasp the meaning and salience of self-concept, they had better examine closely what self-concept is and to what extent it matters.

As already noted, the vast majority of psychological studies conducted under the banner of self-concept over the past thirty years or so has actually been about global self-esteem and its expected correlations with various socio-moral and educational factors. The initial hypothesis – sometimes dressed up in textbooks almost as a truism requiring no corroborating evidence – was that high global self-esteem would be positively and even causally correlated with pro-social behaviour in general and educational achievement in particular. Hence, the urgent need to 'boost' self-esteem. This mantra quickly spread to the school arena and became the rallying cry of progressive educators. In the 1980s–1990s, the magic words 'lack of self-esteem' thus became an all-purpose explanation for educational underachievement and disengagement from schoolwork. Conversely, the cultivation of self-esteem became the first business of educators.

Not only educators were taken in; self-esteem gradually established itself as the core item on psychology's general 'enhancement agenda' – an agenda stating that psychological conditions for the effective functioning of human beings can be usefully heightened or enhanced (Cigman, 2008). A search of PsycINFO (January 1985–May 2006), using the search term 'self-esteem', resulted in no less than 11,313 abstracts. I assume that readers are aware of the grandiose claims that have been made in the name of this overarching agenda (see, e.g., Branden, 1969) and the copious research that has been conducted to establish the relevant correlations. According to Branden and his followers, low self-esteem lies at the bottom of almost every personal and social ill, ranging from excessive masturbation to serial killings! High self-esteem needs to be injected into young people in the home and the school to vaccinate them against those ills and to carve out a safe path for them through school, work and life in general. The most notorious example of the smug and attitudinising – although no doubt well-meaning – efforts of the self-esteem movement was the establishment of a state-funded 'Self-Esteem Task Force' in California, which was meant to concentrate on ways of improving self-esteem as a 'unifying concept to reframe American problem solving' (see, e.g., Stout, 2000, p. 13). Although by the early 1980s self-esteem had become a household term in academic circles, especially in Britain and the USA, the public had scarcely taken notice. A search of 300 UK newspapers in 1980 did not locate a single use of the term (see Furedi, 2004, p. 3). That was all to change soon, however; and by the turn of the century, the popular media abounded in references to self-esteem as our new Balm of Gilead. Gradually, the self-esteem movement spawned its own cottage industry, making millions, offering everything from self-help manuals to jewellery specifically designed to help people soak up self-esteem.

The assumption of young people's vulnerable self, constantly in danger of a dearth of reflexive esteem if they experience frustration, hardship or difficulty, had obvious educational ramifications (see Damon, 1995; Stout, 2000). Tough school work could be stifling; the same applied to teachers' criticisms and corrections. Everybody was supposed to feel good at school at all times, and self-affirming, sycophantic messages proliferated ('I am great; you are great, no matter what'). As the fashion pundits would put it, this preoccupation with self-esteem was 'so much 1990s'. In the wake of harsh criticisms urged against the self-esteem movement in recent years, the pendulum has swung radically. The ferocious generalisations of the 1990s, the grandiose and extravagant claims made in the name of global self-esteem, ultimately resulted in its ironic overkill. Although some media pundits and populists continue to man the barricades of (global) self-esteem – witness Oprah Winfrey, whose shows still contain copious references to people's destructive self-disesteem – the movement has, to all intents and purposes, struck its flag in academic circles. How long that news will take to percolate through to the public is another story. In any case, I review and enter the debate on global self-esteem in the following section.

Prior to that, something more needs to be said about how James's famous formulation of global self-esteem (1890, chap. 10), as constituting the ratio of people's successes to their 'pretensions', has been operationalised in psychology. Empirical psychologists need yardsticks before they can take measurements. Those yardsticks are concepts defined in terms of theoretically constructed measurements. Although most of the approximately 200 instruments that have been devised to measure the ratio of successes to pretensions/aspirations take their cue from James' basic insight, it oversimplifies matters to talk about a unitary social science conception. Rather, we see at least two such conceptions and corresponding instruments in the literature. Despite the fact that the second of those conceptions or instruments has predominated lately, it is instructive to say a few things at the outset about the other one.

The first type of instrument asks us to rate ourselves (say, on a scale from 1 to 10) compared to other people of our age and sex on 'competences' that people generally care about, such as intelligence, social skills, athletic ability and physical attractiveness. The scores are then added to create a total score (see, e.g., Swann, 1996, pp. 221–23). Instruments of this kind have been faulted in two ways. The first fault is that the measure does not necessarily capture all the relevant variables. There may well be additional 'competences' about which people care deeply; and people may even care little, if at all, about how they score on the factors measured. Consider a monk who rated himself low on intelligence and physical attractiveness, but who felt that he had reached union with the spiritual principle of the universe and was therefore content with his success ratio. As James himself noted, people vary widely in the goals upon which they 'stake salvation' (1890, p. 310), and lack of success in an area in which one has no 'pretensions' (e.g., Greek for James) will not erode global self-esteem. Put briefly, self-esteem requires a background notion of what individuals deem significant for themselves. The second fault of this type of instrument lies in its ability to measure only the evaluative component of self-esteem, while ignoring the conative/affective one. There is a world of difference between *evaluating* oneself high or low on certain characteristics compared with other people and *desiring* those characteristics oneself. Think of a pretty teenage student who is good at sports and estimates herself realistically as having high athletic ability and physical attractiveness. Yet she loathes those characteristics and abilities because they prevent other people from appreciating her in the way she would really like: as a computer nerd. It would be counterintuitive to claim that her high self-esteem score reflected her true self-esteem. As David Dewhurst aptly puts it: 'One may make a correct estimate of one's qualities and capabilities without feeling positively towards oneself, and this positive, affective component is an essential ingredient in self-esteem' (1991, p. 4). What seems to be missing in this type of instrument is the *emotional* element. A parallel mistake has been made by some emotion theorists who have tried to define emotions exclusively with regard to evaluative beliefs (for example, Nussbaum, 2001), thereby overlooking the Aristotelian insight that unless pleasure or pain is attached to the relevant cognition, no emotion is elicited.

Psychologists are, of course, at liberty to construct whatever concept they like and whatever instrument. The fact that 'self-esteem' does not have a clearly specified meaning in ordinary language notwithstanding, I think we have to agree with Nicholas Emler (2001, p. 7) that self-esteem is a matter of an *emotional attitude* rather than mere belief. The second type of instrument is meant to measure precisely such an 'attitude' – global conative self-esteem – and it is this that gives us the prevailing social science conception of self-esteem. The classic example is the Rosenberg scale (1965) that, for a while at least, became the standard in self-esteem research (see Emler, 2001, p. 5). The scale consists of 10 statements dealing with one's overall feelings about oneself, with which one is asked to 'strongly agree', 'agree', 'disagree' or 'strongly disagree'. Five of those statements indicate pleasant feelings about one's perceptions of one's qualities and achievements, and five indicate painful feelings. Although essentially in line with James' formulation, Rosenberg's scale and other measures of the same ilk assume that global self-esteem has a tripartite structure: It involves (1) one's overall life goals, (2) one's estimate of the achievement of those goals and (3), most important, one's attitude toward this estimated achievement. Yet what information about the purported psychological status of self-esteem is actually yielded here? 'Attitude' is a notoriously ambiguous term. Does the social science conception imply, for instance, that self-esteem is a full-blown emotion? I have rarely seen that question addressed, let alone answered, in the social science literature, but I revisit it in the final section of this chapter.

5.2. The Debate about Global Self-Esteem

To recapitulate, self-esteem was not long ago the Holy Grail of much psychological and educational research, hailed both as an essential social vaccine and as a panacea for an array of personal and educational ills. Every flow has its ebb, however, and in recent years we have seen the ideal of (indiscriminately) boosted self-esteem come under sustained attack. It is helpful to initiate our inquiry with Ruth Cigman's account of the four 'homes' to which the concept of self-esteem has been thought to belong and between which it tends to migrate, not always legitimately (Cigman, 2004, pp. 92–93) – typically expanding and metamorphosising as it leaves one home for the next. I am prompted to think here of the life cycle of the butterfly, whose larva hatches from an original small egg, then pupates and finally metamorphosises into a full-grown adult. The 'egg' of self-esteem research is the *social scientific* concept of one's personal satisfaction with the global ratio of one's achievements to aspirations. The *therapy* concept, or the 'larva', of self-esteem is this first concept, coupled with the assumption that a number of gruelling psychological problems are connected to low self-esteem and that they will benefit from therapeutic treatment. The concept then 'pupates' into that of the *self-help* industry, where every psychological and social problem afflicting humanity can be traced to low self-esteem – or so the self-help gurus enthuse. The concept finally reaches full 'maturity', as it leaves the self-help manuals and enters the world of *education*, where the chief or overall aim of education, formal no less than informal, becomes reduced to that of shoring up students' self-esteem. Perhaps it would be more apt to talk about four *conceptions* of the same concept rather than four distinct concepts, because they all start from the same 'egg', but different contours and layers of complexity are added. The crucial question will then be: Which of those conceptions, if any, are logically and morally acceptable? The recent backlash against global self-esteem has seen a battery of criticisms crowding in from various quarters. I divide them, for convenience's sake, into educational, ethical, philosophical and psychological criticisms.

Educational critics argue that the self-esteem movement has wreaked havoc on educational standards and 'dumbed down' the curriculum. Eminent child psychologist William Damon (1995) was among the first to sound a healthy counterpoint to the self-esteem industry's colonisation of education. First, transparently undeserved flattery is demotivating rather than motivating, condescending rather than uplifting. More precisely, if self-esteem is understood simply as satisfaction with the ratio of achievements to aspirations, the easiest way to enhance self-esteem is by diminishing the aspirations and dulling educational standards. The catch there, however, is the 'devaluation of the currency': If students are rewarded for achievements that are fake and independent of effort, they quickly learn to enjoy self-esteem without the effort. And although the house of such (deluded) educational self-esteem may be easy to build, it is draughty to live in and liable to fall once students enter the 'real' (read: meritocratic) outside world (Damon, 1995; Stout, 2000; Smith, 2002). Second, it is not true that what one loses on true attainment, is made up in an enhanced self. A diminution of educational standards may boost short-term positive feelings, but it damages students' long-term self-image and wellbeing, as well as the interests of society at large (Damon, 1995). Even the current high priest of 'positive psychology', Martin Seligman – who has recently made headlines in Great Britain as the person commissioned to cure Scotland of its 'epidemic of pessimism' – anticipated as much in 1995 (pp. 33–34), when he wrote that 'trying to achieve the feeling side of self-esteem directly, before achieving good commerce with the world, confuses profoundly the means and the end'. All in all, it can in no way be the role of the teacher to indiscriminately 'boost' self-esteem (Smith, 2002; Cigman, 2004).

Ethicists also started to complain that the concept of self-esteem lacked an objective moral grounding – which then prompted a number of searching questions: Given that self-esteem instruments merely measure subjective self-reported satisfaction, may not, amongst the individuals epitomising high self-esteem, lurk the big-headed bully, the smug drug baron and the Machiavellian tyrant (cf. Kristjánsson, 2007, chap. 6)? Does the ideal of high self-esteem promote anything but that bland, shallow, goal-driven character type, allegedly championed by positive psychology (Miller, 2008)? Does the empty praise bestowed upon students as a result of the feel-good philosophy not teach them hypocrisy rather than a true valuing of themselves and others (Stout, 2000)?

I leave it to readers to ponder those ethical questions, but turn next to some deeper *philosophical* worries about the very notion of (global) self-esteem. Richard Smith places little stock in this notion, and in fact deems the concept seriously flawed (2002, 2006). Smith distinguishes between 'instrumentalist' and 'non-instrumentalist' claims made in the name of self-esteem. On an instrumentalist reading, raising self-esteem is considered valuable because it makes children better learners; on a non-instrumentalist reading, self-esteem is seen as a distinct educational aim, perhaps even the ultimate aim of all education (2002, p. 91). Smith tenders two main arguments against the instrumentalist reading, which are basically subtle versions of the educational objections delineated above. One is the familiar one about the effects of empty cajolery in devaluating the currency of praise; the other focuses on the corrosive influence that self-esteem worship has had on present-day ideas about 'personalised learning', where undue (in Smith's, words, 'chilling') attention is being paid to giving students tasks pitched at precisely their current level of aptitude in order not to have their fragile self-esteem wounded should they fail. Nevertheless, Smith leaves some room for instrumental self-esteem as one goal of education among many, if it is not sought directly or exclusively. He refrains, however, from explaining clearly what kind of self-esteem he has in mind – surely not one hatched from the rotten 'egg' that James bequeathed to us.

Smith objects even more strenuously – and this time from a more exclusively philosophical perspective – to a non-instrumental reading of self-esteem. He smells a rat when exploring the original 'egg': the social science conception of self-esteem. He argues (and another philosopher of education, Cigman, concurs) that global self-esteem, as measured by social scientists, is an artificially created notion without a home in ordinary language. Most seriously, it obliterates important distinctions made in everyday talk among different kinds of self-description. We may describe a person as being mild, quiet, meek, self-effacing, lacking in self-confidence, shy, humble or diffident, for instance. But we would never – unless we had read too many self-help manuals for our own good – dream of describing a person as having 'low self-esteem'. Similarly, in ordinary language, we have a range of terms to describe excessive, unreasonable self-esteem: smugness, conceit, arrogance, pomposity, grandiosity, bravado, big-headedness. The notion of 'high self-esteem' runs those differences promiscuously together (Smith, 2002, 2006; Cigman, 2004). The general complaint here is that 'global self-esteem' is a banal construct which obscures our rich ordinary-language repertoire of self-evaluation concepts and dislodges any proper criteria for distinguishing between reasonable and unreasonable feelings about oneself.

A second and related philosophical problem is the abandonment of truth. If all that is aimed for is psychological effectiveness and subjective satisfaction, then why care whether people assess their achievements accurately or not (or, as self-realists would put it, if self-concept fits self)? Self-deceptions may even become preferable to truths that genuinely reflect achievements. Daniel Statman, for instance, seriously considers the systematic inculcation of self-deceptions as a viable option in schools (1993, p. 61). But by trading substance for image, we have replaced the time-honoured educational ideal of a truth-seeking self with a narcissistic and cynical chimera-seeking self (cf. Stout, 2000).

As mentioned, Cigman (2004) concurs with Smith in rejecting the social science conception of global self-esteem, although she embraces more explicitly a subtler version of self-esteem as educationally salient, even claiming that it may sometimes be pursued directly. She calls it 'situated self-esteem': our thick, 'ordinary evaluative concept' of self-belief (2004, p. 95). Indeed, Cigman considers the worst permutations of the concept of self-esteem to have taken place in the 'home' of the self-help industry rather than in the educational arena. Cigman makes two notable empirical claims in her writings on self-esteem. One is that, although we should try to cultivate reasonable, realistic self-esteem in ourselves and others, this requirement does not apply to young children; for developmental reasons, they constitute an exception. What young children need to guard them against the potential hazards of failure is 'basic self-esteem': a sense of 'boundless self-worth'. Such basic self-esteem derives primarily from the childhood experience of being loved and liked. Even when it means that children think they are capable of much more than they really are, it would be self-defeating to try to relieve them of their delusions. It is one of the many roles of the teacher to promote such 'healthy' basic self-esteem in students. Most important, the teacher needs to engage those students who feel everything about themselves is worthless and useless (Cigman, 2001).

Cigman's second claim is that people such as school bullies, who tend to score high on typical psychological self-report measures of self-esteem, are often fraudsters trying to disguise their inferiority complexes as bravado. Thus, deep-rooted feelings of self-doubt and self-loathing may be camouflaged as high self-esteem in self-esteem questionnaires, as the self-doubters fake positive answers in order to feel better about themselves momentarily (Cigman, 2004).

The potential allure of all these philosophical criticisms notwithstanding, it was not until the publication of comprehensive meta-analyses of the actual findings of *psychological* research into global self-esteem and its various alleged correlates that the self-esteem movement finally started to lose ground (see especially Emler, 2001; Baumeister et al., 2003). Those results have been well documented in the academic and popular literature (even making headlines in magazines such as *Newsweek*), and I need only rehearse them in a brief outline. The crucial finding is that the expected correlations between high global self-esteem and salient positively valenced factors, such as above-average school achievement and pro-social behaviour, have failed to materialise in the empirical research. Null findings abound, in fact; and if any consistent correlation exists, it seems to be between high self-esteem, on the one hand, and various types of risky and anti-social behaviour on the other.

More specifically, only weak correlations (less than 0.2) exist between low *educational achievement* and low global self-esteem. Nor is high global self-esteem connected to long-term educational success. Most of the evidence suggests that global self-esteem has no impact on subsequent educational performance, and that attempts to boost it can even be counter-productive. Rather, both factors may be influenced by a prior shared variable, such as family background; and in some cases, improved school performance has been shown to enhance self-esteem, as one might expect. Some links have been established with *alcohol and drug abuse*; yet they were not, as hypothesised, between low self-esteem and alcohol/drug abuse, but between high self-esteem and such abuse. It seems that high levels of global self-esteem may engender feelings of invulnerability, which in turn encourage risk-taking. Probably for the same reason, *risky sexual behaviour* is linked to high rather than (as expected) low levels of global self-esteem. As for *bullying and school violence*, the perpetrators tend to report higher than average levels of self-esteem. The same applies to students who try to stand up to the bullies, suggesting that high self-esteem may intensify both pro-social and anti-social tendencies. No indications have emerged to strengthen Cigman's thesis that the aggressors are systematically deceiving themselves and others. The two most robust links in the literature have been found between high global self-esteem and *happiness*, and between low global self-esteem and *depression*. This result is unsurprising, as the self-report questionnaires for global self-esteem chart many of the same painful feelings that characterise depressed people (although such feelings tend to fluctuate even more for people who are depressed than they do for those with low self-esteem), and psychiatrists have long known that clinical depression often presents itself as self-disesteem.

As difficult as it may have been for some social scientists to stomach the fact that their work had been hag-ridden for years by a self-esteem fallacy, these results did carry a positive message about psychology's ability to self-correct. Psychology could deconstruct its own constructs, should they fail to have grounding in real experiences. It was not, as some critics had suggested, doomed to perpetuate sleight-of-hand constructs and self-fulfilling prophecies. I expand on that positive note below. But first, a critical response to some of Smith's and Cigman's comments is in order.

In reply to Smith, I would urge that an instrumentalist reading of self-esteem need not include indiscriminate self-esteem an educational goal; rather, it could be 'justified self-esteem' (see below) that should be the objective. Moreover, my study of the recent literature on 'personalised learning' or 'individualised education' in the UK and USA – which I review in Section 10.5 – reveals no unhealthy fascination with preserving students' self-esteem by feeding them on a diet of easy tasks.

Enter Cigman. My first qualm about her discussion concerns a linguistic point. Because Cigman holds that a conception of self-esteem must be coherent and ethically acceptable in order to be legitimate (2004, p. 92), I would suggest that the kind of legitimate self-esteem that she is after should be more usefully referred to as 'justified self-esteem'. This term captures Cigman's two conditions better than does the term 'situated'. *Justified self-esteem* indicates that it is both rationally warranted and morally justifiable (see further in Section 5.5). Consider next Cigman's two empirical claims or hypotheses. Although having little patience with the social science work on self-esteem, she invokes her own armchair thesis about the psychological fraudsters in our midst who dress up their feelings of low self-worth as 'high' self-esteem (psychologically measured). I would respond by saying that empirical psychologists are notoriously adept at exposing fakers. In the case of self-esteem, faked self-esteem has been detected through a variety of subtle methods (see, e.g., Baumeister et al., p. 5). I fault Cigman's fraud hypothesis for implicitly perpetuating one of the myths of the self-help industry: that anti-social behaviour and attitudes must eventually be traceable to low self-esteem. She is thinking of characters such as the school bully who takes out his own inferiority complex on others – or so a common story goes – while consistently (and fraudulently) scoring high on psychological self-esteem tests. The actual psychological evidence seems to provide us with a simpler explanation: The bullies who score high on self-esteem tests probably *do have* high global self-esteem (according to the social science conception), but such self-esteem is not always, as it happens, a good thing to have. (This does not alter the fact that the school bully will almost certainly have low *self-respect*, which is another if not altogether unrelated issue that I discuss in Chapter 7.) Indeed, peer reports and parents' reports of people's global self-esteem seem to correspond substantially with self-reports (see, e.g., DuBois, Felner, Brand, Phillips & Lease, 1996). This fact does not augur well for Cigman's fraud thesis – unless the fraudsters are particularly adept at their trade. Notably, teachers constitute an exception here, as they are singularly bad at guessing their students' levels of self-reported self-esteem (Wickline, 2003). In fact, many teachers seem to be in the grip of the fallacious thesis that educational under-achievement must be indicative of low self-esteem, thus automatically presuming the self-esteem of their badly performing students to be low.

Cigman's other hypothesis – on the reasonableness of unreasonable self-esteem in young children – seems more plausible. Empirical evidence for Cigman's conjecture may come from the very research tradition that she distrusts; the small and infrequent correlations that have been found between high global self-esteem and educational achievement exist primarily in the youngest age group (Marsh & Craven, 2006). I wonder, however, if Cigman's hypothesis needs to be formulated in terms of self-esteem at all. When she describes happy children with 'basic' but unrealistic 'self-esteem', it seems to me that she is describing children not with an inflated view of the ratio of their achievements to aspirations – or at least not children who are bursting with enthusiasm *because* of such a view – but rather children with an abundance of self-confidence. Their self-confidence may well be – partly at least – the result of a strong sense of *self-worth*, inspired in them by the love and attention of parents and other caregivers (although inborn individual differences in temperamental dispositions should not be forgotten either). Considerations of self-worth take us beyond mere self-concept, however, into the realm of the actual full self. I return to that issue, and to Cigman's second hypothesis, in Section 5.4.

To close this section with Smith's and Cigman's linguistic objection, I accept that both social scientific and philosophical investigations should take ordinary language as their starting point. I totally agree with warnings against the 'I-am-the-king-of-the-Romans-and-above-grammar' tendencies of some radically operationalist social scientists. Researchers may have good reasons for departing from ordinary language, however, or for sharpening it to a finer edge. Everyday usage may fail to honour significant distinctions that emerge only from a thorough, fine-grained analysis. Some concepts in everyday use (take 'freedom') are too ambiguous to serve as research material and do stand in need of conceptual regimentation. Others (take 'nervous breakdown') are not scientifically useful, full stop. The invocation of operationalist neologisms may even be necessary for particular purposes (take 'IQ' as measured by IQ tests). Sometimes, as in the case of self-esteem, a clearly specified meaning may be missing in ordinary language (it is not as if we could go into the field and ask the real self-esteem to please stand up); and in such cases, more radical conceptual regimentation may be required. All in all, compliance to ordinary language is one important consideration among many in conceptual studies, but all such studies will, by necessity, involve critical revisions of idiomatic expressions if we want them to serve useful theoretical purposes.

What is the scientific status of the notion of global self-esteem in this context? Have psychologists succeeded in locating something singular in the prodigious plurality of sundry notions that nest within that of self-concept? If by this we mean whether or not they have identified a natural-kind concept, the answer is obviously no. If the claim is the more modest one, however – that they have specified a cluster concept with reasonable defining features, general intuitive appeal and at least some *prima facie* explanatory force in making sense of human experiences – I think we should give the psychologists the benefit of doubt and agree that global self-esteem had, until recently that is, a promissory status not inferior to that of many related but better established open-textured psychological concepts. This acceptance of conceptual serviceability does not imply that global self-esteem could automatically be granted a powerful mediating influence on human behaviour. The common claim that high global self-esteem is fundamental to educational achievement, psychological health and rewarding relationships never amounted to more than a slogan in the absence of empirical investigation.

For philosophers of education such as Smith and Cigman, the key question is whether or not the social science conception turned out to have any educational salience. Unlike Smith and Cigman, I answer that question in the positive. Indeed, I think that we have little reason to baulk at the social science conception of global self-esteem, but considerable reason to welcome all the empirical research that has been conducted in its name, Why? Because the social science conception of self-esteem has provided the necessary ammunition to stem the 'migration' of the self-help conception to its educational 'home'. More specifically, the freight heaped on global self-esteem in that home turned out to be elusive. Smith and Cigman may want to argue that this is a negative conclusion that bolsters their case for the dispensability of the social science conception. Let us not forget, however, that from a scientific perspective, null or weak findings are often as enlightening as strong findings are. The conclusion that global self-esteem, as measured by Rosenberg-type self-report instruments, matters little for sociomoral functioning in general and educational achievement in particular is, indeed, an educationally salient conclusion.

To recap: An intuitively appealing idea – the idea that one's self-concept, understood as the global estimation of one's relative successes, is a significant life variable – has turned out to be untenable. The only way to learn that was through careful scientific experimentation. And there, James's construct of global self-esteem proved enormously useful, if not exactly in the 'positive' way that he and most subsequent theorists had predicted.

5.3. Domain-Specific Self-Esteem and Self-Confidence

What should now happen, after the implosion of global self-esteem, to the powerful and pervasive intuition that one's self-concept has significant bearing on educational achievement and general wellbeing? The most unyielding response would be to dispose of this intuition altogether. In shunning one kind of idea, however, we must be careful not to run to the opposite extreme. The idea that what we believe ourselves to be worthy and capable of is irrelevant to sociomoral functioning may be just as dogmatic and short-sighted as is the idea that it is the only thing which matters. To be sure, if self-concept is equated with global self-esteem, as has often been done in the past, we are stuck with the counter-intuitive implication that self-concept does not matter at all. If, however, we understand self-concept (as I have done in this book) as the totality of an individual's attitudes towards himself or herself, involving a number of distinct aspects or dimensions, then various candidates for research other than global self-esteem will emerge.

I happen to think that those facets of self-concept that have the greatest relevance for our success in life are *domain-specific self-esteem* (one's self-esteem as a philosophy student for one's philosophy studies, for instance) and *self-confidence*. Cigman may want to argue that I am simply presenting bits of my own favoured armchair psychology. However, a hypothesis on the relevance of domain-specific self-esteem is more than a pipe dream. In fact, prior to and particularly after the publication of the meta-analyses demolishing global self-esteem, psychologists have turned their attention towards this facet of self-concept. A formidable mountain of literature already exists displaying relevant research findings, especially as they relate to educational and clinical variables. Taken together, this body of research seems to show that although little if any correlation exists between academic and non-academic components, academic achievement is highly correlated with academic self-esteem, and achievement in specific academic fields even more highly correlated with self-esteem in those fields. What is more, the causal chain, when probed, does not lead merely from academic achievement to academic self-esteem, as could have been expected, but also leads in the other direction. This finding carries significant practical implications for educators: Domain-specific performance and domain-specific self-esteem seem to be reciprocally related and mutually reinforcing variables, and teachers may be well advised to spend time improving them both. That said, recent research concurs with common sense in that the gains of merely enhancing self-esteem without improving performance are likely to be short lived, as are the gains of enhancing self-esteem out of proportion with actual performance (see Marsh & Craven, 2006, for an extensive overview; Marsh, Trautwein, Lüdtke, Köller & Baumert, 2006, for an impressive individual study; cf. also Swann, Chang-Schneider & McClarty, 2007).

Self-confidence is another facet of self-concept. Self-confidence embodies belief and optimism in one's capacity to succeed at a given task. Folk psychology teaches us that, given the same level of ability, people who firmly believe in their ability to accomplish a given task are more likely to be able to accomplish it than are those who doubt their ability. Folk psychology must be taken with a grain of salt; its 'educated guesses' often turn out, on close inspection, to be half-truths or truths and a half. One of the callings of academic psychology is to subject such teachings to rigorous empirical investigation either to support or refute them. In this case, however, the folk-psychology hypothesis seems to be close to the truth. The psychology literature is replete with findings of a strong correlation between self-confidence and life success (Bandura, 1997, chap. 6). Jeff Valentine's meta-analysis (2001), for instance, found a much stronger link between self-confidence and school performance than between global self-esteem and school performance. As a long-time teacher educator, I find that conclusion to tally well with the reports of my teacher trainees who complain that one of the most pervasive problems they encounter on their field trips are students' doubts that they can perform the tasks that will be expected of them (lack of self-confidence). I also surmise that if we eavesdropped on teachers' conversations, we would more often hear them mention their students' lack of self-confidence than their lack of global self-esteem.

We must be cautious not to smuggle in through the side window considerations that have just been kicked out the main door. How can self-confidence be so vital to achievement if global self-esteem matters so little? It requires only a moment's reflection, however, to realise that the contours and implications of self-confidence are radically different from those of self-esteem. Having a low opinion of the present ratio of one's achievements to aspirations does not mean that one doubts one's ability to improve that ratio in due course. Conversely, having high global self-esteem here and now does not mean that one judges oneself to be capable of maintaining one's present standing or improving it. For example, there is no contradiction in my believing firmly in my ability, if I try hard enough, to succeed at learning a new language even though I have little esteem in my mastery of foreign languages here and now. Conversely, I may lack confidence in further ventures at learning new languages (say, because I am too old), although I am pleased with my current ability to speak many. Self-confidence is concerned with what one hopes to accomplish; self-esteem is concerned with what one believes oneself to have accomplished. Self-confidence is not a concept reared in the same abstract discourse on self-value as self-esteem is; at the same time it is less artificial, more earthbound. All teachers and sport coaches know what it means for their students and athletes to be brimming with or wanting in confidence; only those in the thralls of the global self-esteem fallacy will care if they have 'high global self-esteem'.

'Self-efficacy' – or, more precisely, 'perceived self-efficacy' – is the typical psychological jargon of the day for self-confidence. Social cognitivist Albert Bandura (1997) is the father of perceived-self-efficacy research, which has already an extensive line of descent. I prefer to avoid unnecessary jargon and simply talk about research on *self-confidence* – a term which has a comfortable home in common parlance.

But it is instructive to understand why Bandura and his colleagues prefer the cumbersome neologism *perceived self-efficacy*. The first reason given by them is that self-confidence is commonly run together with self-esteem. That may well be true (see, e.g., Bandura, 1997, p. 12; Furedi, 2004, p. 159). It is usually more serviceable in conceptual analyses, however, to try to clarify existing concepts rather than to create new ones. The second reason is that the type of self-confidence Bandura is interested in and takes to be a significant correlate of achievement is domain-specific or item-specific self-confidence. The term 'self-confidence' in ordinary language is, by contrast, commonly understood globally, just as self-esteem typically is in psychological research (or so Bandura claims, 1997, pp. 40, 50). Two things may be said in response: (a) Not all self-efficacy theorists follow Bandura in construing the term non-globally – witness, for instance, Schwarzer and Jerusalem's (1995) global self-efficacy scale, which is eerily reminiscent of typical global self-esteem measures. (b) If what we are interested in is domain-specific self-confidence, then we can simply say 'domain-specific self-confidence'. It is no more cumbersome than 'perceived self-efficacy' and has the additional advantage of respecting ordinary language. This is why I think it is wise to overrule Bandura's self-imposed division between perceived self-efficacy and self-confidence, and simply rely on the latter term, hereafter in this chapter to be understood as *domain-specific* self-confidence.

Bandura's book (1997) is a tome, and I cannot do justice to all its subtleties here. Most importantly, Bandura understands self-confidence as a belief in one's capabilities to organise and execute the courses of action required to produce a given attainment. The book weaves together theoretical and empirical considerations to show that the self-confidence of a person (P) vis-à-vis a task (T) – a student's self-confidence with respect to a given assignment, for instance – substantially influences the course of action P chooses to pursue, how much effort P puts forth, how long P perseveres in the face of obstacles and failures, the levels of stress P experiences in coping with T and, ultimately, the likelihood of P's accomplishing T (1997, p. 3). Bandura argues that self-confidence is cultivated through 'enactive mastery experiences', 'vicarious experiences' provided by role models, 'verbal persuasion and allied types of social influences' and 'physiological and affective states' (1997, chap. 3).

I particularly recommend Bandura's book to parents and educators. Of special interest for them will be his discussion of the growth of self-confidence through the transitional experiences of adolescence – the time when many students have lost their early eagerness to try their luck at every suggested school project, believing instead that they are useless at this and that – and what parents and teachers can do to guide them through this make-or-break period (1997, pp. 177–84). Furthermore, Bandura is keenly aware of the extent to which educators are able to stimulate self-confidence in students only if they possess enough of it themselves (1997, pp. 240–43). Although the illusions of the self-esteem industry are gradually falling into desuetude, we may confidently hope that restoring attention to the need to inspire realistic self-confidence in young people can have a positive impact on their lives. Such inspiration will have to do, however, with advice pertaining to exercise and time on task, realistic comparisons and goal settings, stepwise approximations, non-depressive interpretations of results and the development of the relevant emotional virtues of persistence and courage – rather than global self-aggrandising episodes of 'I am great and I can do anything'.

5.4. Beyond Mere Self-Concept: Implicit Self-Esteem

Where do these considerations leave Cigman's 'losers', who think they are bad at everything (Cigman, 2004, p. 105), lacking as they are in what she calls 'basic self-esteem' (Cigman, 2001)? Is it possible to help them improve their self-concepts? Of course, that is primarily an empirical question: Can children with a consistently low self-esteem in all or almost all life-domains really be helped? My own armchair psychology tells me that they often can, but I do not want to indulge it here out of season. Instead I simply make three preliminary observations. The first is that many people who seem to be plagued by deep insecurities and self-doubts all their lives actually do quite well – witness Abraham Lincoln, to mention a somewhat hackneyed example (see, e.g., Roland and Foxx, 2003, p. 271). We should not always take declarations of self-inadequacy at face value. Second, some of the children Cigman mentions may be suffering from clinical depression, an ailment that seems to afflict more and more young people. Parents and teachers must be alert to this possibility and see to it that such children receive the relevant medical attention. Third, low self-confidence may often be mistaken for low self-esteem; and I suggested earlier that Cigman might have been guilty of that mistake. If so, the low self-confidence of the children she describes could well be caused by their lack of *self-worth*. People with a strong sense of self-worth believe that they possess a self potentially worthy of its own esteem and the esteem of others. They carry about with them, as William James put it, 'a certain average tone of self-feeling' which is independent of the reasons they have for satisfaction or dissatisfaction (1890, p. 306). Self-worth, then, like self-confidence, is forward looking. But optimistically looking forward to achieving x is not the same as the satisfaction of having achieved x – and it is only the latter that matters for Jamesian self-esteem. So the fall from grace of global self-esteem as a valued educational indicator does not mean that undergirding children's self-worth and firing salvoes of self-confidence into them – even unrealistic self-confidence in the case of young children – cannot be an educational asset.

A lingering sense of doubt remains as to how much of the disagreement between me and Cigman (abetted by Ferkany, 2008, who airs similar concerns to hers) is merely terminological and how much of it is substantive. In order to clear up that doubt, let us retrace our steps a little. Cigman states that the basic self-esteem, on which 'very young children need to coast for a while', is indeed a sense of self-worth, namely 'boundless self-worth', actualised in the 'confidence to act' (2001, pp. 567, 569, 571). She thinks that the social science conception of global self-esteem was a misguided construct from the word go because it lacked any grounding in ordinary language (2004). An 'ordinary' concept of self-esteem can, however, be resurrected – asked to 'please stand up' (2008) – and this concept happily turns out to be that of basic self-esteem. In a similar vein, Ferkany wants to forge a conceptual link between self-esteem and self-confidence. On a 'sophisticated account' of self-esteem, reasonably faithful to ordinary usage, a threshold level of dispositional self-confidence is necessary for high self-esteem; the two go hand in hand. The threshold in question can be crossed only via proper childhood attachment between infants and parents; therefore the 'sophisticated account' of self-esteem is essentially 'attachment theoretic' (Ferkany, 2008).

Now, I have nothing against attachment theory; indeed, I find its insights quite plausible. Similarly, I would concur with Cigman's related emphasis on the need for young children to experience a pervasive, if perhaps not 'boundless', sense of self-worth. What I question, however, is that an ordinary-language notion of self-esteem can be reconstructed to carry all this freight. Recall that 'self-esteem' was almost never used in ordinary language before the 1980s. It is an essentially artificial construct. Psychologists did well to devise two operationalist variants of this construct; one of them, global self-esteem, failed in the end to prove its mettle, but domain-specific self-esteem seems to offer more promise. 'Self-confidence' and 'self-worth' are, however, terms reared through generations of language users and cannot simply be specified on a whim. Moreover, we have good reasons – as I have explained – for keeping them logically distinct from self-esteem.

So far, then, the disagreements between Cigman/Ferkany and me seem to be essentially terminological. Nevertheless, raising those disagreements here is useful, for they connect naturally to a territory that is more theoretically controversial and perilous. (I do not know exactly what would be Cigman's and Ferkany's preferred routes through that territory, so I refrain from speculating on how they would react to the following considerations.) I have to this point treated the issue under discussion as simply that of exploring which facets of self-concept matter most for wellbeing. As a self-realist, I wonder, however, if some of these facets, such as 'sense of self-worth' and one's 'average tone of self-feeling', do not have more to do with one's actual full self than one's self-concept. That possibility is rarely if ever considered in the literature because it is predominantly anti-self-realist; self is simply automatically equated with self-concept. The facets that I mentioned involve beliefs that may be hidden from the agent's own view. Not that I want to exclude the possibility that beliefs may be temporarily unarticulated and inexplicit and still belong to self-concept. However, when we start exploring aspects of people's core character states that are, by their very nature implicit rather than explicit, I think we have good reason – given that we believe in a distinction between self and self-concept – to consider those aspects as belonging to the former rather than the latter; namely, as entering selfhood not via self-concept but independent of self-concept. What I have primarily in mind here is the currently active research on what some psychologists call – somewhat infelicitously – 'implicit self-esteem'. It bears striking resemblance both to Cigman's 'basic self-esteem' and Ferkany's 'attachment-theoretic self-esteem'.

Contrary to explicit self-esteem, on which I have concentrated so far and which is captured via self-reports and other explicit measurements techniques, implicit self-esteem has to do with affect that is elicited automatically via cognitive priming tasks and other ingenious 'implicit' measures (Bosson & Prewitt-Freilino, 2007). Those measures, which are meant to tap self-evaluations that cannot be accessed via conscious introspection, include the 'name letter test' (in which participants rate their liking for various letters, including those of their own names), the 'implicit association test' (in which participants are asked to combine self-related categorisations with a number of negative and positive stimuli) and the 'implicit evaluation test' (in which participants are asked to evaluate a series of positive or negative target words which are either preceded by self-related or non-self-related primes). The general idea is to tease out each participant's unconscious network of associations between representations of the self and negative or positive evaluations (Koole & DeHart, 2007). The underlying theoretical assumption is similar to that of attachment theory: that children develop unconscious beliefs about their own selves based on interactions with primary caregivers – beliefs, in particular, about whether or not they are worthy of love and esteem – which persist into adulthood. This assumption has been tested and corroborated in a number of studies by implicit-self-esteem theorists (see Koole & DeHart, 2007, for a review).

In a sense, this assumption is not new. More than 40 years ago, educational psychologist David Ausubel wrote about the 'intrinsic self-esteem' that flows from unconditional parental acceptance, and the learned helplessness that can result from lack of such acceptance (1968, pp. 401–407). Findings demonstrate how people retain their style of attachment from infancy to adulthood (see, e.g., Waters, Merrick, Treboux, Crowell & Albersheim, 2000), and special attention has been paid in the literature to the impact of the quality of the early parent–child relationship for the experience of self-conscious emotions later in life (Lagattuta & Thompson, 2007).

More original are some of the recent specific findings by implicit-self-esteem theorists and the implications that seem to follow from them. One significant finding is that the correlation between explicit and implicit self-esteem is low (although slightly higher for women than men). Another finding indicates that high implicit self-esteem forms a buffer against low explicit self-esteem, providing the 'sufferers' of the latter with 'a glimmer of hope'. Yet another finding shows people exhibiting narcissism to be characterised by extremely high implicit self-esteem (rooted perhaps in parental overvaluation) combined with relatively low explicit self-esteem (see further in Bosson & Prewitt-Freilino, 2007; Koole & DeHart, 2007). Most importantly for present purposes, implicit self-esteem – which I would be tempted to call a person's sense of self-worth – presents itself as an enduring character state, much more than does explicit self-esteem, which can fluctuate considerably in response to circumstantial variables. As defined by the implicit-self-esteem theorists themselves, this sense of self-worth is *ex hypothesi* hidden from our conscious view. A mirror that cannot mirror is not a real mirror. This is why I think it is misleading to think of implicit self-esteem as a specific facet of self-concept (and indeed to call it 'self-esteem', which makes people think of it in the same breath as explicit self-esteem). It is more rewarding – from a self-realist perspective at least – to consider it on par with the various other emotion-based core traits that, while outside the purview of self-concept, make up our actual full self.

5.5. Self-Esteem, Emotion and Value

Turning finally to self-concept again, instantiated via explicit self-esteem and self-confidence, various questions remain as to its nature and purpose. What kind of a psychological entity is self-esteem? I have already pointed out that it does not merely comprise beliefs. The belief that I am good at maths does not give me high domain-specific self-esteem as a maths student if the affective element (my caring about being good at maths) is missing. Self-esteem is at least partly concerned with how I *feel* about myself. If self-esteem constitutes a cognition plus affect, however, we seem to have entered the realm of emotions. Does self-esteem, then, represent a specific kind of emotion(s), and if so, which emotion(s)? Pride and shame may seem the most likely candidates. Recall from Chapter 4 that Keshen referred to them as 'self-esteem feelings' (1996, p. 4). Brown and Marshall (2001) have, in fact, found a strong correlation between high self-esteem and pride, and between low self-esteem and shame – much stronger than between self-esteem and non-self-conscious emotions. Correlations can indicate causal relations, but also logical relationships in disguise. Does self-esteem perhaps correlate so strongly with pride and shame because it simply *is* pride (when it is high) and shame (when it is low)?

There are episodic emotions and there are dispositional emotions. Scheff has proposed that self-esteem be seen as an *episodic* emotion of pride (when high) and shame (when low) – and that we are thus 'virtually always in a state of pride or shame' (cited in Tracy & Robins, 2007b, p. 187). This proposal, however, runs into difficulty. Although my pride swells when I achieve a high grade on a maths test, my maths self-esteem can still be, on average, low. More seriously, it is simply both empirically and logically impossible that a person with high self-esteem is constantly in a state of pride: empirically, because we know from everyday experience that no one is constantly in a state of a particular episodic emotion, and logically, because if one were constantly in the state of an episodic emotion, it would, *ex hypothesi*, be nonepisodic.

A more plausible proposal would be that self-esteem constitutes *dispositional* emotions: tendencies to experience pride or shame regularly. In favour of that proposal would be a fact noted in Section 4.3 – that in English at least, the language of pride does not provide any locution to cover dispositional pride. That X is a proud person does not mean that X has a strong tendency to experience pride, but rather that X is sensitive to pride-or-shame-fuelling experiences (namely that X is prideful) or that X is a self-respectful person. Perhaps 'high self-esteem' is the term that fills this lacuna? There are two considerations that speak against that possibility. The first is that high self-esteem, as measured by Rosenberg-type scales, for instance, neither measures nor aspires to measure a disposition; it merely measures one's feelings about one's perceived standing at the moment. And second, whereas it is conceptually true that compassionate people possess compassion as a stable character state (*hexis*, in the Aristotelian model) – for that is what 'being compassionate' means – it may or may not be true that people with high self-esteem possess self-esteem as a stable character state. If they do, it has yet to be demonstrated through psychological research. To date such research indicates precisely that the kind of self-esteem under discussion here as belonging to self-concept (explicit self-esteem) fluctuates much more than does the kind of implicit self-esteem (namely sense of self-worth) that we possess as an emotion-grounded character state.

We seem to be running out of emotional candidates, then. Surely, self-esteem is not a mere *mood*, because moods are typically specified as objectless states, but in so far as self-esteem incorporates affective states, they clearly have formal objects. My maths self-esteem is *about* my maths achievements, for example; it is not merely an objectless mood of 'pride' about nothing in particular. Martha Nussbaum has suggested, however, that a special category of emotions resides between dispositional emotions and moods. She calls them *background emotions* (2001, chap. 1). Background emotions are persisting affective states, which lurk in the backseat of our psyche and pervade our characters, but which may go unnoticed unless certain conditions bring them into consciousness. They possess the intentionality that moods lack, but also the fluctuations in appearance and intensity that distinguish them from dispositional emotions. Notice that some theorists use the term 'mood' not to denote objectless emotional states, but rather to denote highly generalised emotional appraisals of the 'existential backgrounds' of our lives (Lazarus, 1994). On such an understanding, the background emotions that I have in mind are best described as moods.

David Hume may provide guidance here, as before. A cleverly orchestrated interpretation of Hume's view on an agent's sense of power, produced recently by Brown and Hooper (2008), lends considerable backbone to the suggestion that self-esteem be best understood as a *background emotion* of pride (when high) or shame (when low). According to Brown and Hooper's analysis, Hume (1978) explains how the anticipation of future pleasures is itself pleasurable, thus reinforcing the 'passion' of pride as a background concern. Although the episodic experience of pride subsides, a deep-rooted 'sense of power' to procure similar future episodes remains. This sense of power retrospectively encapsulates past pleasures and anticipates future ones. Thus, episodic experiences of the self-conscious emotions possess self-reinforcing and self-perpetuating qualities that gradually carve out more and more persistent backgrounds for themselves. These backgrounds then become the emotional hotbeds of our self-esteem – and, as already argued, such emotion-grounded self-esteem turns out to be important for human flourishing as long as it is domain-specific rather than global.

If this Humean explanation holds true, as I am inclined to believe it does, it provides nothing less than the missing link between self-esteem and emotion. To remain faithful to the proposed conceptual taxonomy of self-conscious emotions (see Section 4.3), which is slightly more nuanced than that of Hume, we need to amend the above thesis slightly: High self-esteem is constituted not only by the background emotion of pride, but also the background emotion of self-satisfaction (concerning outcomes that reflect positively on one's self, although one is not responsible for them). Similarly, low self-esteem involves not only shame as a background emotion, but also self-disappointment, such as when one's self-esteem is lowered because of being ugly by nature; physical appearance is after all the domain that has turned out to correlate most highly with global self-esteem at every developmental level (Harter, 1999, pp. 158–59; cf. also Deonna & Teroni's persuasive criticism of the claim that low self-esteem is *only* about shame, 2009).

Although the self-conscious emotions are not at issue in *self-confidence*, a similar explanation could be made to work there as well. Self-confidence is not only a belief about future successes; it is a belief tied to optimistic courage (if the self-confidence is high) or pessimistic fear (if it is low). Yet high self-confidence constitutes neither episodic courage nor dispositional courage in the ordinary sense. If we think of it as a background emotion of (domain-specific) courage to meet new challenges, however – that has been reinforced in the manner that Hume envisaged for pride – we arrive at the explanation that we need without the additional baggage of understanding self-confidence as either an occurrent emotional state or a steady disposition. Such background-emotion accounts of self-esteem and self-confidence, respectively, further secure my 'alternative' emotion-based paradigm of selfhood. Emotions, then, have been shown to be constitutive not only of our actual full self, but also of our self-concept – an important milestone in the forging of the link between self and emotion aimed at in this study and, by implication, of a link between self research and emotion research.

Can background emotions of this type constitute moral virtues in the same sense as dispositional emotions can? Elizabeth Telfer claims that self-esteem cannot be considered a virtue, because whereas virtues are permanent traits, self-esteem is an attitude to oneself that a person can possess in different degrees at different times: 'Whether we think it is a good attitude or not will depend on whether we think it is justified in a particular case' (1995, p. 115). Nevertheless, recall that Aristotle refused to call *megalopsychia* a virtue unless the actual moral worth of the *megalopsychoi* was accompanied by the corresponding domain-specific self-esteem predicated upon that moral worth; we could call it 'background' pride in their own moral attainments. (Notably, some translators of Aristotle prefer to translate *megalopsychia* simply as 'pride'!) The mere correspondence with reality or reasonableness of the self-esteem does not suffice, however; Aristotle's losers, who lack moral worth and esteem themselves *correctly* as lacking moral worth, are obviously not morally virtuous (Aristotle, 1985, pp. 97–104 [1123a33–1125a35]). For self-esteem to constitute moral virtue, therefore, in the Aristotelian schema, it must be concurrently reasonable *and* morally up to scratch.

This observation takes us right back to the practicalities of my earlier discussion of justified self-esteem. Cigman (2004) argued for a type of self-esteem that educators should help promote: what she called 'situated self-esteem' and what I preferred to call 'justified self-esteem'. What precisely does such self-esteem involve? The empirical research canvassed in Section 5.2 helps us to formulate an initial answer to that question. Baumeister and his colleagues reasonably conclude on the basis of their analysis that the type of self-esteem for which we should aim is a domain-specific one 'that accurately reflects capabilities and interpersonal characteristics' and that would, for instance, help students to know what courses to take in school or what occupations to pursue. Although a favourable view of the self is preferable to an unfavourable one, such a view should be promoted only 'on the basis of performing well and acting morally' (Baumeister et al., pp. 38–39). Talk about psychological research never carrying normative implications! The global self-esteem movement placed students inside a cocoon of low expectations and abundant but hollow rewards. After its demise, we can safely return to a more classic conception of students as thriving on wholesome ambition, and not being in danger of becoming over-burdened, overstressed or overwhelmed if we expect them to achieve. As Damon correctly notes, young people make the greatest progress when they are given demanding challenges and opportunities to prove themselves (1995, pp. 22 and 84).

Once the conception of global self-esteem has been laid to rest, we can begin to explore the nuts and bolts of domain-specific justified self-esteem more fruitfully – in school contexts, for instance. The teacher's role with regard to students' domain-specific self-esteem would be to help them (1) to set themselves worthwhile and morally acceptable goals in areas of school work, (2) to estimate their achievements correctly and (3) to experience proper satisfaction with their achievements: that is, bring the feeling component of self-esteem into alignment with the proper estimations, and to establish pride and courage as background emotions related to school work (cf. Keshen, 1996, pp. 6–15 on the self-concept of the 'reasonable' person). The goals in (1) will be primarily the school subjects and various practical and social skills that schoolwork requires. Justified self-esteem matters in those domain-specific areas for the simple practical reason that students who overestimate or underestimate their achievements or who feel overly or deficiently satisfied with those achievements do not make good learners. Needless to say, assisting students in achieving a correct estimate of and proper satisfaction with their school achievements will not always augment self-esteem; it may reduce domain-specific self-esteem for some of them. But it is better for students' future learning to know where they stand than for them to live in a fool's paradise. Although I have taken school as an example here, similar implications would obviously follow for other domains.

Why is justified domain-specific self-esteem morally important, then? For moral philosophers of an Aristotelian bent, it is important in so far it constitutes or is conducive to emotion-grounded moral virtues, which in turn constitute or are conducive to *eudaimonia*, the highest human good. For Humeans, it is important as a pervasive and potent background emotion of pride, both because of Hume's pride-produces-self thesis and because self-constituting pride is subsequently the 'surest guardian of every virtue' (1972, p. 276). The differences between the general Humean and Aristotelian moral ontologies not-withstanding, these explanations more or less concur.

It there anything more to say about the value of self-esteem? Contemporary psychologists think there is; many of them are keenly interested in its value as an adaptive evolutionary mechanism. Leary and Baumeister believe, for instance, that because 'it is nearly impossible to imagine an otherwise healthy and well-adjusted person who is truly indifferent to self-esteem' (2000, p. 1), an evolutionary account is required to explain its salience. Philosophers tend to be rather wary of such accounts (see, e.g., Kristjánsson, 2002, pp. 206–207), although it must be admitted that their understanding of evolutionary theory often fails to go far enough to buttress their discomfort with its arguments. The first reason for this philosophical uneasiness is the propensity of evolutionary explanations to collapse into the *historical fallacy* of confounding moral genealogy and moral justification. A second, related, reason is the *moral irrelevance* of some evolutionary accounts of morality. It is not difficult, for instance, to imagine a plausible evolutionary account of the adaptive value of *Schadenfreude* (pleasure at other people's undeserved bad fortune) and the certain hardness of heart that goes with it. Yet, such an account would not offer any good moral reason to experience *Schadenfreude*. The third reason is the danger of *explanatory over-crowding*: After explaining how self-esteem can impact *eudaimonia*, do we really need a further explanation of why it is important? The fourth reason is the highly *speculative nature* of many evolutionary 'just-so stories', which renders them impervious to possible refutations. They are, so to speak, too clever for their own good, and even the alleged abstractness of philosophical doctrines pales by comparison.

A number of evolutionary accounts of the value of self-esteem have been produced (for an overview, see Leary & Baumeister, 2000, pp. 6–8). I merely mention two. So-called *terror management theory* likens the value of self-esteem to that of a security blanket diverting our attention from the inevitability of our own mortality. This theory mixes evolutionary elements with existentialist concerns – an unusual mixture – about the creation of 'bad faith' and other self-protecting mechanisms, shielding us against insufferable truths about our destiny as free and mortal beings. By seeing ourselves as meaningful, success-ful agents in an ongoing cultural drama, we palliate the severity of the death threat (see Arndt, Schimel & Cox, 2007). Correlational research does show self-esteem to be negatively correlated with death anxiety, among other things. The problem here, however, is not so much the dearth of corroborative evidence as its overabundance. One would nat-urally expect most positive psychological states, not only self-esteem, to be negatively correlated with death anxiety, which could tell us some-thing general and profound about the human condition, but very little specifically about the value of self-esteem.

Sociometer theory claims that self-esteem serves as a subjective mon-itor of our relational evaluations: the degree to which we think other people regard us as valuable and worthy of esteem. Put differently, self-esteem forms a sociometer system – instilled in us through evolutionary selection – that monitors the quality of our actual and potential inter-personal relationships, especially within near groups. Self-esteem, then, is not seen only as being *influenced by* other people's appraisals, but is seen as being *about* precisely those appraisals – our relational value in the eyes of others (Leary & Baumeister, 2000; Leary, 2007a). Leary finds it 'difficult to imagine', from an evolutionary standpoint, 'what sort of selection pressures would have led human beings to be concerned about their own self-evaluations unless those evaluations were linked to important, reproductively meaningful outcomes' (2007b, p. 47). Most moral philosophers would probably find it baffling that anyone should conceive of this issue in such a way, but let us leave this remark out of further consideration to focus instead on the empirical evidence.

If self-esteem has, as I have argued, to do with pride or shame as background emotions, then those emotions are, according to soci-ometer theory, not really about the self, except in an oblique way, but rather about interpersonal relationships (see Leary, 2007a, p. 333). This claim would seem to contradict much of the received wisdom about self-conscious emotions (recall Chapter 4) – which does not mean soci-ometer theory is necessarily any worse, for that matter. Sociometer theorists such as Leary and Baumeister do provide empirical find-ings showing that public events exert a stronger effect on self-esteem than do private events. Failures known to others lower our self-esteem more than do failures known only to ourselves; being perceived by others in an undesired fashion can embarrass us, even when we believe that those perceptions are inaccurate; other people generate feelings of guilt and shame in us, even when we know deep down that we have done nothing wrong (see examples in Leary & Baumeister, 2000; Leary, 2007a).

Such findings should not surprise anyone who is at least moderately sensitive to the social embeddedness of selfhood in general and self-concept in particular. More disconcerting is the claim that when people experience self-conscious self-esteem-constituting emotions simply from thinking about or evaluating themselves in their own minds, they must inevitably have *internalised* the evaluations of others. 'Internalised', here, is clearly distinct from simply having learnt from others to evaluate oneself and having one's evaluations 'seconded' by them in the Humean sense discussed in Section 2.5. This is a much stricter condition. Or, as Leary puts it, the 'necessary and sufficient cause of self-conscious emotions is the real or imagined appraisal of other people' (2007a, p. 330). The difficulty with this contention is not so much that it rubs up against our everyday experiences of purely private self-appraisals, which I think it does but is difficult to demonstrate empirically (cf. Deonna & Teroni, 2008). The problem is rather that this contention, which is meant to be a scientific hypothesis of an evolutionary theory as distinct from a philosophical suggestion, seems to be irrefutable and hence unscientific. For what possible qualities could a self-evaluation ever present that would prove that it did not originate from the internalisation of other people's evaluations? In any case, as a philosophical cobbler, I shall stick to my last and rest content with my earlier conclusions about the nature and moral value of justified domain-specific self-esteem, rather than being drawn into further speculations as to its adaptive origin and value.

6. The Self As Moral Character

6.1. The Situationist Challenge

It is time to turn our focus again from self-concept to the actual full self, in whose existence self-realists believe. Self-realists tend to be moral objectivists, as explained in Section 1.2. Among the tenets of such objectivism is the *psychological* assumption that human beings are capable of forming intentions to honour objective moral properties, and to do so, with time, by developing stable, self-shaping, virtuous dispositions. Aristotle says of such dispositions that 'no human achievement has the stability of activities that express virtue, since these seem to be more enduring even than our knowledge of the sciences'. The virtuous person is indeed no human 'chameleon, insecurely based', but rather a human who 'keeps the character he has throughout his life' – even in the face of severe misfortunes – 'good, foursquare and blameless' (1985, pp. 25–26 [1100b1–35]).

Most moral philosophers have assumed that, on this issue at least, Aristotle should be trusted. Persons have moral characters, and those characters dispose them to good or evil deeds. Folk psychology concurs; in everyday conversation, we typically explain and predict actions on the basis of people's long-term personality traits – blissfully prized commodities in our fractured times. Similarly, virtue ethics, so prominent in today's ethical discourse, focuses on the cultivation of moral virtues *qua* stable dispositions conducive to human flourishing. And in education circles, character education – a close cousin of virtue ethics and sharing many of the same assumptions – has become not so much the flavour of the month as the flavour of the past decade.

Dispositionism (or globalism with respect to character traits) is not an undisputed thesis, however. Many social psychologists will have none of it. They consider dispositionism to be refutable by empirical evidence. In recent years, spearheaded by Gilbert Harman (1999) and John Doris (1998, 2002), a number of philosophers have followed suit, launching a sustained attack on residues of dispositionism in ethics and moral education. This challenge has a rallying cry: *situationism*. According to situationism, there is no such thing as character in its etymological sense of an indelible mark impressed on an object. People have no robust traits; how they act varies with the situation. If this is true, all the suspects in the story – folk psychology, virtue ethics and character education – are guilty of the same 'fundamental attribution error' (Harman, 1999, p. 327). The chief villain, however, is Aristotle: the prime instigator of the error. Character attributions rest on the tenets of an Aristotelian psychology that is some 2,500 years old, and, from a scientific perspective, out of the ark (see Doris, 2002, p. ix). The rejection of dispositionism will therefore have devastating ramifications for the neo-Aristotelian theory prominent in moral philosophy for the past quarter century (see Doris, 1998, pp. 504–505). Aristotle-inspired folk psychology finally goes down the same drain as Aristotelian cosmology did 500 years ago; virtue ethics will be shown to be going nowhere fast; and from an educational perspective, if there is no such thing as character, then character education is also an illusion (Harman, 1999, p. 328).

Recall that Aristotle did not distinguish between moral character and moral selfhood. Although I believe such a distinction can be made – on the assumption that one's character may undergo non-radical changes while leaving one's selfhood intact (see Section 1.1) – it is clear that without moral character, there is no moral selfhood either (as the latter is a subset of the former). An attack on Aristotle's notion of moral character is therefore an attack on the 'alternative' paradigm's notion of moral selfhood espoused in this book. Hence, it must be attended to here and answered.

Judging from the number of rejoinders to the situationist challenge, situationism seems to have repelled more moral philosophers than it has attracted. There is a steadily growing mountain of such rejoinders (see, e.g., Flanagan, 1991, chap. 14; Athanassoulis, 2001; Miller, 2003; Kamtekar, 2004; Goldie, 2004; Sabini & Silver, 2005; Fleming, 2006; Webber, 2006). Arguably, this literature has now reached what qualitative researchers call a 'saturation point': the point at which the addition of new participants fails to provide new and significant information. I do not aspire to lift the saturation point in this chapter by producing new objections to situationism. Rather, my aim is threefold. First,

I propose what I consider to be a helpful classification of the existing objections under four main headings: 'the methodological objection', 'the moral dilemma objection', 'the bullet-biting objection' and 'the anti-behaviouristic objection'. The last two objections draw essentially on Aristotelian sources. I argue, however, that the anti-behaviouristic objection in particular has so far deployed but a miniscule part of the available Aristotelian arsenal. My second aim is to resuscitate a more powerful Aristotelian version of this objection by fleshing it out through varied illustrative examples of human conduct – thus deepening the current discourse on situationism. My third and final aim is to explore some of the implications of such resuscitation for our understanding of the salience of moral character and moral selfhood, particularly with regard to its *emotional basis*. Prior to all of this, however, is a brief rehearsal of some of the basic ingredients of the situationist challenge is in order.

6.2. The Psychological Experiments and Their Alleged Implications

The psychological experiments that social psychologists and, later, moral philosophers have used as grist for the situationist mill are, I trust, familiar to most readers after repeated discussions in both academic journals and the popular media, and require only the briefest of rehearsals. I focus here on the four experiments most commonly cited:

Honesty Experiment. Over 8,000 schoolchildren were placed in situations in which they could (a) cheat on artificially created tests by peeking or asking friends, (b) fake records or cheat at party games, (c) steal change left on a table and (d) lie about their conduct. The mean correlation across behaviour types (a)–(d) was only 0.23. Furthermore, no significant correlation was found between the children's behaviour and their knowledge of the Ten Commandments or the Boy Scout Code. The researchers (Hartshorne & May, 1928) concluded that there is no such thing as cross-situational honesty, and, indeed, no such thing as character. This experiment, conducted in the 1920s, is by far the oldest of this type and the one which has had the clearest practical repercussions. It influenced Kohlberg's moral-reasoning approach and gave succour to his dismissal of traditional character building as a 'bag of virtues' – thereby influencing the content of moral education for decades, until the renascence of character education in the 1990s.

Dime Experiment. In this experiment, performed in the 1970s, the subjects were adults making calls from public telephones in US shopping malls. Some of the subjects found a dime secretly left in the phone by the experimenter; others did not. As the subjects left the phone booths, a confederate of the experimenter 'accidentally' dropped a folder full of papers on the floor. As it turned out, most of the subjects who had found a dime stopped to help the confederate pick up the papers, but only one out of 25 participants who did not find a dime offered help. The experimenters (Isen and Levin, 1972) hypothesised that finding a dime improved the subjects' mood, and that their good mood – rather than any consistent character trait – prompted the helping behaviour.

Good Samaritans Experiment. When it comes to responding to the needs of a sick person, does it matter what religious views people hold, or whether they are preparing a talk on a religious or a secular theme? Not according to this experiment, performed in the 1970s. Whether seminary students believed that they were on their way to deliver a talk on the parable of the Good Samaritan or on a practical topic had no significant impact on their stopping to help a 'sick' confederate. However, the experimenters (Darley & Batson, 1973) found that whereas 63% of subjects who did not consider themselves to be in a hurry to reach their destination offered help, only 10% of hurried participants helped. Again, a situational factor seemed to be the crucial variable.

Milgram Experiment. The most famous of the four, this experiment from the 1960s focused on a fictitious learning–memory test in which the 'learners' were strapped to chairs and supposedly given electric shocks by the 'teachers' each time they made a mistake on a learning task. The 'teachers' sat in an adjacent room and administered the shocks by pushing a button. All the subjects recruited for the experiment as 'teachers' knew beforehand what was considered to be a safe, moderate, strong, intense and life-threatening voltage. The experimenter instructed the subjects, with increasingly forceful verbal prods, to give shocks of higher voltage after each mistake made by the learners. Contrary to prior predictions by their peers, all the subjects went at least to the 'intense' level, and two-thirds went all the way to the end of the (fictitious) shock series, ignoring cries of increased agony emanating from the learners. Only 2.5% of unprodded subjects went all the way, however. The experimenter (Milgram, 1974) saw this as an explanation of the apparently irrational obedience to authority shown, for instance, by Nazi soldiers during World War II.

Recent years have witnessed a burgeoning literature on the moral implications of those psychological experiments. Ethical situationists claim that people's behaviour is essentially situation-dependent rather than character dependent. Undue freight has been heaped on the idea of a fixed component, moral character or moral selfhood, which simply does not seem to be operative in the experiments; people are not as set in their ways as we used to think; and we have systematically underappreciated the salience of situational factors. The results of these experiments, then, are deemed *at least* sufficient to shake our previously imperturbable confidence in the existence of consistent cross-situational dispositions, and to call for 'a certain redirection of our ethical attention' (Doris, 1998, p. 505) – *at most* even sufficient to eliminate the very ideas of moral character and selfhood, and to damn the entire fields of virtue ethics and character education. Harman (1999) is the one who draws the most radical implications from the experiments, by rejecting the notion of character altogether, at least in its everyday sense.

In slightly more technical terms, situationists do not typically deny that people have dispositions to behaviours that are stable from this day to the next within a range of reasonably similar situations – the correlations between children's behaviours listed within each group (a)–(d) in the *Honesty Experiment*, for instance, was relatively high. What they do deny is that people possess dispositions which are robustly consistent among diverse situations; even more do they deny the strong reading of the unity-of-the-virtues thesis (discussed briefly in Section 3.3) that one virtue entails all the others. In other words, whereas some stability remains (for 'local', 'situation-specific' dispositions), two other core elements of globalism about character traits – 'robustness' and 'evaluative integrity' – are rejected (Doris, 2002, pp. 22–26). The cobweb that most urgently needs to be blown away is said to be the 'fundamental attribution error', committed in equal measure by folk psychologists and academics: the error of explaining and predicting people's behaviour via robust character traits.

Although situationism is meant to hit primarily at the assumption of robust traits of moral character or selfhood, it does not leave mere personality traits untouched either. Staple textbooks in personality psychology tell us that personality traits are enduring states, forming broad or generalised patterns across a range of situations. Situationism obviously denies the existence of such traits. Harman, for instance, explicitly mentions 'talkativeness' as one of the supposedly imaginary global dispositions (1999, p. 316), and in psychological circles, the four experiments described are more often invoked as part of an ongoing feud between social psychologists and personality psychologists on the existence of a firm and enduring individual personality than they are as ammunition in a debate about specifically moral characteristics. Many moderate psychologists from both camps reject the dichotomy, however, claiming that *both* situational and personality variables are crucial determinants of behaviour (see, e.g., Funder, 1999, p. 37).

As noted, situationists direct their animadversions specifically against the apotheosis of Aristotle's virtue theory in contemporary moral philosophy and moral education. It is obviously not the naturalistic streak in Aristotelian ethics that they resent. They are all for letting moral philosophy meet social psychology and sundry other empirical disciplines. What they do object to are the specifics of the Aristotelian story, which they consider factually wrong. Aristotelian virtue theory and Aristotle-inspired character education are faulty not because they are anchored in psychology but because they are anchored in a flawed psychology. There is no clash of two research cultures here such as the one I explored in Chapter 3. In Doris's own words, situationism 'is not *radically revisionary*, generally problematising ethical thought, but *conservatively revisionary*, undermining only particular – and dispensable – features of ethical thought associated with Aristotelian characterological psychology' (Doris, 1998, p. 513).

Noticeably, in this regard, situationism does not involve a complete rupture with the idea of human dispositions. Although cross-situational dispositions, such as global compassion, go overboard, intra-situational dispositions, such as consistent 'dime-finding, dropped-paper compassion', remain (Doris, 1998, p. 514). Furthermore, situationists acknowledge the fact that many people *appear* to possess global dispositions by virtue of having been diligent enough in selecting and modifying the situations to which they could be exposed. If I assume the role of a devoted husband, for example, and carefully avoid situations in which my devotion can be tested, then I may be able to deceive myself and others into considering it a global character trait (see, e.g., Harman, 1999 p. 320). If done self-deceptively, situationists do not recommend such self-inuring strategies, however. Indeed, in the situationist literature, much is made of the way in which misguided attributions of global characterological traits to oneself or others produce deceit, disappointment, prejudice and mawkish hero worship.

On the other hand, situationists strongly recommend deliberate (un-self-deceived, if you will) situation selection as a strategy in moral education. We should teach children to avoid situations in which they are likely to get into trouble, arrange social institutions such that outlets for temptations are limited and manipulate our own social settings so that they become propitious to decent behaviour. I should not, for instance, accept the invitation of a flirtatious colleague when my spouse is out of town, in the belief that I can control my impulses when it comes to the crunch (Doris, 1998, pp. 516–17). Apart from this advice, situationists have little patience with what currently goes by the name of moral education. Take character education, which revolves around the notion of character building, and where character is understood to include a sense of personal integrity, enduring consistency and steadfastness of purpose (see, e.g., McLaughlin & Halstead, 1999, pp. 134–35). The situationist response here is Harman's blunt and scathing remark that 'there is no such thing as character building' (1999, p. 328).

6.3. Two Initial Objections to Situationism

Let me first review two common objections to situationism that are not specifically Aristotelian: 'the methodological objection' and 'the moral dilemma objection'.

According to the *methodological objection*, there is something individually wrong with the way in which each of the situationism-supporting experiments has been conducted or interpreted. Consider first the *Honesty Experiment*. The subjects in this experiment were children, and it is no news that children's characters are more malleable than are those of adults. More saliently, it may well be that the to-be-researched dimension of 'honesty versus dishonesty' existed only in the heads of the experimenters, not in the heads of the children. Did the children necessarily consider lying, stealing and cheating as instances of a common underlying principle? Child psychologist William Damon has studied the method employed in this experiment and his verdict is one of damning indictment. When examining children's behaviour, Damon points out, we must try to understand its significance within the context of the child's own world and developmental level rather than cherry picking our favourite adult conceptualisation. Children have their own social lives and social roles, and they may interpret interpersonal events differently than adults do. There is no good reason to think that the subjects in this experiment understood that copying obscure answers to bizarre tests or breaking silly rules in games was to be considered 'cheating', let alone 'dishonesty'. Perhaps, if the children realised that they were being tested, they thought that the test was one of helpfulness to friends, loyalty and cooperation – in which case they would have being playing a straight bat and scored high. From the perspective of current child psychology, the experimenters committed pedestrian errors (Damon, 1988, pp. 6–9).

Turning to the *Dime Experiment*, it seems to show that trivial matters, such as minor mood swings, may affect behaviour. But do they affect morally important behaviour, such as helping someone in dire need? That *Dime Experiment* demonstrates only that they affect morally insignificant behaviour which is, in any case, not part of one's daily grind: Failing to pick up a stranger's dropped papers is hardly an important manifestation of moral failings (see Sabini & Silver, 2005, pp. 539–540).

The *Milgram Experiment* has generated considerably more nuanced methodological discussion. The unpreparedness of the subjects, the relentless pressure exerted on them by the experimenter, the fast pace of the experiment (which gave the subject's behaviour a knee-jerk quality), and the stepwise, slippery slope nature of the subjects' decisions have all been mentioned as possible mitigating factors. In their careful scrutiny of this experiment, Sabini and Silver conclude that the disturbance it may cause to our conception of character will at most be 'local', not 'global'. It does reveal two specific weaknesses to which most people happen to be prone: the tendency to yield more or less unquestioningly to the commands of articulate, domineering 'institutional experts', and to act like Romans when in Rome in order to avoid embarrassment, thereby following uncritically what other apparently reasonable people around them seem to be doing (Sabini & Silver, 2005, 550–61). The uncomfortable facts that few people have a spoon long enough to sup with the devil, and that many can bear adversity but few contempt, do not undermine any folk psychology about character, as they are already part and parcel of such psychology.

These methodological qualms notwithstanding, it may be too optimistic to think that all psychological experiments which seem conducive to situationism can be shown to fall prey to methodological errors. I have seen no such objection urged against the *Good Samaritans Experiment*, for example, apart from the fact that it has not been repeated. A second objection, however, cuts deeper to the core of what is at stake here morally. According to the *moral dilemma objection*, none of the four psychological experiments place subjects in our typical day-to-day choice situations in which the imperatives of a virtue compete with those of a vice or of a neutral state. Rather, they place subjects in situations in which they face the pressure of competing virtue imperatives. Such dilemma situations, requiring one to walk a tightrope between two virtues and not but contravene one or both of them, constitute that perilous terrain where virtue ethics – be it Aristotelian or modern – encounters its severest trials. Sometimes the diminution of one virtue can coherently and with impunity be set off against the proper manifestation of another, as when a temperate person decides to suspend temperance momentarily by accepting a huge slice of creamy cake from an elderly grandmother – for saying no would be cruel to the old lady. Other cases remain, however, in which choice is inherently tragic. Situationists focus on experiments relating to isolated and out-of-the-ordinary dilemma situations and conclude from them that people do not possess robust virtues. What they should be doing instead is gauging behavioural consistencies over extended periods involving everyday situations.

In the *Honesty Experiment*, for example, it may have been the children's pride, loyalty and helpfulness rather than their dishonesty that they pitted against honesty and which, in the end, eclipsed it (see Doris, 1988, p. 8). In the *Good Samaritans Experiment*, attending to the virtue of appropriate punctuality is at least a mitigating concern (see Kamtekar, 2004, p. 481). And in the *Milgram Experiment*, one must bear in mind that cooperativeness in group enterprises and a certain deference to appropriate authority are virtuous up to a point (Kamtekar, 2004, p. 473). That the subjects took those virtues too far is, in retrospect, not to be doubted, but we should not forget that they were the hapless victims of an artificially created situation which was always likely to overstrain human nature or at least bring it close to tipping point. Moreover, taking a virtue too far is one thing; being positively vicious (here: cruel to peers) is another.

On a particularist reading of virtue ethics that is currently popular, moral theory does not provide us with an algorithm to adjudicate the imperatives of conflicting virtues in dilemma situations. There is no yardstick – no single currency – to summarise and codify the variously dimensioned vectors of those imperatives; instead we must rely on some sort of intuitive artistry in such cases. And it is possible that equally virtuous persons will make radically different choices, all equally good. Some virtue ethicists consider it to be a strength, rather than a weakness, of modern virtue ethics and 'entirely to its credit' that it does not furnish us with any general decision procedure to apply theory to particular cases (Hursthouse, 1995). It would be instructive to explore the relationship between situationism and particularism. Although the former is essentially a psychological thesis and the latter a moral one, one could well imagine an argument to the effect that, because of the inherent particularity of morality, the fact that people's moral decisions always turn out to be situation-specific may not be such a bad thing after all. This is not a line of thought that I will not pursue further here, however.

Some moral particularists have been eager to enlist Aristotle as their ally (e.g., McDowell, 1996; Dunne, 1993). The trouble for them is that in Aristotle's view, *phronesis* adjudicates moral conflicts, and it relies not only upon situational appreciation but also upon general moral truths. Thus, when Aristotle uses examples, he does not abandon generalisations and tell us to attend only to the particularities of the situation; rather he describes the generalisations we should seek (on Aristotle as a moral generalist, see, e.g., Irwin, 2000; Kristjánsson, 2007, chap. 11). It may, therefore, be urged that in so far as the moral dilemma objection stems from a brand of modern virtue ethics that renounces moral generalism and instead embraces claims of moral particularism, it does not really constitute an Aristotelian response to situationism.

6.4. The Two Aristotelian Objections to Situationism

How should Aristotelians react to situationism? I think they should do so by dint of two objections: 'the bullet-biting objection' and 'the anti-behaviouristic objection'. The former objection is correctly anticipated by Doris as follows:

> The fact that many people failed morally in the observed situations tells us little about the adequacy of Aristotelian descriptive psychology, since such disappointing demographics are exactly what the virtue theorist would expect. Indeed, a virtue-based approach can explain the situationist data: it is precisely because so few people are truly virtuous that we see the results that we do (1998, p. 511. Cf. Fleming, 2006, pp. 41–42; Miller, 2003, pp. 378–79).

In the *Nicomachean Ethics*, Aristotle proposes a complicated if unsystematically explicated stage theory of moral development, ranging from the level of 'the many' (including children and other moral learners) through the levels of 'the soft', 'the resistant', 'the incontinent' and 'the continent', to that of the 'fully virtuous' (see Kristjánsson, 2007, chap. 2.2). Aristotle forthrightly acknowledges in a couple of places that 'most people' are placed between the levels of the incontinent and the continent (1985, pp. 190 and 197 [1150a15 and 1152a25–6]). Aristotle must be referring there to adult citizens; it would be out of line with his description of the level of 'the many' to hold that this level is not the one where most people (including children, labourers and slaves, in his system) are placed. In any case, most people cannot be counted upon to respond virtuously in morally tricky situations, for only a small minority has reached the level of full virtue. Far from being a *reductio* of Aristotelian characterological explanations, the results of the psychological experiment turn out to be exactly what coherent Aristotelians would expect. And far from pointing to the poverty of character building, the results underscore the need for sustained and intense education of that sort (see, e.g., Miller, 2003, pp. 370 and 385). This objection is felicitously referred to 'bullet-biting'. Not only does it embrace with ease the allegedly embarrassing facts thrown at it, it positively relishes the data from the experiments – which tend to show that 20–30% of people actually possess robustly virtuous traits – as (happily) indicating a bigger minority than could have been expected (see, e.g., Sabini & Silver, 2005, pp. 542–544).

Doris latches onto Aristotle's point that virtuous persons will never behave basely (1998, p. 506; cf. Aristotle, 1985, pp. 25–26 and 115 [1100b19–34 and 1128b22–32]). However, Howard Curzer's (2005) studied reading of the relevant portions of Aristotle's corpus clearly brings to light that this point is an idealisation which Aristotle modifies in various ways. If he did not, we would be unable to explain the various passages which indicate that virtue comes in degrees; that full virtue is still inferior to god-like heroic virtue; and that virtuous people sometimes act wrongly, while remaining virtuous. Indeed, Curzer identifies at least seven distinct ways in which fully virtuous persons can, by Aristotle's lights, act out of character without being displaced from their superior level. This observation further substantiates the bullet-biting objection: Not only are most people insufficiently virtuous, even the fully virtuous can have tiny glitches in their characters.

I return to the bullet-biting objection in the final section, when I consider Doris's rejoinders, but it is now time to explore the second, and more profound Aristotelian objection: the *anti-behaviouristic* one. For a start, Harman describes an Aristotelian character trait as a 'relatively long-term stable disposition to act in distinctive ways': an honest person being a person disposed to act honestly, and so forth (1999, p. 317). This understanding is in harmony with the 'standard' self-paradigm's notion of selfhood as constituted by dispositional actions. Many Aristotelian commentators have pointed out, however, that this is a crude behaviouristic understanding which has little to do with the modern virtue ethical conception of character, let alone the Aristotelian one. So even if social psychologists succeed in convincing us that people do not possess character traits *qua* robust behavioural dispositions, it does not mean that people do not possess character in the more nuanced Aristotelian sense, which – as we have seen in previous chapters – is holistic and inclusive of judgement, emotion and manner, as well as action (see e.g. Athanassoulis, 2001, p. 218; Kamtekar, 2004, pp. 460 and 477; Webber, 2006).

Some critics have fleshed out this objection by noting that, owing to their behaviouristic bias, situationists would be prone to confusing the virtuous with the continent and the vicious with the incontinent, although the actions or inactions of those persons would issue from radically different motivations (Athanassoulis, 2001, p. 218; Goldie, 2004, pp. 72–73). I believe that the anti-behaviouristic objectors are on the right track. I also believe, however, that this objection has been seriously underdeveloped. After explaining the difference between the reactions of the virtuous, continent, incontinent and vicious in a given case, for instance, Goldie comments that this 'just about completes the list' (2004, p. 73). To do justice to the subtleties of Aristotle's character distinctions – and thus to appreciate the full power of the possible Aristotelian response – a more fine-grained analysis is needed.

Let us begin by considering the following scenario: A number of persons, who are on their way home from work and waiting at a bus stop, are approached by a scantily clad girl who asks them, with tears in her eyes, to give her 80p so that she can take the bus home. This girl does not look like a typical street person or druggie: There is certain awkwardness in her demeanour, indicating that she is not street-smart, and she is young – hardly a teenager yet. The way she looks indicates that she may just have undergone some terrible experience. Let us now look at a number of variations in what could follow:

P$_1$ does not care a whit about the girl's predicament. He has a rule about never giving to beggars or to charity. He considers it a waste of money. He shakes his head at the girl.

P$_2$ likes to be seen and hailed as a generous person. He waits until more passengers come to the bus stop, then he ostentatiously hands the girl the 80p.

P$_3$ feels incredibly sad to see the state this girl is in. Although he occupies a low-paying post and has barely enough money to live on, he passionately thrusts a 50-pound note into the girl's palm.

P_4 might have given the girl 80p if he had been in a good mood. After a bad day at work, however, he is out of sorts and says no.

P_5 feels compassion towards the girl. However, just before handing her the money, he realises that he may be seen to be accosting her. He immediately hesitates and decides to say no.

P_6 often behaves generously towards strangers in need. However, he recalls his wife's stern complaints last night about his spending money too freely. After contemplating for a while, he decides not to give the girl 80p.

P_7 would normally give money under such circumstances. However, he had been planning all day to try his luck at a slot machine on the way home. He only has a pound in cash on him, so he decides that giving 80p away is not a good idea this time.

P_8 is having family problems and is in a bad mood. He does not feel a hint of compassion towards the girl. However, being a person of principles – one of which is behaving generously – he hands her the coins.

P_9 feels compassion towards the girl. Without the need for any deliberation, he searches his pockets for coins and hands them to the girl with a warm glow of pleasure.

P_{10} is himself extremely poor. He does not know how to feed his family until the end of the month, and today he only has a pound left to buy bread for them. Yet he unhesitatingly hands the girl his one pound.

If this had been a psychological experiment of people's generosity, we can envisage the outcome: P_2, P_3, P_8, P_9 and P_{10} would be deemed generous and the rest ungenerous, based on their displayed actions or inactions. If their behaviour were to be compared to their behaviour in other, differently designed, experiments, lo and behold, correlations would likely be low, and the notion of character infirmed once again. The Aristotelian response would be to refuse the very gambit offered by such behaviouristic measurements as an exercise in intellectual bullying. In contrast, consider the following analysis as an alternative:

P_1 is consistently deficient in giving and thus ungenerous (Aristotle, 1985, pp. 91–93 [1121b13–1122a17]). P_2 is a stable giver, but he does not give for the right reasons. He is the kind of person who typically decides to do without generosity in order to practise charity. In plain terms, he possesses the character of 'vanity' (Aristotle, 1985, pp. 103–104 [1125a27–35]). P_3 is excessive in giving and thus 'wasteful' rather than generous (Aristotle, 1985, pp. 90–91 [1121a10–1121b13]). P_4 is at the level of 'the many'. They 'live by their [non-reason-informed] feelings' and 'have not even a notion of what is fine' and hence 'truly pleasant' (Aristotle, 1985, p. 292 [1179b11–17]). P_5 belongs to 'the soft'. They have some grasp of the virtuous thing to do in given circumstances, but they fail to heed it if doing so is accompanied by any hint of pain (Aristotle, 1985, pp. 190–91 [1150a13–1150b7]). P_6 is 'resistant'. The resistant possess only a limited degree of control against painful appetites, even when these go against morality (Aristotle, 1985, pp. 190–91 [1150a13–37]). P_7 is 'incontinent'. The incontinent have managed to overcome the thrust of the painful appetites that prevent many people from aiming at the good. They are easily overcome by pleasant counter-moral appetites, however: they fail in many cases to abide by reason, 'because of too much [enjoyment]' (Aristotle, 1985, pp. 173–96 [1145a34–1151b33]). P_8 is continent. The continent have managed to overcome permanently both painful and pleasant counter-moral appetites and are able to do the right thing. They are fully self-controlled and listen diligently to reason. Yet they are far from being virtuous; self-control is not the ideal state, because continent persons still have base appetites, and merely force themselves to act as they should (Aristotle, 1985, pp. 173–96 [1145a34–1151b33]). P_9 is truly generous, possessing the virtue in full measure. Full virtue is achieved only when one's appetites and emotions have both become reasonable and morally fitting – when they 'share in reason', in the strong sense of 'agreeing with reason'. The virtuous persons' perceptions of moral salience silence considerations that remain active for the continent person (Aristotle, 1985, p. 32 [1102b25–9]). P_{10} is also generous. It is 'definitely proper to the generous person to exceed so much in giving that he leaves less for himself, since it is proper to a generous person not to look out for himself' (Aristotle, 1985, p. 88 [1120b4–6]). A parallel example is of the virtue of mildness [with respect to anger]: The mild person 'seems to err more in the direction of deficiency [of anger], since the mild person is ready to pardon', see p. 105 [1125b35–1126a3]; cf. Curzer, 2005). Aristotle's point is that, for at least a number of people, some virtues require – as a matter of psychological fact – their own intermittent excess for them to continue to exist as virtues. Generosity is one of them: To be generous to a fault may require, so to speak, being at times faultily (namely excessively) generous.

On this Aristotelian analysis, five out of those ten persons possess 'firm and unchanging' states of character (Aristotle, 1985, p. 40

[1105a30–34]): P_1 is ungenerous (*qua* deficit); P_2 is ungenerous (*qua* vanity); P_3 is ungenerous (*qua* excess); P_9 is generous full stop; and P_{10} is generous also because he hits the relevant medial target often enough, although he has a small – but psychologically excusable – glitch in his virtuous character. The rest of these people do not possess 'firm and unchanging' character states. Their souls have not become stably responsive to reason, either right reason (leading to virtue) or wrong reason (leading to vice). Their personae are still too fickle and erratic – too easily swayed by non-reason-infused feelings – to constitute character. However, if all is well, they are progressing towards character.

It is particularly salutary to consider why, in this Aristotelian picture, three of the five persons who actually give the girl the money she requests would not count as generous. Generous persons are, according to Aristotle, good users of riches; they give the proper amounts to the right people, at the right time and for the right reason. In general, they aim at what is fine in giving, and they take pleasure in it, just as they take pleasure in other virtuous activities. However, they do not give *in order to* take pleasure in the giving or in being seen by others as good givers, like the vainglorious P_2 did; their pleasure simply supervenes upon and completes the virtuous activity. Nor do they carelessly throw away their own possessions or overburden themselves and their families, like the do-gooder P_3 did; for this would make them less able to continue giving in the future. And in the case of P_8, he lacks the right frame of mind to be considered truly generous. For P_2, think of the slimy lawyer, Clamence, in Camus's story *The Fall*; for P_3, think of the over-zealous David in Nick Hornby's *How to Be Good*; for P_8, think of Kant's 'person of moral worth', on what used to be the canonical interpretation, as a person whose goodness would be compromised by a co-operating inclination (for thicker examples from the literary sources, see Kristjánsson, 2007, chap. 9).

From an Aristotelian perspective, the trouble with a behaviouristic interpretation of the these story variations is not only that it fails to identify the generous and the ungenerous persons; more significantly, it tells us next to nothing about who possesses character and who does not.

6.5. Rejoinders and Implications

Doris anticipates both the bullet-biting objection and the anti-behaviouristic objection and tries to meet them. I think his rejoinders misfire. Consider first Doris's response to the bullet-biting objection, which he refers to as 'the argument from rarity' (1998, p. 512; cf. Miller's response, pp. 380–81). (1) Doris doubts that 'reflection on a few extraordinary individuals' facilities ethically desirable behaviour. (2) He notes that character training is, on virtue-based accounts, typically about inculcation rather than 'reflection on a rarefied ideal'. (3) He complains that if the virtues touted in virtue-based moral theories cannot be appealed to in the explanation and prediction of behaviour, those theories become too 'empirically modest' to retain their current appeal.

Running quickly through possible Aristotelian responses, they should, I submit, take the following form. (1) Although Aristotle would admit that full virtue is comparatively rare (cf. Aristotle, 1985, p. 213 [1126b24]), it is not the privileged province of 'a few extraordinary individuals'. If 20–30% of people possess robust character traits – witness some of the staple psychological experiments – that is already a considerable subset of the population. Doris may be thinking here of heroic virtue rather than ordinary full virtue. (2) The claim that virtue educators are not concerned about reflection on ideals does not stick in Aristotle's case. He characterises a special emotional virtue, called 'emulousness': distress at the apparent presence among others of things honoured and possible for a person to acquire, with the distress arising not from the fact that another has them, but that the emulator does not (Aristotle, 1991, p. 161 [1388a30–35]). Aristotle insists that this is one of two virtues specific to young moral learners, the other being – let us recall – shamefulness. Role-modelling on ideals is thus an essential Aristotelian strategy of moral education, along with habituation, just as it has become in recent character-education accounts. (3) If Aristotle's virtue theory fails to satisfy the demands of the behavioural sciences for predictive validity, this may say more about the limits of predictivism as a model of social inquiry than it says about the limits of his virtue theory. Incidentally, I do not think that the current appeal of such a theory lies essentially in its predictive value. But, in any case, as I note at the end of this section, Aristotelianism is compatible with scientific methods for investigating character.

Doris refers to the anti-behaviouristic objection as an 'intellectualist account', according to which the virtuous person is typified by a 'distinctive outlook' – some goings on 'within the head' – rather than reliable overt behaviours. Doris cavils at such an account for two distinct reasons. First, he finds it morally strange (and not 'the most inspiring epitaph') to say of someone that 'his ethical perceptions were unfailingly admirable, although he behaved only averagely'. Second, he points out that the alleged outlook of virtuous persons may also turn out to exhibit situational variability, just as other capacities and dispositions do, and thus be tarred with the same brush as overt behaviours (Doris, 1998, pp. 509–11).

In order to respond to Doris, we need first to consider what is to be understood by the 'distinctive outlook' of a virtuous person. As we saw in Section 1.3, the typical Aristotelian virtue will be a complex character state (*hexis*), at the core of which lies moral sensitivity, exhibited through emotional reactions, to goings-on in the agent's world. Whether a felt emotion should be acted upon or not is always a separate question, however. The answer to that question must take various situational factors into account and be adjudicated through the intellectual virtue of *phronesis*. Moreover, the description of a given virtue is not fully exhausted by characterising its underlying emotional sensitivity and the range of possible actions to which it can give rise. Virtuous persons also comport themselves in certain distinctive ways which reverberate through all their attitudes and conduct; what matters is not only what they feel and do but also the manner in which they feel and do it. The *megalopsychoi*, for instance, exude an aura of dignity and moral superiority which distinguishes them from other persons possessing virtues (Aristotle, 1985, pp. 97–104 [1123b34–1125a35]). This is why each *hexis* is truly a complex state, rather than a mere disposition to feel and act. In our little story, the actors could, from a crude behaviouristic perspective, only give or not give the girl the money she requested. From an Aristotelian perspective, they could *feel* in a number of different ways about the giving or not giving and – although this was not clearly revealed in the thinly described variations – give or not give in a radically different *manner*.

It was thus an *emotional factor* which turned out to be the distinguishing one in the Aristotelian analysis of the ten persons. Is that an 'intellectualist' idiosyncrasy? I very much doubt that it is. Consider once again the *Milgram Experiment*. The participants were subjected to overtaxing pressures to which most of them succumbed. They did not behave well. Yet, at the same time, they displayed 'striking reactions of emotional strain' – and later many of them reported significant levels of regret and post-traumatic stress. When relieved of the pressure to toe the line, only 20% continued to administer maximum-level shocks (cited in Webber, 2006, p. 199). Moreover, although no correlation was found between the subjects' decisions to quit or not quit pushing the button and their Kohlbergian stages of moral reasoning, a clear demarcation was evidenced when subjects were asked at the end of the experiments about the *desire* they had felt to quit. The stages of moral reasoning were clearly related to behavioural independence in feeling and judgement, although not, under those taxing circumstances, to independence in action (cited in Blasi, 1980, p. 37). It is no wonder, then, that the one factor in the famous Big Five Personality Trait Model (see, e.g., Goldberg, 1993) that most clearly zooms in on moral characteristics (namely, agreeableness, as it is somewhat infelicitously called there) is measured by asking respondents to assess themselves in relation to their emotions – if they have soft hearts, sympathise with others' feelings, feel concern for others and so forth – rather than to their actions. The personality psychologists who designed this model seem to have realised that the clearest distinguishing factor between personality types is emotion. It is that same insight that prompts me to regard dispositional *emotions*, rather than dispositional *actions*, as the main constitutive element in moral selfhood in the 'alternative' self-paradigm.

To return to Aristotle, recall that the kind of moral education he describes in greatest detail is emotion education. For him, the process of affective sensitisation plays a decisive role in the gradual consolidation of moral character, thus forming an indispensable starting point of any formal or informal programme of character education. Aristotle would agree with Doris that situation selection and modification constitutes an important facet of such a sensitisation process – but he would not neglect more cognitively complex strategies. To be sure, it would be empirically conceivable that emotions turn out to exhibit the same situational variations as actions – as was Doris's sceptical suggestion. The empirical evidence so far, however, seems to check that scepticism; emotional inclinations have more permanence and robustness than our actions do (in addition to sources already cited, see Ben-Ze'ev, 2000, pp. 88–89, on affective traits; Keller & Edelstein, 1993, on the significance of moral feelings in self-development; and the extensive literature on Big Five personality research).

But that brings us to Doris's other complaint about the anti-behaviouristic objection. If emotional factors are really the touchstones for measuring moral character, could we not end up with the bizarre implication of someone's ethical perception being deemed unfailingly admirable, although he behaves only sub-optimally? Aristotle has an answer to this. He says that wellbeing is an 'activity' rather than a 'state'; for if it were not, someone could enjoy it and yet 'be asleep for his whole life, living the life of a plant' (1985, p. 281 [1176a33–36]). Furthermore, 'Olympic prises are not for the finest and strongest, but for contestants, since it is only these who win; so also in life [only] the fine and good people who act correctly win the prise' (1985, p. 20 [1099a4–6]). Contrary to much of contemporary virtue ethics, there is no presumption of the 'primacy of character' here; rather, the tree is known by its fruit. Being endowed with a good character is, for Aristotle, clearly not praiseworthy as such; what matters is how it is manifested through specific performances. One could even read him as saying that attributing 'good character' to a person who fails to exemplify it in his deeds is a logical mistake.

Are these claims incompatible with an emphasis on moral character as emotional sensitivity and moral perception? Indeed not. The point being made in the analysis of my ten scenarios was that only an understanding of people's motivational structure can truly tell us whether they behave virtuously or viciously; and, moreover, whether or not they possess character in the first place. The emotional reactions leading up to the decision to act or not to act, and the reactive attitudes the person experiences after the decision has been made are indispensable data for us to evaluate the moral propriety of the act and of the agent (cf. Montada, 1993). Each action or inaction of our ten persons in Section 6.4 had to be understood as *that* action or inaction guided by *that* emotional make-up; otherwise we could not know if it exhibited the virtue of generosity.

If the anti-behaviouristic objection succeeds in revealing the poverty of the standard psychological experiments on character, what implications does this have for the ideal measurement of character? Kamtekar suggests that social psychologists should engage in more painstaking research into the considerations that experimental subjects have in mind when making moral decisions: the inner mediating events (2004, p. 476). We should not assume, however, that subjects have privileged access to their inner lives or that they are always better at predicting their emotional rather than their behavioural reactions. Indeed, people often make wrong forecasts about how they will respond emotionally to a given future event. For instance, recent research indicates that although people tend to predict that they will be very upset by blatant racial acts or comments, they actually show little emotional distress when this occurs (Kawakami, Dunn, Karmali & Dovidio, 2009). So once again we need more objective criteria. And it is precisely here that the suggestions made at the end of Chapter 2 come to the fore again: about alternative methods to mere self-reports for accessing people's full selves rather than merely their self-concepts. Brain scans and hormonal analyses were among the suggested options there – and those would be particularly apt in identifying underlying emotions. There is something quintessentially Aristotelian about such suggestions, given Aristotle's keen awareness of the physical, as well as the cognitive, components of emotion.

What now has been said suffices, I submit, to parry Doris's rejoinders to the two Aristotelian objections. More generally, I hope to have fleshed out a more substantive response to situationism than has so far been advanced in repeated attempts to deflect the situationist challenge. Aristotelian characterology is not at death's door; there is quite a lot of life in the old dog yet. For precisely that reason, situationism leaves the 'alternative' paradigm's notion of moral selfhood untouched. Indeed, the identification of the *emotional basis of character* has strengthened rather than weakened it. We can carry on undauntingly with our quest to understand its workings.

7. Self-Respect

7.1. Self-Respect Instead of Self-Esteem?

Chapter 5 chartered the rise and fall of global self-esteem as a salient sociomoral and educational variable. In a suggestive article, psychologists Roland and Foxx (2003) have argued that the star of global self-esteem in psychological and educational research should now be eclipsed by that of self-respect. Coming from psychologists, this is a quite a radical proposal, not only because of the scant attention that has been paid to self-respect in psychological, as opposed to philosophical circles, but also because, in philosophical discourse, self-respect has traditionally been associated with people's actual full selves rather than with their self-concepts – and it is usually only the latter that has interested contemporary psychologists. The aim of this chapter is to gauge the aptness of this proposal, to ameliorate certain shortcomings in it and to develop it further. In order to do so, I need to respond to two competing pulls: the philosophical one of elucidating the notion of self-respect, and the psychological one of suggesting ways for conducting empirical research into self-respect. Although it is difficult to respond adequately to both pulls simultaneously, it is worth a try, given the interdisciplinary remit of this book.

The radical nature of Roland and Foxx's proposal can be seen by comparing the respective numbers of abstracts yielded by PsycINFO (1985–May 2006) when using the search terms 'self-esteem' and 'self-respect'. Whereas the former results in no less than 11,313 abstracts (let us recall), the latter turns up only 239. Put bluntly, self-respect has yet to rivet the attention of psychologists; moreover – tellingly – few if any of those 239 abstracts point to any empirical research on self-respect. In their 2003 article, Roland and Foxx claim to have found no 'scientific studies' (p. 279) of self-respect. To be sure, showing that self-respect provides a lean counterpart to self-esteem in recent psychological research is not indicative of the futility of research into self-respect; the current research focus may simply be wrong. That is more or less what Roland and Foxx argue: Now that the 'self-esteem fallacy' has been exposed, it is time to explore 'the couch on which the cushion of self-esteem resides'. More specifically, they propose that 'a relationship exists between self-respect and self-esteem such that self-respecting individuals may experience either high or low levels of self-esteem and individuals with high levels of self-esteem may or may not possess self-respect'. They hypothesise that this relationship could explain, inter alia, why people reporting low levels of self-esteem often fail to exhibit the expected psychological or social dysfunction: because such people may have a secure seat on their 'couch' (the self-shaping moral principles to which they aspire) although the 'cushion' (the satisfaction with their attainment) happens to be missing (2003, pp. 247, 268, 271). Those people would then occupy a position similar to Aristotle's 'pusillanimous' persons in his taxonomy of the non-*megalopsychoi* – those who are morally worthy but do not think of themselves in that way.

With regard to psychology's typical characterisation of self-esteem as one's level of satisfaction with the global ratio of achievements to aspirations, a shift of research focus from self-esteem to self-respect would mean that closer attention be paid to the nature and content of the relevant 'aspirations' but less to the reported subjective satisfaction. Any remaining concern with the 'ratio' part would focus on domain-specific, rather than global, self-esteem – namely, exclusively on that type of self-esteem which is predicated upon self-respect. How happy are people with the attainment of their self-respect-grounding aspirations?

Before I continue, a terminological warning must be sounded. In certain contexts in everyday English, the locutions 'self-respect' and 'respect oneself' are used to signify 'self-esteem' and 'esteeming oneself' in so far as this esteem is grounded upon self-respect (witness the phrase 'I could never respect myself again if I did that'). To account for this fact, some philosophers (Sachs, 1981; Massey, 1983; Telfer, 1995) have suggested that self-respect be called 'conative' or 'objective' self-respect when it refers to the objects of the relevant self-aspirations (Roland and Foxx's 'couch'), but 'appraisal', 'estimative' or 'subjective' self-respect when it refers to self-esteem predicated upon self-respect (Roland and Foxx's 'cushion'). I shall overlook those vagaries of ordinary language in what follows and simply continue to talk about self-respect versus self-esteem. Yet it is worth mentioning here how those vagaries seem to have confused John Rawls when famously, in his *Theory of Justice*, he invoked 'self-respect or (self-esteem)' – as if these concepts were synonymous – and called it 'perhaps the most important primary good' (1973, p. 386), subsequently arguing that the central importance of securing self-respect in society justifies the lexical priority of liberty in his theory. Contained in the Rawlsian notion of 'self-respect (or self-esteem)' is our sense of our own value plus our self-confidence, which indicates that what he is after is the subjective notion of self-esteem rather than the objective one of self-respect (see, e.g., Massey, 1983). This usage creates certain problems for Rawls's account, however, because it is difficult to understand how esteeming one's self-respect can be a relevant moral primary good per se without regard for the moral content of the esteemed self-respect. If Rawls had posited self-respect as the primary good, however, it would have jeopardised his notion of primary goods as existing independently of any particular 'comprehensive' moral doctrine. Rawls may inadvertently have helped himself to the ambiguities of ordinary language to 'veil' this potential dilemma.

Returning to Roland and Foxx's proposal, should social science turn its empirical compass to self-respect and (possibly) the associated domain-specific self-esteem, after having forsaken global self-esteem? I assume that many educationists would take well to such a suggestion. It seems more intuitively plausible that there exists a positive correlation – and even a causal connection – between self-respect and school achievement than between global self-esteem and school achievement. Perhaps high self-respect can help keep students focused and working hard, inducing them not to let their talents lie fallow. It has been suggested, moreover, that self-respect is easier to achieve than are many other educational competences – improving one's maths score, for instance (Nesbitt, 1993). Philosophers are unlikely to protest at such a change of compass either. After all, self-respect has a more secure grounding in ordinary parlance than does global self-esteem (at least prior to the self-esteem industry's colonisation of the public media) and can draw on long-running discursive traditions in the philosophical literature. Furthermore, self-respect may provide precisely what self-esteem is lacking from a moral point of view: an objective basis for or true measure of moral worth. It is common in the philosophical literature to see self-respect referred to as the guardian of the other moral virtues: the column of true majesty in human beings which preserves commendable character traits and contributes to the continuation of morality. Roland and Foxx note that 'objectivity is what differentiates self-respect from self-esteem', and that it is the presence of a 'moral code' in self-respect which provides its objective components (2003, pp. 269, 282).

Self-respect will be of special interest to *self-realists*. Despite the occasional irregularities of ordinary language mentioned above, self-respect is not essentially a belief concept. Although the belief that one can do things (supported by background courage) makes one self-confident, the belief that one has strong self-respect does not make one self-respectful, any more than the belief that one is a good driver makes one a good driver. Indeed, we even tend to suspect people of hypocrisy or a pharisaical attitude rather than self-respect if they *believe* that their self-respect is high. Still, the self that is referred to in the concept of self-respect seems to be the same self that is at issue in the concepts of self-esteem and self-confidence: the unitary self of everyday moral and social encounters, as opposed to a metaphysical, perceptual or material self (see Chapter 2). Furthermore, although self-respect obviously involves a host of beliefs relating to the self – beliefs about what is worthy for the self to think or do – these are not beliefs *about* the self in the same sense as beliefs about self-esteem or self-confidence are. We have thus good reason to think of self-respect as belonging to one's actual full self, not only one's self-concept.

7.2. Psychological Misgivings about Self-Respect

The people having to carry out the relevant measurements of psychological constructs are empirical *psychologists*, and I suspect that many of them would not be as enamoured of Roland and Foxx's proposal as their colleagues in philosophy and education. Let me touch here upon three doubts that psychologists may entertain: an aversion to the concept of morality, the difficulty of operationalising self-respect such that it would result in meaningful correlates, and the probability that self-respect is not a single concept. First, self-respect is a moral concept and, as Roland and Foxx note, some psychologists are made uneasy by issues of morality, even to the point of being averse to the very word 'morality' with its connotations of a 'holier-than-thou' attitude. The chasm between social scientists who (allegedly) trade only in the descriptive and moral philosophers who trade in the normative is, after all, long-standing and difficult to bridge, as we saw in Chapter 3.

Nevertheless, two simple observations may allay some of doubts of empirical psychologists and persuade them to tread on the moral terrain with less trepidation.

The first observation is that normativity does not necessarily entail relativity. Judgments such as 'It is good to teach children honesty' or 'It is morally wrong to have sexual relations with children' do not so much evaluate the world of description as describe the world of evaluation. Although they are value-laden, they are neither inherently relative (to place or time), nor merely subjectively true. This much at least will be acknowledged by those who subscribe to some form of moral naturalism, whether Aristotelian *eudaimonism*, or an evolutionary perspective on morality such as that to which Roland and Foxx allude (2003, p. 280). Roland and Foxx also note helpfully the existence of ethnographic evidence for the universality of prosocial behaviour (2003, p. 280). The second observation is that normativity does not necessarily entail prescription. Doing research based on a moral concept and possibly finding correlations between its normative components and positively or negatively valenced psychosocial variables does not mean that empirical psychologists have turned themselves into moralists: have started to prescribe rather than describe. As I pointed out in response to David Carr's moralism in Section 3.5, describing a positive outcome is not the same as prescribing it. For example, even if the normative components of self-respect turned out to have positively valenced correlates, such findings would not by themselves prescribe those components, except to persons who *wanted* to be moral and to embrace those components in the first place. I will leave the 'we-are-not-moralists'-qualm out of further scrutiny in what follows.

The second doubt entertained by psychologists, at least those of a more discerning nature, would concern whether or not the notion of self-respect could be operationalised in such a way that nonlogical, and hence nontrivial, correlations could be found between it and such salient psychological and social variables as school achievement and prosocial behaviour. Even if correlations were found, they could well be logical – if the measured components of self-respect included those very characteristics (say, diligence in school work) that informed the other variables to be explored, for instance. More generally speaking, empirical research on self-respect cannot get off the ground without a careful and critical analysis of its components, which would surely mean some notable tightening of our popular notion of 'self-respect' as it exists in ordinary language.

The third possible doubt relates to an unresolved issue in the area of self-respect: Does ordinary language and the philosophical literature recognise a single concept of self-respect, two or more overlapping concepts, or even radically distinct concepts? If there is, in fact, more than one concept, the preliminary task must be the selection of one to form the basis of the empirical research and the providing of good reasons for that choice.

I would not want to be understood as being mired in a positivistic conception of methodology which refuses to accept as 'scientific' any construct that cannot be operationalised and measured. Obviously, there are established qualitative research paradigms within social science which would not require prior consensus on the meaning of the research term and would not aspire to measure it in any way. Consider, for example, possible phenomenological studies into people's understandings of self-respect, or case studies of exemplary individuals who have been widely thought to possess self-respect (cf. Colby & Damon, 1992). However, I understand Roland and Foxx's suggestion about replacing self-esteem with self-respect in psychological research to mean replacing it (*also* if not necessarily *only*) within the discursive field in which self-esteem has been studied most assiduously. That discursive field happens to be a quantitative one. And in that field, the best reason for psychological investigation of a variable is considered to be the expectation that interesting and illuminating correlations – and better yet, causal connections – will be found between that variable and others; whereas an important scientific reason for psychologists *not* to investigate a variable is that it cannot be adequately operationalised.

Roland and Foxx have done well to spark attention to the salience of self-respect and to suggest it as a possible topic of exploration after the demise of global self-esteem. Pointing to self-respect in that way, however, has merely the status of a promissory note. To establish whether or not the note can be paid off, the second and third doubts that psychologists may entertain (the probability that self-respect is not a single concept and the difficulty of operationalising self-respect) must be subjected to a more thorough analysis than the two authors undertake in their article. I try to do so in the following sections.

7.3. Kantian or Aristotelian Self-Respect?

A quick and superficial glance at what contemporary philosophers have written about self-respect may create the impression that they are all contributions to a unitary discourse about a single concept. Philosophers thus seem to agree that self-respect is a complex character state involving a disposition not to act or feel in a manner unworthy of oneself: a disposition to shun behaviour and emotions that one views as contemptible, degrading or otherwise immoral. A person with a sense of self-respect is intimately attached to a project, code or status that provides a standard of worthy conduct, a line beyond which he or she simply does not pass. The person is committed to this standard, confident that by and large they are the right commitments and tries to live accordingly (see, e.g., Kristjánsson, 2002, chap. 3.1, for various references to the philosophical literature). Apart from a few situationists (recall Chapter 6), philosophers also seem to agree, at least implicitly, that there is no such thing as 'domain-specific self-respect': A person who, say, behaves self-respectfully within the family circle but un-self-respectfully outside of it will simply be considered to lack self-respect. Self-respect is thus understood holistically as a global trait of one's character (see, e.g., Russell, 2005, p. 104). If our behaviour were as fickle and erratic as situationists claim, there really would be no such thing as self-respect.

When one probes more deeply into what stands behind the relatively converging formulations of self-respect, however, considerable divergence begins to emerge. Roland and Foxx are aware of the fact that current discussions of self-respect are grounded in different historical traditions, and they make a reasonable attempt at grouping those discussions with respect to their originators and historical precedents from Aristotle to Kant (2003, pp. 248–58). Unfortunately, their taxonomical groundwork seems to betray an inadequate grasp of just how radical some of the internal divisions are – as can be divined from the fact that those divisions do not survive to the latter and more substantive part of their article in which they explore the differences between self-esteem and self-respect and the use that psychologists could make of the latter. Indeed, in this latter section the authors quietly ignore their earlier rhetoric about different philosophical conceptions of self-respect and clandestinely help themselves to one such conception, namely the Kantian one. They claim, for instance, that 'cognition and the law of respect for persons would be considered the predominant properties of self-respect' and that 'self-regulation and self-control is an integral component of a self-respect system' (pp. 269, 273). Moreover, in the very abstract of their article they say that 'autonomy is central to self-respect' (p. 247). This is all well and good on a Kantian conception, but it fits an Aristotelian conception only tangentially, if at all.

Table 7.1. *Contrasts between the Kantian and the Aristotelian Concepts of Self-Respect*

	Kantian Self-Respect	Aristotelian Self-Respect
a) *Moral basis of self-respect*	Dignity of persons as ends in themselves	Virtues as ends
b) *Psychological processes involved*	Cognitive	Cognitive and affective
c) *Relation to desires*	Self-control	Moralisation
d) *Extension to others*	Members of the kingdom of ends	*Philia*
e) *Concern for others*	Their human rights	Their *eudaimonia*
f) *Formation/maintenance of self-respect*	Autonomous	Heteronomous plus autonomous
g) *Moral worth of persons*	Equal	Unequal
h) *Basis of morality*	Rational (formal)	Substantive (non-formal)
i) *Possible loss of self-respect*	Internal	Internal or external
j) *Excessive self-respect*	Impossible	Possible

Indeed, after delving through the contemporary philosophical literature on self-respect, I have become convinced that there are two main concepts of self-respect at work there which can be characterised, broadly, as Kantian and Aristotelian. Notice that I say 'concepts' rather than 'conceptions'; I do not believe that these are simply contestable conceptions of the same concept revolving around a common core. Rather, I consider them to be radically divergent notions. Notice also that I say 'Kantian' and 'Aristotelian', rather than 'Kant's' and 'Aristotle's'. In recent years, we have witnessed various attempts to undermine the traditional distinction between Kant as a moral formalist and Aristotle as a moral naturalist, by naturalising (or de-formalising) the former and formalising (or de-naturalising) the latter (see, e.g., Korsgaard, 1996; McDowell, 1996). Although I think that those interpretive manoeuvres are ultimately misguided, this is not the place to argue the point. Rather, let us rely on the traditional analyses distilled from Kant's (1967) and Aristotle's (1985) main ethical works and the views customarily trotted out under the banners of 'Kantianism' and 'Aristotelianism'.

I first unpack in Table 7.1 what I take to be some of the fundamental differences between the Kantian and the Aristotelian approach to self-respect, and then expand upon each difference. Although this list is by no means exhaustive, I have singled out those differences that I consider most germane to the task of contrasting the two concepts. I leave it to readers to explore the extent to which the lines of descent of various contemporary accounts of self-respect can be traced to either the Kantian or the Aristotelian approach. Readers will be helped in that pursuit by Roland and Foxx's categorisations (2003, pp. 250–58); indeed, I hope that the following comparisons will throw a clearer light on what precisely it is in such modern accounts as those of Sachs (1981) that makes them Kantian, and in such as those of Telfer (1995) that makes them Aristotelian.

(a) *Moral basis of self-respect.* Personhood and its inherent dignity form the core of Kantian moral philosophy. Persons are ends in themselves, by virtue of their ability to rationalise, think and choose, and must respect themselves and others as such. Meanwhile, recall that in the Aristotelian system, *eudaimonia* forms the core of morality. Persons achieve *eudaimonia*, and come to deserve dignity, in so far as they actualise the moral and intellectual *eudaimonia*-constituting virtues. Persons are entitled to respect themselves and others not as ends in themselves, but only to the extent that they have mastered the virtues, which are the real ends. Simply invoking one's personhood or humanity does not count. 'Respect' (including 'self-respect') has in general a more earthbound and less detached understanding in the Aristotelian than the Kantian model (see *(b)*).

(b) *Psychological processes involved.* According to the Kantian concept, conformity to a pure rational principle (namely, his well-known categorical imperative) is essential to human agency and to morality. Emotions are, on the other hand, intruders in the realm of reason. The psychological processes which guide true self-respect are thus exclusively cognitive in a narrow sense. In contrast, the assumption that emotional dispositions also constitute virtues is – as I have repeatedly stressed – essential to Aristotle's virtue theory, just as it is to the 'alternative' self-paradigm proposed in this book. People can be fully virtuous only if they are disposed to experience emotions in the correct medial way on a regular basis. Guiding their self-respect will be not only pure cognitive processes and beliefs, but also emotions such as pride and antecedent shame, which prevent them from engaging in behaviour that may jeopardise their self-respect.

(c) *Relation to desires.* Virtue is, in the Kantian model, about strength of will. Reason must therefore constrain desires. It is not enough to try to sublimate and purify the desires, for it would still remain possible that they might run amok and counter to reason. For Kant, the disposition to overcome conative obstacles to moral behaviour through an act of will is an ineradicable feature of human nature: The self-respectful person is essentially the self-controlled person. In the Aristotelian system, desires belong to the irrational part of the soul. Policing them through self-control is, however, only a second-best tack – a semi-virtue at most – for the self-controlled person still has base desires. Truly virtuous persons have infused their desires with reason, thereby moralising them. 'Generous' Kantians who force themselves to give money to the poor in deference to the moral law, for instance (and whose moral virtues are compromised rather than enhanced by the presence of co-operating inclinations), count only as 'resistant' or 'continent' in the Aristotelian model. The truly generous Aristotelians give money to the poor because they truly want to; they are emotionally disposed to do so (see Chapter 6). In contrast to the bifurcated nature of Kantian agents, Aristotelian self-respectful persons are essentially at one with themselves: manifestations of their own properly felt desires.

(d) *Extension to others*. Once Kantian agents have understood their uniqueness as rational agents and the dignity that such a status necessarily involves, they extend their respect for themselves to respect for other rational beings, belonging to the same kingdom of ends, where each being must be treated as an end in itself and never as a means to an end. This extension is again purely cognitive; there are no emotions (such as compassion or kindness) involved. For Aristotle, it is an empirical fact that the virtues are essential to our own good; they help us to fulfil what is central to us. Applying the virtues is therefore necessary to our own interest. But the virtues require precisely that we pursue the good of others in the ways required by morality; indeed, the greatest virtues are those most beneficial to others. This assumption is best revealed in Aristotle's discussion of true self-love as involving love of others, with the two developing together inseparably. Self-respectful persons extend their respect to others through the process of *philia*: of friendship and (non-erotic) love, which incorporate various other-regarding emotions. Indeed, self-respect may turn out to be the very maturity that makes a character capable of self-love and, hence, of loving others (see further in Russell, 2005, p. 119).

(e) *Concern for others*. After extending our self-respect to others, the Kantian concern for others rests primarily on their human rights. As members of the kingdom of ends, human beings are entitled to certain inalienable rights, and respect for others means respecting those rights. The indebtedness of modern liberalism, and of the Western liberal self-concept, to Kant is obvious here: The human good is defined in terms of the right, which in this case leaves us with a relatively thin notion of the common good. In Aristotle's view, concern for others is expressed through our concern for their *eudaimonia*. We want them to be able to actualise their essential human capabilities. Respect for others thus implies a thick conception of the common good, a direct descendant of which is the moral position nowadays referred to as 'the capabilities view' (often connected to the works of Amartya Sen, and of Martha Nussbaum before her liberal turn a decade ago).

(f) *Formation/maintenance of self-respect*. The Kantian rational will is essentially autonomous and free in the sense that it is the original author of the law that binds it (the categorical imperative) and the constant protector of that same law. It is not only negatively free (from external influence) but, more importantly, positively free as its own author, and this freedom to choose its own law has inherent worth. Autonomy is, therefore, nothing less than the lifeblood of Kantian self-respect – but *pace* Roland and Foxx, not of *all* self-respect. Aristotle does not possess a corresponding notion of 'will', nor does he have at his disposal a concept of 'autonomy' in the modern sense. The Aristotelian self, just like the Humean one, is derived from and essentially sustained through social recognition, and to that extent it is 'heteronomous' in the Kantian sense. To be sure, fully self-respectful persons have developed their own *phronesis*, and the decisions they take are, in that sense, 'their own'. This does not make their choices intrinsically valuable, however, but only extrinsically so (in so far as they are morally right and conducive to *eudaimonia*); and in any case, all choice is embedded. It takes place within a framework of moral upbringing that is itself unchosen and non-autonomous.

(g) *Moral worth of persons*. For Kantians, all persons deserve equal respect and may respect themselves equally, by virtue of their rationality, irrespective of their contingent characteristics. This is a far cry from the Aristotelian model, in which people are of unequal moral worth – and have unequally good reasons for respecting themselves – based on their actual respective attainment of moral and intellectual virtues. Immoral persons, therefore, have no good reasons for respecting themselves here and now, although they would have good reasons for improving themselves in such ways that they would be worthy of self-respect and the respect of others (provided they could fathom the need for such improvements). In the Kantian model, the idea of a person's worthlessness is inconceivable; for Aristotelians, in contrast, there can be persons who have no moral worth (and even realise this fact themselves).

(h) *Basis of morality.* As we have seen, both the Kantian and the Aristotelian concepts of self-respect have their bases in morality. In that sense they concur. But the problem is that morality is understood here in very different ways. For Kantians, the basis of morality itself is the 'good will', the only thing good without qualification, and good-willed actions are good because of the way they are willed – in virtue of the formal qualities of choice. For Aristotle, in contrast, good-willed actions are good because they exemplify the virtues, many of which are irreducibly moral. Kant is therefore a moral formalist (rationalist), whereas Aristotle is a moral substantivist (naturalist).

(i) *Possible loss of self-respect.* If Kantian agents lose their self-respect, it will be solely for internal reasons: for failing to exercise their own good will. Total loss of self-respect is impossible, however, as long as they remain rational agents. From the Aristotelian viewpoint, persons can lose their self-respect for internal reasons (negligence, carelessness or simply choosing to be bad), but also for external reasons. Lack of what is currently known as 'moral luck' – various externalities that are necessary for the good life – can thus deprive us of the necessary conditions for self-respect. Aristotle would be quick to point out, however, that these would have to be extreme deprivations and, moreover, that persons can avoid becoming totally miserable as long as they retain their equanimity in the face of adversity. But these caveats do not change the fact that total loss of self-respect is possible, in the Aristotelian model, for either internal and or external reasons.

(j) *Excessive self-respect.* This notion is perplexing for Kantians – witness Sachs's refusal to accept this possibility (1981, pp. 348–49): How can a person's will be too good? How can persons overestimate the worth of their rationality? For Aristotelians, there is nothing perplexing about this notion. Persons who make stronger demands on themselves than they can live up to as natural beings, who set their moral stakes too high, have excessive self-respect. Self-respect, like any other virtue, admits of a golden mean between excess and deficiency.

The Kantian and Aristotelian concepts of self-respect are obviously not diametrical opposites. Both engage with the issue of human dignity and fortitude, and both include a demand for public availability: The self-respectful person must not hide under a bushel – not sit pretty on it, but rather do something with it. Nevertheless, I hope that these comparisons suffice to show that the Kantian and Aristotelian concepts of self-respect are radically distinct on a number of scores and that it is futile to attempt to wrench from the two some sort of unified account of self-respect, or to disregard the differences with impunity. This can be seen, for instance, in the previously noted shift from *a concept* of self-respect in Roland and Foxx's article to what is actually *the Kantian concept*. These differences need to be preserved and engaged rather than overlooked. But which of the two concepts is preferable, then? Which should form the basis of psychological research into self-respect? These are, of course, tricky questions. The Kantian concept will recommend itself naturally to liberals, whereas communitarians and like-minded people will favour the Aristotelian one. The general reservations that communitarians entertain about the thin liberal notion of the good and the disembeddedness of the liberal self-concept will certainly transfer into their assessment of Kantian self-respect. Nevertheless, we should bear in mind that the rampant disputes that raged between liberals and communitarians twenty-odd years ago have gradually subsided. In any case, I offer three *practical* reasons for my belief that social scientists should consider measuring Aristotelian rather than Kantian self-respect.

First, Aristotelian self-respect falls neatly into line with contemporary virtue ethics which, whether we like it or not, is the currently most fashionable moral theory in academic circles. Moreover, ample anecdotal evidence seems to suggest that virtue ethics – with all its down-to-earth references to human virtues and vices, flourishing and follies – holds strong appeal for the general public, much more so, at least, than the Kantian discourse, which tends to be pitched at a relatively high level of abstraction. Second, Aristotelian self-respect acknowledges the psychological and moral salience of the emotions (their affective as well as cognitive features), which is in full accordance with respectable contemporary research trends in psychology and philosophy, and also, of course, with the 'alternative' self-paradigm for which I have been arguing. Third, the Aristotelian notion of excessive self-respect will appear more intuitively plausible to most people than does the Kantian denial of this possibility. This is, in fact, precisely what laypeople tend to refer to as *perfectionism*, a syndrome which can, according to folk psychology, be a disabling condition. It should be noted however, that 'perfectionism' in this lay sense is not the same as 'moral perfectionism' (a respectable philosophical outlook). Readers may find these reasons variously weighty. I consider them, at least, when taken together, weighty enough to warrant further scrutiny into possible measures of Aristotelian self-respect.

7.4. Measuring the Components of Aristotelian Self-Respect

Roland and Foxx make no bones about psychological research into self-respect being in its infancy. If self-respect is to supplant the now much-maligned global esteem in quantitative psychological research, the concept must be strengthened, its main components demarcated and made operational. Roland and Foxx devote only a single short paragraph to the potentially measurable components of self-respect (2003, p. 281). Some of those components, such as 'self-control', 'humility' and a life plan based on 'moral law', are not parts of the Aristotelian concept. Others, such as 'behaviors that demonstrate respect for others', seem too vague, as they stand, to serve as guidelines for instrument design. It may be that Roland and Foxx give questions of measurement such short shrift because they are more interested in the future uses of self-respect for psychological *therapy* – helping therapists engage in character-building moral discourse with their clients (see 2003, pp. 275–82) – than for psychological measurement of the kind which proliferated in recent decades for global self-esteem. Nevertheless, even if the future uses of self-respect were to be predominantly therapeutic, one would think that some standards for measuring clients' self-respect would also be required to monitor the benefits of the relevant therapeutic interventions.

In the preceding section, I claimed that psychologists would first have to choose between Kantian and Aristotelian self-respect as the one to be measured. Assuming that my reasons for favouring the latter are accepted, our earlier glimpse of it must now be enhanced. My exploration focused on the areas of discordance between the Aristotelian concept of self-respect and the Kantian one; now it is time to say more about its actual components. We need not be overly deterred there by the fact that Aristotle's corpus does not contain any term equivalent to 'self-respect' in contemporary English; a clear concept of self-respect can be teased, and has been teased, out of his account of 'great-mindedness' (*megalopsychia*) and its surrounding virtues (see, e.g., Kristjánsson, 2002, chap. 3; Russell, 2005; recall also my character description of Socrates as an icon of self-respect in Section 1.1).

The first component of Aristotelian self-respect is *command of all the moral virtues*, including the purely emotional ones. It is not clear to what extent ordinary language places constraints, moral or otherwise, upon the content of a person's self-respect. One can think of people setting themselves idiosyncratic standards, unrelated to anything that others would value, and I presume that it would not be at odds with ordinary language to say that those people possessed their own sort of self-respect. On the Aristotelian understanding, however, self-respect cannot be divorced from (other) universally grounded and acknowledged moral virtues. It is a higher-order virtue which makes those other virtues greater and 'does not arise without them' (1985, p. 99 [1124a1–3]). Russell explains this unique status of self-respect, as simultaneously being a separate virtue and a consummation of the other virtues, by noting that self-respect and (other) moral virtues shape each other: One 'must start with some form of self-respect in order to develop a person of virtue, and as a person so develops, the self that he respects changes into a person that is more and more worthy of his own respect' (2005, p. 105). The painful feeling when one occasionally 'loses self-respect' may help secure the characterological foundations of true self-respect, just as painful feelings of remorse attest to and strengthen one's sense of duty (cf. Telfer, 1995, p. 114). Nevertheless, for full Aristotelian virtue (exhibited by the *megalopsychoi*), what is required is not only actions and emotions that are robustly worthy morally, but also proper self-esteem predicated upon this foundation. By Aristotle's lights, if there ever was a magic bullet that could transform a young person's life, it would be a pill coated not with global self-esteem but with such proper domain-specific self-esteem linked to the proper self-respect. Furthermore, I mentioned earlier that in the Aristotelian model, those virtues are considered greatest which are most beneficial to others. Amongst those are (in addition to *megalopsychia* itself) justice, courage and generosity. Measures of Aristotelian self-respect thus need to capture both a person's overall mastery of moral virtues and, more specifically, a person's exhibition of the greatest virtues.

The second component of Aristotelian self-respect is the emotion of *pridefulness*. Self-respectful persons do not only possess *pride* as an episodic, dispositional and background emotion, they also have an acute sense of their own dignity; they are, so to speak, proud of their own worthiness and expect recognition of it from others. They are also liable to shame, not only if they fail to live up to their own standards but also if they feel that the external recognition they deserve is not forthcoming (see further in Kristjánsson, 2002, chaps. 3–4). Measures of Aristotelian self-respect need to capture this self-respectful person's sense of pridefulness.

The third component of Aristotelian self-respect is *strength of character*. By that I mean that self-respectful persons have steadfast convictions, as well as the courage of those convictions. They nail their colours to the mast and stand up for themselves, always willing to defend their convictions with fortitude – even to the point of their own physical peril – but unwilling to overlook insults or to compromise simply for the sake of compromise (see further in Russell, 2005). Measures of Aristotelian self-respect need to capture this fortitude and strength of character (which must, as already noted, not be confounded with Kantian self-control).

The fourth component of Aristotelian self-respect is *stability of character*. Self-respect is a continuing, global trait of one character as a whole (see Russell, 2005, p. 104). Self-respectful persons can be trusted to react consistently under similar circumstances. In that way, they display maturity of character. While not exempt from the occasional error, they do not have regular 'off days' or exhibit systematic moral bias in dealing with different people. In Chapter 6, we saw how such an ideal is not compromised by the threat of 'moral situationism', as stability is to be measured essentially by one's *emotional reactions* rather than one's behavioural reactions in unusual circumstances. Measures of Aristotelian self-respect need to capture the self-respectful person's emotional consistency and maturity of character.

I consider those four components to be necessary conditions of (Aristotelian) self-respect, in terms of which the concept can be analysed. Of course each of them may be studied in psychological research as a separate variable, just as there is already an abundance of investigations of particular moral attitudes. For a psychological study to be one of self-respect, however, the four components would have to be studied conjunctively. Some allowances must be made if the subjects of measured self-respect are children. Children cannot be expected to show the same emotional stability and maturity of character as adults, for example. Some writers interpret Aristotle's account as saying that children cannot possess virtue at all (see, e.g., Welchman, 2005, p. 150) and therefore lack self-respect. That is too drastic a conclusion. As mentioned in Chapter 6, Aristotle goes out of his way to introduce emotional virtues specific to young people: emulousness and shamefulness. He also describes some morally praiseworthy characteristics that virtuous adults should ideally possess but that come more easily to young people for reasons of developmental psychology: open-mindedness, optimism, trust, courage, guilelessness and friendship.

And he unflinchingly refers to these characteristics as 'virtues' (1991, pp. 165–66 [1389a16–b3]). I see no particular problem in measuring these virtues, as well as children's pridefulness and (relative) strength of character, should the aim be, say, to explore the link between self-respect and school performance.

7.5. The Objectivity of Self-Respect Revisited

Let us finally return to Roland and Foxx's contention that it is 'objectivity' which differentiates self-respect from self-esteem (2003, p. 282). Measures of self-esteem typically rely on self-reported subjective feelings that are likely to contain substantial biases (see, e.g., Baumeister, Campbell, Krueger & Vohs, 2003, pp. 7–8). That consideration, coupled with the fact that measures of global self-esteem have failed to yield significant correlations, makes self-respect an attractive alternative research option. Measures of the components of Aristotelian self-respect, delineated above, should utilise the potential advantage of objectivity. Self-reports – particularly of the 'How much self-respect do you feel that you possess?' kind – would then be avoided. Rather, the focus would be on instruments and experiments to determine whether or not people actually possess the components in question (and those components could, subsequently, be examined with regard to possible correlates). I am not an empirical psychologist, and it hardly behoves me to advise experts on the back roads and byways of instrumental and experimental design. I hope I may be forgiven, however, for sounding warnings about potential pitfalls that philosophers commonly encounter when examining empirical research into morality.

The first common pitfall arises from trying to measure people's moral maturity via responses to far-fetched moral dilemmas – scenarios that they are unlikely to encounter in their daily lives. As noted in Chapter 4, this is precisely what was wrong with Kohlberg's research instruments and what gave rise to his bleak stage theory of moral development (1981). The theory may better be termed one of moral underdevelopment, especially with regard to children who tend to score badly when the scenarios to which they are asked to respond lie outside their immediate world of experience (see further in Kristjánsson, 2002, pp. 184–86). Even if self-respect involves – at least in adults – the stable and committed exhibition of moral virtue, the stability of virtue will be partly dependent upon the stability of daily experiences, and when people are prompted to go beyond those experiences, their self-respect may – as we saw in some of the experiments described in Chapter 6 – flounder for awhile, taking time to adjust. What can be learned from those experiments is that when people are confronted, without allies in alien circumstances, with a view of things exceedingly different from their own, and even pressured by those whom they consider figures of authority to act in certain ways, the majority cannot be trusted to follow the dictates of their self-respect. So if prospective instruments for measuring self-respect are to rely on responses to morally charged scenarios, it is advisable to make those scenarios as this-worldly and realistic as possible.

The other pitfall that I want to mention is the behaviouristic fallacy of simply judging persons' self-respect from the way they behave; witness, for instance, Roland and Foxx's contention that in order to measure self-respect, we need to define and observe 'behaviors that are respectful towards the self and others' (2003, p. 272). As I have already emphasised, self-respect is a character state, not merely a behaviour trait. For Aristotle, for example, the merely self-controlled altruist is lacking in self-respect in comparison with the willing and emotionally engaged altruist, even if both perform the same actions. Psychologists studying (Aristotelian) self-respect thus need to try to gauge the emotional and motivational bases of self-respect (cf. again Chapter 6).

Whatever methods are chosen in the end, I think we could reasonably expect empirical psychologists to come up with findings of people's self-respect that would be more valid than those for, say, global self-esteem, given the objectivity of the components of self-respect. Once such findings have been established, the next step would be to look for potential correlates of low and high self-respect. Variables which have been studied in relation to global self-esteem – including school performance, risky sexual behaviour, and drug/alcohol abuse – immediately come to mind. Given my earlier account of the components of Aristotelian self-respect, we could expect such studies to provide non-trivial conclusions. The same would not apply to general 'prosocial behaviour', however, because such behaviour is already included in the first component of self-respect (command of moral virtues).

Now that research into global self-esteem in psychology and education has lost its lustre, I hope that the considerations explored in this chapter may help pave the way for future psychological research into self-respect and its correlates. As I have emphasised, researchers must not avoid taking a stand on the type of self-respect being studied: Aristotelian or Kantian. Nor should they shirk a detailed analysis of the objective components of self-respect (given that what is being studied is a full realist self rather than mere self-concept) and their manifestations in moral emotion and moral character.

8. Multicultural Selves

8.1. Culture-Specific Self-Concepts?

After having devoted Chapters 6 and 7 to workings of the self that are not essentially related to self-concept, I now pick up the thread from Chapter 5 and resume an exploration of the beliefs that people hold in relation to themselves. Some social scientists resent the word 'self-concept', because that word seems to connote that the sets of people's self-conceptions – although obviously *token*-different from individual to individual – possess some *type*-universal form or structure. In contrast, a number of empirical findings, recorded by social scientists, indicate that there are two essentially different types of self-concepts abroad in the world – two essentially different sets of self-conceptions, if you like: those of an *interdependent* self-culture and those of an *independent* self-culture. What is typically added to the story, then, is that these self-conceptions are conceptually and practically irreconcilable or even incommensurable. Human beings inhabit not a single moral and psychological world but two radically different worlds.

I noted in Section 1.2 how such a culture-specific view of self-concepts threatens to undermine the moral objectivism that is the *modus operandi* of much of what exists in the name of moral philosophy. The trouble is not so much the existence of self-conceptions that are type-different rather than token-different, but rather the additional assumption that there is no standpoint, practical or ideal, from which those conflicting types could be harmonised. If the latter is true, the view of the two mutually exclusive self-conceptions may truly cause greater mischief to the idea of an objective morality than old-fashioned cultural relativism and moral situationism ever did. Moreover, it would also jeopardise my proposed 'alternative' self-paradigm in so far as it is a paradigm relating to our allegedly universal human nature. For the self-conscious emotions which I delineated in Chapter 4 and related to self-esteem in Chapter 5 – emotions that are both *about* the self and *in/of* the self – are, according to the two-self-cultures view, radically culture-specific all the way down. There is, for instance, no universal human pride or shame of the kind that I have been describing.

It is a matter of some surprise and disappointment that the challenge of the two-cultures view has gone mostly unheeded by moral philosophers of an objectivist bent, preoccupied as they have been recently with the perils of moral situationism (Chapter 6). In the words of Robert C. Solomon, it is unfortunate that 'so few of our most prestigious philosophers and philosophy journals' have joined in the discussion of the two self-conceptions, 'rife as it is with conceptual confusions' (Solomon, 1999, p. 181). The aim of this chapter is to begin to rectify this imbalance. The method employed is predominantly that of analysing the relevant social scientific research and critically exploring its moral and psychological implications, beginning in the following section with a review of the two-cultures view.

8.2. Interdependent versus Independent Self-Concepts

Hazel Rose Markus and Shinobu Kitayama's (1991) construal of interdependent (Eastern/traditional/collectivist) versus independent (Western/liberal/individualist) self-conceptions is undoubtedly one of the most influential works in late twentieth century social psychology, with far-reaching implications in many areas, including moral philosophy and emotion theory. These conceptions, it turns out, involve not only different psychological self-images, but also radically divergent ways of feeling, seeing, acting and being in the world. Markus and Kitayama's juxtapositioning of the Western bounded, unique, self-contained and segregated liberal self-concept with the Eastern fluid, connected, holistic and less-differentiated traditional self-concept is based on a whole mountain of social scientific research. Since the publication of their article, mountains more have been added of analyses and supporting (and, in some cases, conflicting) findings. At first blush, at least, Markus and Kitayama's construals have seemed to many academics from diverse disciplines to make conceptual sense, to fit in with previous theories, both social scientific and philosophical (such as Charles Taylor's 1989 genealogy of the Western self), and to account for much of the relevant data (see, e.g., Wang & Chaudhary, 2006, and

Table 8.1. *Contrasts between Traditional and Western/Liberal Self-Conceptions*

	Traditional Self	Western/Liberal Self
a) Formation/nature	Relational, other-entwined, embedded	Unitary, other-independent, disembedded
b) Development	Outwardness, towards a mixture of heteronomy and autonomy through cultural submersion	Inwardness, towards full autonomy through crisis, self-exploration and self-enhancement
c) Relation to the good	Appreciator of external values, thick notion of the good	Creator of own values, thin notion of the good
d) Ultimate goal	Self-respect, moralisation or control of emotions, harmony	Self-esteem, emotionalisation, self-expression
e) Pathology	Hyper-identity, excessive self-respect	Self-fragmentation, loss of meaning and self-esteem
f) Beneficiaries	Traditionalists, monoculturalists, religious fundamentalists	Therapists, spin-doctors, big businesses and other merchants of happiness

Matsumoto, 1999 – although Matsumoto considers the initial appeal to be illusory).

Self-concepts involve inter alia beliefs about the nature and trajectory of our selves: what we are, how we develop and where we end up if all is well. Table 8.1 summarises some of the basic ingredients of the conceptual framework in question, focusing on the alleged differences between traditional and Western self-conceptions regarding a) the formation/nature of the self, b) its development, c) its relationship to external goods, d) its ultimate goal, e) its possible pathology and f) the main beneficiaries of the respective self-conceptions (cf. Markus & Kitayama's own somewhat differently focused summary, 1991, p. 230).

a) Formation/nature. According to the traditional understanding, a person's self is formulated within and through a web of relationships, especially kinship. Its nature is defined by this web rather than by a unique autobiographical history. There is no way – either psychologically or ontologically speaking – to set those relationships aside and still retain one's identity. The self is thus considered other-entwined and culturally embedded from its first moments of self-awareness. This does not mean that particular ends, commitments and attachments acquired through the communal genesis of the self cannot later be reflected upon by the individual, called into question and perhaps revised if necessary. It simply means that, without irreparable psychological damage, one cannot achieve independence from the totality of one's existential relations. One's actions are understood against the backdrop of those relations as being 'situationally bound' (Markus and Kitayama, 1991, pp. 225, 232) rather than the results of personal intentions (which may point to a link between interdependent self-conceptions and moral situationism).

Markus and Kitayama see a vast gulf between this traditional conception and the Western liberal conception, which stresses other-independence: that each person is an island, that we are essentially on our own, notwithstanding our social and natural background. The idea is not so much that unchosen and unexamined personal attachments do not enter into the formation of individual identity in childhood, but rather that any such attachments, and indeed the very web of relationships that embeds one originally in a sociocultural context, can be voluntarily eradicated as individuals find their own bearings within themselves. The world is essentially composed of 'me' – wrapped up in an inner space – versus 'all others'; not of 'us' and some particular 'others'. My actions are the results of *my* intentions and *my* dispositions.

b) Development. If all goes well, in the traditional conception, the self develops towards a stronger and stronger sense of its relational nature by strengthening its outward ties to family, culture and tradition. Traditional self-development thus follows an interdependent pathway. Consider Aristotle's idea of moral development, which involves early habituation into common virtues through heteronomously guided repetition and modelling on moral exemplars, followed by growing individual appreciation and mastery of the virtues, yet without the individual ever reaching what moderns would refer to as 'full' or 'strong' autonomy (Winch, 2005). There is no joy in life greater than being initiated into worthwhile communal projects – moral, social, aesthetic – that facilitate social harmony and obliterate rather than reinforce the distinction between the individual and the group. Knowledge about others is ultimately more elaborate and specific than is knowledge about oneself. No fate is more terrible than ostracisation.

Compare this idea of an interdependent pathway with the Western conception of the self's independent pathway to maturity. Individuals are encouraged to realise a life plan that is arrived at autonomously, by gradually cutting ties to tradition and significant others and 'finding themselves' through an inward gaze. To do so, they must attend to their private beliefs, hone their critical faculties and nourish their suspicions of dependency. They must not only locate their proper place in moral space, but must also radically reorientate themselves and invent their own space. As Charles Taylor observes in his description of the genealogy of the Western self, modern liberals have exalted the notion of 'leaving home' to a cultural icon and a measurement of individual salvation. All healthy young people must leave their parental and cultural backgrounds to make their 'authentic' ways in the world (Taylor, 1989, p. 39). In order to 'redeem' oneself in due course, one must experience a 'fall' from comfortable but mistaken grace and must suffer a period of self-diminution (nagging self-doubt and drastic self-exploration) before one can convalesce: reaffirming and enhancing the self.

c) Relation to the good. The traditional self is a self that learns to recognise and identify with the good as an objective, inter-human reality. The 'good' refers not only to the common social good *qua* the value of public institutions and communal enterprises, but also to the moral good, which comprises universal virtues such as personal justice, honesty and sympathy. They are taken to be 'strongly evaluated goods' (Taylor, 1989), to which we should commit ourselves regardless of our actual preferences: goods which are not invented by us but are somewhere out there, and towards which competent, wise and experienced judges can guide us.

By way of contrast, the current Western self-concept posits a notion of the good which, except for subjective values (chosen by but not constitutive of the self), comprises only ultra-thin universal values (procedural values of majority rule, basic human rights, freedom and private property) that bind all rational agents as the formal conditions of choice. Apart from those, the whole world becomes a marketplace of subjective values between which we can reasonably choose more or less as we please, as long as those values are autonomously arrived at, reflexively organised, consistent with one another and instrumentally conducive to our overall chosen life plan (hence, 'authentic'), and as long as they are not harmful to other people's life plans. The Western self is thus understood first and foremost as a choosing self, which discovers values by inventing them (Taylor, 1989, p. 22; cf. Giddens, 1991, p. 80). Society and morality have no independent value, except in so far as they are venues freely entered by individual bearers of rights. Tellingly, what causes greater worry to Western liberals than the allegedly outdated call by moral substantivists for a return to thick universal values, is the threat posed by postmodernism, which rejects even the thin formal rights posited by liberalism.

d) Ultimate goal. As can be inferred so far, the traditional self is considered to have realised its full potential when it has found its proper place within the web of existential relations that create and sustain it. 'Interpersonal harmony' and 'group solidarity' are the terms most felicitously used to describe this goal (Wang & Chaudhary, 2006, p. 327). The mature self respects itself as the possessor of virtues; it esteems itself for the strength and stability of its character; and it expects recognition of its accomplishments from the in-group via deserved honours bestowed upon it. In general, the self is valued because (and in so far as) it is, in fact, valuable. The self's emotions have, ideally, become moralised (imbued with appropriate reason) or, second-best, self-controlled (policed by reason). 'Such voluntary control of the inner attributes constitutes the core of becoming mature' (Markus & Kitayama, 1991, p. 227).

Lacking this thick substantive notion of the moral good, the most important accomplishment of the liberal self is not self-respect, but rather self-esteem: the (now infamous) estimation of the ratio of its global achievements to its aspiration. The litmus test of success here is a feel-good factor: If you feel good about yourself, you are doing well. Selves are considered valuable because (and in so far as) they are valued. 'Positive' (read: pleasant) emotions make the individual happy and should be fully expressed rather than kept at bay. Indeed, there is nothing considered wrong, and much perceived to be right, with emotionalising the whole of personal and public discourse. This strong emphasis on self-esteem cannot be understood independently of a moral culture which sees individualistic, subjective wellbeing as the ultimate goal in life, and understands it in terms of 'loving' and 'esteeming' oneself. Hence, also – as we saw in Chapter 7 – the scant interest in self-respect which focuses on objective wellbeing.

After people have 'found themselves' (see *b) Development*), they need to learn to accept what they have found and to express it. Charles Taylor calls Western culture a culture of 'expressivism' – an ideal incomprehensible to pre-moderns (1989, pp. 374 and 376). Through self-expression, we re-enhance the self, which inevitably diminished during the period of self-discovery. At best, we do something world-shaking, perhaps on the sports field, which guarantees a Warholian 15-minute dose of fame. We do this not because fame is important in itself, but because it demonstrates self-expression to the hilt. Otherwise, as Postman (1985) suggested, we merely amuse ourselves to death; or, if the self is still shaking, undergo therapy and achieve redemption. Art becomes the most valued specific expressive outlet, more than, for example, academic accomplishment, because expressing oneself through art – or even creating oneself as a work of art – involves full subjective disclosure, available to everyone irrespective of IQ, and does not carry with it any burdensome connotation of external truth.

e) Pathology. Both the traditional and the Western self have their potential pathologies. The possible perversion of the traditional self into hyper-identity – loss of individuality, uncritical conformism, susceptibility to authoritarianism – has been well documented. The danger here is that the self starts to live not only *in* but *for* the community. Another danger is that of excessive self-respect, a situation in which the traditional self becomes unduly obsessed with its own image in the eyes of others, leading to extreme forms of pridefulness and perfectionism.

The liberal self runs the risk of an irrevocable loss of meaning. Once bases of communal identification have been eroded, the question of whether the liberal self ever manages to construct a new basis for itself becomes partly one of 'moral luck'. Taylor talks about the potential loss of 'resonance, depth or richness' (1989, p. 501). The inward turn leaves the self vulnerable to fragmentation; the power to deconstruct previous allegiances and to engender (temporary) alienation may spiral out of control and foreclose any attempts to carve out a new core that is 'truly yours'. I return to and flesh out some of those potential self-pathologies in Chapter 9.

f) Beneficiaries. Who benefits most from those two respective conceptions of the self? In the case of the traditional self, the beneficiaries are obviously the custodians of the cultural order with which that self identifies. If anyone is going to abuse the benefits accruing to the traditional conception, the persons who can are the religious fundamentalists and bigoted traditionalists.

Who benefits, on the other hand, from the Western cult of the vulnerable and diminished self? First in line are quack therapists and counsellors, taking care to portray every stage in the life course of the self as presenting such grave risks that constant therapeutic intervention is required. Every existential problem is seen as potentially requiring a diagnosis and treatment, in order to help us get in touch with ourselves. Even 'Christ the saviour' has become 'Christ the counsellor' (see Furedi, 2004, p. 17, citing Archbishop Carey) and illness has become hip, at least when it involves an existential crisis that can be 'healed' with external help. Another group of beneficiaries – according to Furedi (2004) at least – are the politicians, whose lives are made considerably easier by being able to treat people as clients rather than citizens. They stand to gain, no less than the therapists, from the valorisation of the help-seeking self and from the writing off of intimate personal relationships as potentially self-encumbering and emotionally hazardous: 'If you and your family cannot sort out your personal issues, then we, the politicians, can do it for you'. Hence, the steady emotionalisation of political discourse and the increasing intervention into, and rigid regulation of, personal space. The third beneficiary is big business, selling us happiness to mend our broken selves, and preferring, of course, a weak self to a strong one.

8.3 Four Initial Responses and Why They Fail

How should moral philosophers react to this conceptualisation? Let us explore four possible responses. The *first* response is to admit that the epistemological condition behind moral objectivism has been undermined, and to embrace cultural relativism instead. It is unlikely, however, that the objectivist philosophical majority will be won over so easily, not merely because of the standard moral and logical paradoxes that make relativism so difficult to stomach, but because of specific problems attached to the types of relativism – typically referred to as 'postmodern' – that have recently taken advantage of destabilising or voiding the notion of transcultural moral selfhood.

As described in relation to anti-self-realism in Section 2.2, postmodern relativism comes in two distinct guises. One is playful or uncritical postmodernism, which puts the very notion of a personal sense of self 'under erasure' (Hall, 1996). When translated into everyday language, this seems to mean that the human self is a radically multiple self, containing a random collage of possible identities between which each individual can choose at will at any given moment. What emerges is not only a culturally relativised self-conception – as in Markus and Kitayama (1991) – but a more radically protean and fleeting one. Unfortunately, to think that we can simply decide on a whim who we are contravenes an abundance of psychological research on the rugged change-resistance of our self-conceptions (see further in Chapter 10).

More relevant to our present concerns is the second type of postmodern self-theory: that of critical postmodernism, better known as 'identity theory'. Gergen (1991), we recall, considered identity theory to be a natural outgrowth of playful postmodernism grown tedious. Critical postmodernists abandon the fragmentation of their uncritical predecessors through the establishment of socially constructed, collective self-identities. It does not require a great leap of the imagination to envisage how moral relativism inspired by critical postmodernism could take on board insights from Markus and Kitayama's conceptualisations. Human beings would then be seen as historically conditioned to adopt one of the two self-conceptions – an interdependent self versus an independent self – without any hope of a common ground. Criticisms of critical postmodernism, however, are legion. One set of criticisms is typically levied against the postmodern rejection of transcultural variables and its reification of cultures as exceptional and unique – like Leibniz's monads. Another set of objections relates to its determinism concerning social identities. It is odd to claim, on the one hand, that selfhood is socially constructed all the way down and, on the other, that – despite the increased cultural connections and complexities of today's world – each individual is deterministically bound by a single social self-identity at any given time. Critical postmodernism thus seems liable to perversion into the very 'vices' it was created to resist: essentialism and monoculturalism (cf. Luzzati, 2005). A similar tendency to absolutise the relative can be seen in the suggestion of some postmodernists that an interdependent self-conception is somehow 'better' than an independent one (Markus & Kitayama, 1991, p. 228). All in all, although postmodernists of every type will champion the dislocation of the idea of a unifying moral selfhood, neither playful nor critical postmodernism holds much prospect of translating the two-self-cultures view into a respectable relativist position. Admittedly, this does not show that the data in question could not be used to support a more coherent form of relativism – but that form has then not yet been worked out in the literature.

The *second* possible response to the two-self-cultures view is to admit that there are two basic self-concepts, and hence two basic socio-moral perspectives, but to reject the relativistic implication by claiming that these two perspectives can indeed be compared and that, as it turns out, one of them is, across the board, morally superior to the other. The idea that a conception of oneself as a moral agent as extensive and with as many ramifications as that of either the interdependent or the independent self-concept can simply be found wanting and expendable, hook, line and sinker, may grate on modern sensibilities. More specifically, it will no doubt be called reactionary, imperial and offensive. As philosophers well know, however, views that are reactionary, imperial and offensive may nevertheless turn out to be true. Yet in this case, it strains credulity to think that one of these two conceptions can simply be out-argued and eliminated with impunity. As mentioned in the previous section, both self-concepts possess their own characteristic pathologies. It seems obvious that both also have their own characteristic advantages. Take school work, for example: The disciplined, unquestioning acceptance of received wisdoms evoked by an interdependent self-concept will facilitate primary drill-learning, but will, in contrast, wreak havoc on secondary and tertiary studies in which the critical attitudes of an independent self-concept become invaluable. Similarly, it seems too extreme to suggest that the unfaltering group solidarity espoused by the interdependent self-concept and the critical stance towards the group view promulgated by the independent self-concept cannot both, under different circumstances, count as moral requirements. The most promising response here would be to reject the gambit offered by the interdependent-versus-independent-self-concepts dichotomy and to envisage a best-of-both-worlds scenario where some relatively painless accommodation could be found between the requirements of the two, or where items from both might be picked eclectically, in turn, to suit the demands of different situations. It would be getting ahead of the argument to say more about this fond hope at this stage; it will be explored later in this chapter. At all events, such a hope runs counter to most of the literature exploring the two-cultures view, where it tends to be taken for granted that the two self-concepts represent mutually exclusive all-or-nothing moral options.

The *third* possible response is to go back to the drawing board and question some of the methodological and substantive assumptions behind the two-cultures view. Are these alleged two self-cultures perhaps over-simplifications or even fictions (Solomon, 1999, p. 191)? Doubts that have been raised in the literature concern over-hasty generalisations, historical inaccuracies, alleged methodological flaws and the existence of divergent empirical evidence. Some social scientists warn against simplistic stereotyping of societies that are by no means internally homogeneous. There are significant sub-cultural differences within both so-called interdependent and independent self-cultures; and individual variations, as well as gender differences and class differences, must not be overlooked (Spiro, 1993; Killen & Wainryb, 2000).

These warnings are well taken; there is, for example, a certain sense in which Confucianism can be called 'individualistic' in so far as it is concerned with an individual's development of his or her creative potentialities. The difference with Western conceptions, however, still lies in the Western (liberal) insistence that no particular substantive ends (such as Confucian filial relationships) can be considered necessary components of the good life. In the West, the alleged heartland of the independent self-concept, numerous well-known philosophers in the post-Enlightenment era have underscored the other-dependence of the self: Hegel, Schopenhauer, Heidegger and even that hyper-individualist Sartre, to mention but a few. Construing the Western/liberal self as a homogenous category also ignores important differences between Mediterranean and Northern European (let alone American Bible-Belt) societies. In some areas that are generally considered to belong to that of an interdependent self-culture, such as South America and Africa, almost no rigorous experimental work on self-conceptions has ever been carried out. The basic logic underlying Markus and Kitayama's theory has also been put into question: Strictly speaking, only national differences tend to be recorded in experimental studies (Japan versus USA, for instance), but the background assumption – namely, that the countries in question are associated with the alleged underlying self-conceptions – goes untested (Matsumoto, 1999). Matsumoto (1999) also produces a number of empirical findings, 18 in fact, out of which 17 suggest that there is little difference between Americans and Japanese on the interdependent–independent variable, and that the Japanese are, if anything, more individualistic than the Americans. Matusmoto, however, notes that even Japanese scholars have come to believe in the received stereotypes, gradually giving them the status of self-fulfilling prophecies.

Overdrawn as some of Markus and Kitayma's distinctions may be, it must be conceded that since the publication of their seminal paper, further corroborative empirical findings have proliferated, and that for every single negative finding produced by sceptics such as Matsumoto, there are twenty positive ones. Of special interest are studies that link the origin of children's self-concepts to the stories told to them by caregivers in interdependent and independent self-cultures, respectively – with stories in the latter tending to focus on the storyteller but in the former on other people (see references in Wang & Chaudhary, 2006). Particularly striking, also, is a comparative study of European-American, and Taiwanese mothers' beliefs about self-esteem, which indicates that while self-esteem looms large in American folk theories about success and happiness, it plays a minor role in Taiwanese folk theories, and is even frowned upon (Miller, Wang, Sandel & Cho, 2002). In Japan and Taiwan, the kind of self-assertions that Americans consider to be the sign of healthy self-concept are taken to be selfishly immature and an invitation to bad luck. The very word for 'self' in Japanese, 'jibun', implies that the self is part of the social realm; in Japanese, Chinese, and Korean, there is not even a word corresponding to the Western notion of self-esteem (Christopher, 1999; Suh & Oishi, 2002). In those countries, crimes and sport achievements are typically explained with reference to contextual variables rather than merely to ascribed personal traits (Lee, Hallahan & Herzog, 1996) – and the list of similar findings is almost endless.

Writ large, the charges typically made against Markus and Kitayama's conceptualisations do not stick all that well: To be sure, Western and Eastern self-concepts are broad templates or idealised cultural scripts which do not account for individual differences, but then this was a caveat entered by the authors themselves (Markus & Kitayama, 1991, p. 226). Moreover, the claim has never been made that a philosophical consensus exists in the West on an independent self-concept, but rather that such a concept has come into being as an overarching folk theory in the wake of converging and mutually reinforcing social developments such as the reformation, the scientific revolution, industrialisation and secularisation. It need not surprise us either if studies comparing young people in Japan and China with their counterparts in Western countries record less clear-cut distinctions between interdependent and independent self-concepts than before; it is well documented that the self-conceptions of many upwardly mobile young people in non-Western societies have now become heavily Westernised. Enough has been said to indicate the spuriousness of the escape route offered by this third response; enough, at least, to dissuade me from relying on it in what follows.

The *fourth* possible response relies on a so-called two-baskets theory of the self. Recall that the problem for objectivist moral theories is that the independent and interdependent self-conceptions seem to present two conflicting perspectives of the self, with no rational resolution in sight. According to the two-baskets theory, what seem to be irreconcilable self-conceptions may in fact be conceptions that exist at different levels of psychological organisation (and, at the same time, different levels of cognitive abstraction) and hence do not compete for the same ground. One version of such a theory is provided by philosophers Wren and Mendoza (2004). They distinguish between people's personal and social identities and renounce the 'orthodox' social psychological discourse, which treats personal identity as an 'epiphenomenon' of social identity. Individuals may have a strong sense of personal self-esteem, for instance, although their self-esteem as members of a social group is low.

What would be the relevance of this observation – well taken as it may be – for questions of interdependent versus independent self-concepts and moral relativity? There are two ways of interpreting it: One is to say that it is exclusively through one's personal identity that one relates to moral properties, and that personal identity connects to independent self-conceptions. Being brought up in an interdependent self-culture may influence one's social identity, but leave one's personal, and hence one's moral, identity intact. This forging of a link between independent self-concepts and personal identity, on the one hand, and interdependent self-concepts and social identity, on the other, does not bear scrutiny, however. The right way to describe a person with an interdependent self-concept, in Markus and Kitayama's understanding, is not as a person with an interdependent *social* self-concept, but as one possessing possibly underneath it a *personal* independent concept, with only the latter being 'moral'. What Markus and Kitayama call an 'interdependent' self-concept is a conception of one's relationships with other people *and* of one's relations to moral value. Such a conception of relatedness appears to take a radically different form in the case of interdependent self-concepts than in the case of independent ones, and to influence one's 'strong evaluations', in Taylor's sense (1989). Those evaluations are *moral* ones: evaluations that ultimately compete at the *same* cognitive and motivational level (cf. Spiecker, Steutel & de Ruyter, 2004; Schwartz, Montgomery & Briones, 2006).

A second interpretation of Wren and Mendoza's claim (with respect to our present purpose) would be to say that personal identity is one's 'essential' or 'true' selfhood, whereas social identity is a constructed identity which may or may not correspond to one's essential selfhood. This interpretation faces two hurdles. The first hurdle is that most of the studies used by Markus and Kitayama in support of their theory focus specifically on 'constructed' identity; they trace people's socially situated *beliefs* about themselves. There is little if any attempt made to gauge, for instance, whether or not people who take themselves to have an interdependent self-concept (as evidenced by the answers they give to questionnaires) actually act in line with such a concept in every-day situations. One troubling aspect of the two-self-cultures literature here – from a philosophical perspective – is its conceptual sloppi-ness. Self-concepts or self-conceptions are also referred to in the lit-erature as 'self-construals', 'self-identities' or even simply 'identities'. There seems, at first glance at least, to be no noticeable concern with keeping distinguishable notions distinct, let alone with any conceptual regimentation. It takes the reader awhile to realise the underlying assumption: the blatantly anti-realist one that 'self' is considered to be synonymous with 'identity' – what you conceive of the self to be.

The *second* hurdle is that Wren and Mendoza themselves are avowed anti-self-realists, emphatically rejecting the existence of any actual 'non-constructed' selfhood. There is 'no determinate, de facto "hidden self" that, like a jack-in-the-box, suddenly reveals itself when conditions are right', they say; rather, all identity is socially constructed, 'antiessen-tialist' identity (Wren & Mendoza, 2004, p. 242). If that were the case, however, personal and social identity would belong in the same bas-ket. Even if they could be kept distinct at some level of psychological organisation (as in the case of personal versus social self-esteem), such a limited two-baskets-view would do little to alleviate the concerns of moral objectivists.

To take stock: If Markus and Kitayama's two self-systems inevit-ably inform people's deepest moral commitments, and if these two systems are really as irreconcilable as they seem, it is not possible to meet the epistemological condition of moral objectivism (that human beings can become acquainted with and understand moral proper-ties in a way that is independent of non-interhuman preferences, per-spectives or points of view; see Section 1.2). The 'alternative' self-paradigm that I have been proposing in this book, based inter alia on universal self-relevant emotions, also seems in jeopardy. No good reasons emerged from the previous section to question the general aptness of Markus and Kitayama's conceptualisations. But the exist-ence of conflicting independent versus interdependent self-concepts is one thing, the question of whether or not they are psychologic-ally and morally irreconcilable is quite another. To engage that issue and to determine if the game is really up for moral objectivists, the implications of the two-cultures view must be subjected to further scrutiny.

8.4 Self-Cultures and Emotion

Notice that there are some conspicuous lacunae in the literature on interdependent and independent selves, hailing as it does from a particular discursive tradition within social psychology or, more specifically, cultural psychology. Little attention is paid to universal aspects of self-development. Theories such as Damon's on the development of justice conceptions (1981) and Hoffman's on the development of empathy/sympathy (2000) – theories which focus on the transcultural features of moral development, irrespective of alleged self-cultures – receive no mention; much less do biological evolutionary theories based on the formula 'culture via nature' (Keller, 2008). Nor is any attempt made to square the alleged culture specificity of moral selfhood with Kohlberg's universal stages of moral development (1981). In general, no attention is paid to the moral education literature, including constructs such as Aristotle's *phronesis*, which seem to offer some prospect of rational resolution of contested intellectual and emotional perspectives. But more will be said about that in the following section.

Markus and Kitayama make much, in their original paper, of the implications of the two-cultures view for *emotion theory*. Yet those implications have not been followed up in the subsequent literature with the intensity that one might have expected. Incidentally, it must be said that the discussion of self-culture-specific emotions is the least persuasive part of their paper (Markus and Kitayama, 1991, pp. 235–39). The authors seem to believe that the rejection of a biological, natural-kind view of emotion implies that emotions are culture-specific. This assumption overlooks the fact that the cognitive theories of emotion to which most contemporary philosophers subscribe and that tend to be seen as the antitheses of natural-kind theories carry no such implication. Indeed, most prominent cognitive theorists of emotion assume that there is considerable agreement in the identity of emotions across cultures otherwise distinct in time and geography, and that it is precisely for this reason that we can understand and appreciate folk tales, literature and works of art from cultures remote from our own (see, e.g., Roberts, 2003, pp. 182–85). In order to show that emotions are culture-specific – with relation to self-cultures, for instance – is not enough to concentrate, as Markus and Kitayama do, on some exotic anomalous emotions. It must be demonstrated that some of the core morally relevant emotions, such as anger, compassion, indignation, pride and shame, are indeed experienced differently in different cultures (being elicited by essentially different situations; having different cognitive consorts and/or valence; being typically felt at different levels of intensity). Most relevant for present purposes would be such relativist accounts of pride and shame: those emotions that are closest to the self and inform our self-esteem as background emotions – or so I have argued.

Mesquita and Karasawa (2004) argue that current accounts of self-conscious emotions fit only self-conceptions in the West and how these emotions are consequently experienced there. They produce empirical evidence showing that Asians consider shame a healthy attitude and have been taught to be self-critical, while having a negative attitude towards experiencing and expressing pride. From such evidence, the authors deduce that pride is not, whereas shame is, congruent with the goals of an interdependent self-concept – and, more generally, that self-conscious emotions do not generalise over cultures.

The problem with many of the cited findings of allegedly type-different emotions across cultures is that it is unclear if what is being measured is their experience or effects. Notice that it is not enough to show that such emotions are exhibited differently in different societies. That seems clearly to be the case (Markus & Kitayama, 1991, pp. 236–37); but the fact that Eastern subjects have be taught to be more inhibited in expressing their pride, for instance, does not mean that they experience it differently. Do they? Is pride, for them, also a positively felt emotion elicited by the belief that they have done something worthy of admiration? The answer seems to be yes. Even Mesquita and Karasawa accept as much, although they are at pains to emphasise that people with interdependent self-concepts do not really experience pride in the Western sense on such occasions but rather social honour – which shifts the locus of responsibility for the positive outcome to the group as a whole (2004, p. 164). But recall that for Aristotle – who in the interdependent-versus-independent-self-concept dichotomy would come down on the side of the interdependent one, as would other pre-Enlightenment Westerners – pride was perhaps the most positively valued emotion (when felt about the proper things). We may or may not believe that 'our' accomplishments are ours alone, or are attributable in large measure to a surrounding group, but those are factual beliefs which do not change the nature of the felt emotion (as pleasant and about a positive accomplishment related to our selves). The beliefs underlying individualist and collectivist pride appear to be token-different rather than type-different beliefs about the exact source of the worthy accomplishment.

No one denies the claim that emotions are socially developed and involve a host of subordinate culture-specific and even person-specific beliefs. I must agree with what seems to be the mainstream view in psychological circles, however: that self-conscious emotion processes are universal at their core (Goetz & Keltner, 2007). They are recognisable by individuals all over the world, even from culturally isolated, non-literate cultures, and are elicited by the same set of underlying core cognitions – although the frequency at which they are felt and the mode of their expression may vary considerably in response to cultural norms (Tracy & Robins, 2004, 2007b, 2007c). The difference between my view and the mainstream psychological one is that whereas the latter sees in the universality of self-conscious emotions the workings of an adaptive mechanism which has given our species certain reproductive advantages (James, 1890, p. 52; Tracy & Robins, 2007b, pp. 191–201), I rest content with seeing in them the construction of emotional dispositions and background self-appraisals that form part of our common and irreducibly moral human *eudaimonia* (recall Section 5.5).

All in all, different self-cultures may produce token-different emotions in different contexts, but not radically type-different emotions felt differently. The emotions experienced in an interdependent self-culture and an independent one are probably often incompatible, given differences in the underlying self-beliefs. But that it not to say that they are incommensurable or irreconcilable.

8.5 The Possibility of Synergic Selfhood – or *Phronesis* Revisited

In order to pursue further questions on the relevance of the two-cultures view for issues of objectivity or relativity, it is – in line with the interdisciplinary perspective of this study – salutary not to abandon the psychological literature, as some philosophers would be inclined to do. Rather, we should delve into it more deeply, and consider material from other fields of social scientific study – especially those having to do with bilingualism and biculturalism.

Until recently, social scientific studies have painted a relatively gloomy picture of the socio-psychological status of people caught up in a struggle between conflicting self-conceptions, such as those of an interdependent and an independent self. In recent years, labour mobility and large-scale migrations of people between distant cultures have become not so much the exception as the rule. There is, consequently, widespread talk of lack of rooted identity; of dislocation or a constant tug-of-war between two cultures; of culture shocks, existential vacuums, and anomie; of not knowing 'how to file all the things that are inside me' (Wren & Mendoza, 2004, p. 260). The upshot is that any kind of double consciousness is seen as inherently problematic. There is no question that for some people it is – witness the case of conflict-ridden suicide bombers that I explore in the following chapter. Popular fiction writers such as Amy Tan have even made a career of describing the painful trade-offs forced upon people torn between two cultural worlds.

Not everyone sees this predicament as a painful ordeal, however. Some individuals describe it as an exhilarating challenge, associated with feelings of pride, achievement and uniqueness (Nguyen & Benet-Martínez, 2007). One can only speculate why such positive accounts have had a disproportionally low profile in the literature in past decades. Perhaps they have been considered less 'juicy'; perhaps they have squared less well with prominent twentieth century research paradigms such as Freudianism, Marxism and poststructuralism, which emphasise intrapersonal and/or interpersonal conflicts, power struggles and enmities; perhaps the well-known linguistic situation of our having a more nuanced vocabulary to describe painful emotions than pleasant ones has also had an impact on research in this area. Whatever the reason, the tide seems now to be turning in favour of more positive characterisations of experiences involving biculturalism and bilingualism. It is to those experiences that we now turn, as they carry implications for questions of moral and emotional relativity.

Bilingualism used to be defined as the native-like control of two languages (Harding & Riley, 1986, p. 22). As native-like control obviously comes in degrees, the earlier definition has been replaced with one which considers bilingualism to involve the regular use of two languages (Mills, 2001). By that definition, no less than half of the world's population is bilingual. The early 1960s marked a watershed in bilingualism studies. Previously stigmatised as educationally handicapped, it turned out that bilinguals scored higher on IQ tests than monolinguals did. Bilingualism had become an educational asset. *Biculturalism* refers to the co-existence (exposure to and internalisation of) of two cultural scripts in the same individual (Nguyen & Benet-Martínez, 2007). Bilingualism and biculturalism often go hand in hand, but they are not necessarily co-extensive; bicultural individuals may be monolingual and bilingual individuals monocultural (Mills, 2001). As it is the existence of different culturally enshrined self-conceptions, rather than different languages, that is our present concern, the focus in what follows will be on biculturalism.

Considerable research has been conducted on the acculturation of individuals exposed to a new and radically different culture. For once, a considerably broad consensus also seems to exist on how to categorise experiences of such acculturation (Berger, 1997; Benet-Martínez, Leu & Lee, 2002; Nguyen & Benet-Martínez, 2007). Those experiences are typically divided into four categories: (a) *separation* (involvement and identification with the original culture only – remaining a 'clinger' or a 'traditionalist'); (b) *marginalisation* (lack of identification and engagement with either culture – being a 'vacillator' or an 'alienator'); (c) *assimilation* (involvement and identification with the new culture only – being an 'eraser' of the original culture); and (d) *integration* (involvement and identification with both cultures – being a true 'integrator' and bicultural). The received wisdom is that (d) is the option most propitious for psychosocial wellbeing, leading to benefits in all areas of life. The notion of 'true integrators' seems, however, to be beset by an unfortunate ambiguity. Sometimes it refers to alternating, chameleon-like individuals who manage to switch their thinking and behaviour in response to situational demands; sometimes to individuals who somehow fuse those demands into a new whole (Nguyen & Benet-Martínez, 2007). This ambiguity gives rise to two contrasting paradigms of bicultural integration which tend to be lumped together in the literature.

One of these paradigms could be termed integration *qua* 'hyphenated identity' or 'compartmentalisation'. It refers to a strategy for the negotiation of two cultural scripts described in recent studies as carrying positive benefits. Individuals who adopt it act not as unified cultural beings but as unions of different cultural beings, diverging and converging to the needs of the moment by engaging in cued cultural frame-switching (Nguyen & Benet-Martínez, 2007). The experiences of the bilingual poet Gomez-Pena are a case in point (cited in Foster, 1996, p. 100):

> English for politics, Spanish for love
> English for praxis, Spanish for theory
> English for survival, Spanish for laughter
> English for time, Spanish for space
> English for art, Spanish for literature.

Different self-conceptions and experiential systems are then organised around the respective cultural scripts – perhaps even stored in separate areas of the cortex (Foster, 1996). The individuals in question may feel united and achieve considerable adjustment skills, helping them to lead reasonably well-rounded lives, even though the feeling of inner unity is little more than a 'sonorous illusion' (Foster, 1996, p. 117). One can question the felicitousness of the label 'bicultural identity integration' (Benet-Martínez et al., 2002) for those human chameleons (the term 'defence mechanism' springs more readily to mind), but the adjustment value of their dilettantism seems to be high. Even if it helps solve existential problems of biculturalism, however, it offers little reprieve for moral objectivists. The existence of successfully hyphenated identities does not so much alleviate as exacerbate the force of moral relativism. Indeed, it adds an experimental gloss to the relativists' claim that there is no interhuman perspective from which to engage external value. When primed and cued in the Roman way, one feels and acts as the Romans; when primed and cued in the Non-Roman way, one responds accordingly. Is there really no more to bicultural integration than that?

A second paradigm, which is gradually emerging from research on bicultural integration, could be termed integration *qua* 'synergic identity'. 'Synergy' was a term famously employed by Maslow (1970), who borrowed it from anthropologist and poet Ruth Benedict, for a broad range of psychological syntheses. Here it refers to the self-conceptions of integrated biculturals who are comfortable in simultaneously engaging both of their cultural backgrounds – of the two self-cultures under discussion in this chapter, for example. They have forged an entirely new, fused identity, a unique configuration which cannot be reduced to its parts. When biculturals negotiate identity in this truly integrated way, they have managed to turn their cultural traditions into objects of higher-order reflection by cognitively juxtaposing them; and they consider their double background not as a mixed blessing but rather as a unique source of interpretative tools for grasping experience. There is no more ambivalence, no more code-switching, but rather full synthesis, characterised by a sense of self-fulfilment (see, in particular, Hong, Wan, No & Chiu, 2007; cf. Berger, 1997). As my own son (who is fully bilingual and arguably also integratively bicultural) put it when he was about 9 years old: 'I feel when I come across a problem that I can sometimes solve it by looking it from above with both my Chinese and Icelandic eyes' – and for him that was both an exciting and empowering experience.

When the synthesis in question involves independent versus inter-dependent self-concepts, Kagitçibasi refers to the successful union of the two as the 'autonomous–relational self' (1996). Lu and Yang's study (2006) seems to indicate that such a union is possible even amongst presumed monoculturals – individuals who have only been exposed geographically to a single language and a single culture. Lu and Yang's research revolves around the 'composite self' that is gradually evolving amongst young Taiwanese people: a dynamic amalgam that construct-ively integrates a traditional interdependent Chinese self-concept and a Western-influenced independent self-concept.

The paradigm of synergic bicultural integration goes hand in hand with a larger trend in cultural psychology in which the cultural–individual relationship is conceived as dialectical, dialogic and critical, and the focus has shifted from the question of how culture moulds the individual to that of how the individual communicatively 'does' culture (Haste & Abrahams, 2008). The potential of a fruitful cross-fertilisation among cultural psychology, developmental psychology and moral philosophy is yet to be fulfilled, unfortunately. Moreover, most of the empirical studies underpinning this paradigm of integra-tion *qua* synergy are relatively recent. Some of the evidence provided in its favour is merely anecdotal, and it is still controversial enough to be conspicuously avoided by theorists who equate bicultural integration with code switching. Yet, if it can be made to work – as will optimist-ically be presumed in what follows – this paradigm is heaven-sent for moral objectivists – at least for those who adhere to Flanagan's prin-ciple of 'minimal psychological realism', which asserts, as we recall, that moral ideals must be feasible 'for creatures like us' (Flanagan, 1991, p. 32). Synergic biculturalism seems to indicate that moral objectivity may indeed be possible for creatures like us.

Let me conclude this section with some further observations about the possible moral ramifications of synergic biculturalism. There is an old Slovak proverb which says that with each newly learned lan-guage one acquires a new soul. The paradigm of bicultural integration as hyphenated identity takes the idea behind this proverb literally. It assumes that bicultural individuals possess multiple souls, or rather *multiple selves*, between which they switch according to need, selves that may involve radically different conceptions of their 'owner's' rela-tionships with moral value and with other people. Jon Elster has subjec-ted theories of multiple selves – hierarchical selves, horizontal selves, parallel selves – to sustained scrutiny and, as I mentioned briefly in Section 1.1, his well-argued conclusion is that, barring pathological cases, talk of multiple selves is a mere metaphorical device which obscures rather than illuminates. Most apparent cases of split or divided selves turn out to be little more than failures of coordination and integration. A single self can, however, accommodate conflicting conceptions – 'contain multitudes' as in Walt Whitman's poem – that is, for instance, what self-deceptions are all about. Such conceptions may even coexist peacefully for a long time, as long as nothing brings them into conflict (Elster, 1986, pp. 3–4). More significantly perhaps, the very possibility of synergic biculturalism suggests a radical move away from the notion of a merely constructed anti-realist self towards the idea of a stable moral (realist) self that reflects upon the available constructions, reflexively organising and adjudicating between them (see, e.g., Illeris, 2003; Schwartz, Montgomery & Briones, 2006). As Jopling claims, the accessibility of different self-conceptions is possible not because the conceptual schemes underlying self-vocabularies are somehow identical at a deeper level but because the selves forging those identities, endowed with a common biological heritage, have faced the same sorts of problems and affordances in coming to grips with the world (Jopling, 1997, p. 264).

This idea of a person's real self (or character) as a psycho-moral anchor and synthesiser is, of course, agreeably Aristotelian. In the Aristotelian schema, it is the intellectual virtue of *phronesis* that oversees this synthesising (recall Section 1.3). Feeding on emotional dispositions cultivated unreflectively in the young moral agent through habituation, *phronesis* – after it kicks is – re-evaluates those dispositions critically and turns them into a unitary whole. The *phronesis* 'concerned with the individual himself seems most of all to be counted as [*phronesis*]', which indicates that *phronesis* is most of all concerned with critical self-cultivation (Aristotle, 1985, pp. 154, 159, 171 [1140b4–6, 1141b30–31, 1144b30–32]). The Aristotelian *phronesis* is used to dealing with the kinds of intellectual and emotional conflict inherent in the contrasting demands of an interdependent and an independent self-concept located within the same (realist) self. *Phronesis* compares the relative weight of competing values and emotions – values and emotions that are incompatible but not incommensurable – with *eudaimonia*: the ultimate good and unconditional end of human beings. This involves reasoning, based on such first principles, about one's appropriate and rational combinations of desires and beliefs (cf. Chappell,

2006). As explained in Section 3.3, a person who has acquired *phronesis* has the wisdom to adjudicate the relative weight of various virtues in conflict situations and to reach a measured verdict. For *phronesis* to work, the divergence of particular values must be set against the background of substantial convergence about the fundamental virtues that make up *eudaimonia*. Contra Prinz (2007, p. 157), I see no indication in the empirical material supporting the two-cultures view that the existence of independent versus interdependent self-concepts violates that condition – say, with regard to the fundamental emotional virtues such as compassion, righteous indignation or even (as already noted) pride.

When experiences of synergic bicultural integration are described as those of an 'inner voice' or a 'third ear' (Illeris, 2003, p. 358; Foster, 1996, p. 99), guiding the self towards a unified mode of acting and being, the Aristotelian will understand that as the workings of the finely tuned radar of *phronesis*. The Jamesian will understand it as the I-self being at the helm, steering Me-self development (Harter, 1999, p. 332). The Confucian, in turn, will understand it as the working of self-reflection: *zi-xing* (Wang & Chaudhary, 2006, p. 333). In modern parlance, *phronesis* or *zi-xing* involves higher-order reflective self-consciousness: the ability to take a second-order volitional attitude toward oneself, as if from the outside, turning the mind towards its own operations (Dennett, 1976, p. 193; Elster, 1986, p. 20). It should be noted, however, that *phronesis* and *zi-xing* do not only require the epistemological condition of moral objectivism to be met, but also the ontological condition: that there really exist moral properties which are independent of any (non-interhuman) preferences, perspectives or points of view. To satisfy the latter condition as well, more work than simply averting the alleged relativistic implications of the two-cultures view must be done. But it is a good place to start.

In summary, the paradigm of synergic bicultural integration that has been explored in this section allows, whereas the paradigm of hyphenated identity does not, for the epistemological condition of moral objectivism to be met. More specifically, it may even pave the way for an (Aristotle-inspired) explanation of *how* it is met, both at the intellectual and – even more importantly for this study – the emotional level. While satisfying Aristotelians and other moral objectivists, it does not undermine the validity of the interdependent-versus-independent-self-concept dichotomy. Nor should it upset its original formulators who, after all, encouraged readers not to despair over the 'lack of generality' implied by the dichotomy, and warned them against embracing the 'conclusion of some anthropologists that culturally divergent individuals inhabit incomparably different worlds' (Markus & Kitayama, 1991, p. 248).

9. Self-Pathologies

9.1. Pathologies of the Actual Full Self and of Self-Concept

Selves have their pathologies, medical as well as moral. Various classic theories in psychology propose that cognitive self-conflicts and self-inconsistencies *produce* emotional problems (see, e.g., Higgins, 1987). That is obviously the 'dominant' self-paradigm's take on the issue. My 'alternative' self-paradigm's suggestion would be that – because selfhood and affect are inseparable – such conflicts and inconsistencies *are* emotional problems.

It would be difficult to identify serious psychological or moral ailments – or indeed psychiatric diseases – that did not involve the self. One well-known model of *addictions* sees them, for instance, as ways of 'escaping the self'. Alcohol and drug abuse as well as eating disorders are then understood as escapist behaviours to avoid distressing self-examinations and self-resolutions (Leary & Baumeister, 2000, pp. 49–50). Another common human ailment, *depression*, which hits about one in six people, has been shown to be most typically caused by serious life events that undermine self-constituting projects – events such as the loss of loved ones, important relationships or occupations (Oatley, 2007). Given the high frequency and pervasiveness of possible psychopathologies of selves, no single chapter could do justice to all of them – at least not if selves are understood in realist terms as actual full selves. I am therefore limiting my focus to a special category of self-pathologies involving *self-concepts* rather than full selves. Again, however, that category is too wide to be explored comprehensively within the confines of one chapter. All I can do is to focus on a few test cases; and I single out three for consideration. The first involves the emotional conflict of different cultural (Western–Eastern) self-concepts – or, as James would have put it, of different 'Me's' (1890, pp. 169–74) – as exemplified in the case of Western-based suicide terrorists. The second involves the excessive medicalisation of Western self-conceptions, typified by the recent expansion of the so-called Attention Deficit (Hyperactivity) Disorder. The third focuses on the rampant hedonism permeating some current Western self-conceptions, as represented, for example, by the 'Hiltonism' of Paris Hilton and her followers.

9.2. The Self-Conflicts of Suicide Terrorists

For an outsider entering the discursive field of suicide bombers and their motivations, it may seem odd how rarely their actions are analysed as 'traditional' suicides and explained via insights from modern suicidology. The explanation which tends to be given for this omission is that the conceptualisation of suicide bombings as acts of suicide would constitute a biased 'outsider'-framing of the acts because the 'insiders', the perpetrators themselves, understand them as acts of martyrdom (see Maiese, 2005). But this explanation does not bear scrutiny. We need to distinguish carefully between issues of conceptualisation and justification in order to avoid a moralistic fallacy. For comparison, the killing of innocent noncombatants in war is *killing*, whether or not the war is justified. Here, suicide bombers commit *suicide*, whether or not they do so in the interest of a higher cause and whether or not they count as villains or martyrs. Modern suicidology, harking back to Émile Durkheim's groundbreaking treatise (1951, originally published 1897), refrains from smuggling normative considerations into its characterisation of *suicide*: a term which refers to any act by the victim – however the victim conceptualises it – which intentionally produces the victim's own death. The failure to plot its path within the expanding field of suicidology is, in my view, a disabling feature of the current discourse on suicide bombing.

Considerable media attention has been paid recently to the psychological profiling of past and prospective suicide bombers. So far the results are mixed, to put it mildly. What has been achieved is essentially the deconstruction of the rigid stereotyping foisted upon us by popular wisdom rather than the construction of a stable and predictable profile (see, e.g., Pape, 2005; Maiese, 2005; Sharpe, 2006). Thus, we know by now that (a) suicide bombers are not typically, and indeed rarely, psychopathological ('nutcases' being carefully weeded out by the recruiters who value reliability); (b) they are not coerced into their acts, either directly or through brainwashing (if we understand brainwashing to include stringent restriction of alternative sources of information); (c) they are not uneducated and illiterate, nor do they have low IQs (quite the opposite, they tend to be better educated and 'brighter' than the average); and (d) they do not typically come from a poor background.

In spite of the significance of those findings about what suicide bombers *are not*, antiterrorist experts have floundered in trying to acquire a purchase on what those bombers *are*. Can we trace any distinct singularity in the plurality of the psychological motivations that drives this type of what seems to most of us to be barbarous and heinous terror? From a psychological perspective, blowing oneself to smithereens obviously cannot be considered as a bolt from the blue, at least not when people are doing it by the hundreds. Yet one may agree with psychologist John Horgan that pure psychological profiling, which does not account for social and ideological conditions, is probably a waste of time (Reynolds, 2006). We need to proceed on a more extended front, and even engage in that proverbial turn-off for academics, boundary-busting scholarship, which avails itself of insights from disciplines such as sociology, philosophy and the history of ideas, as well as psychology.

To synthesise social, philosophical and psychological insights does not mean to move explanations up to an impersonal macro-level. Robert Pape (2005), for one, has basically taken that step by giving up on all personal, motivational explanations in favour of organisational ones. Suicide bombings are then explained as a cost-effective, highly successful organisational strategy to destabilise the social order. This does explain why insurgent groups favour this strategy, but it fails to explain why individuals, persons like you or me, take it on board and decide to sacrifice their own lives. Rather, I submit, we need to combine societal-level examinations and explanations with psychological ones, in order to understand what drives individual suicide bombers.

I must admit to being more interested in the motivations of home-grown Western-based suicide bombers than those from the Near East or Middle East (hereafter referred to as 'Eastern-based'). Stimulating my quest are questions such as the one posed by Mary Sharpe (2006): 'What drove Mohammed Sidique Khan and his 3 friends who grew up in Britain to one day pack a rucksack full of explosives and destroy the lives of 52 innocent people and their own?' There are two reasons why Western-based suicide bombers intrigue me more than their Eastern-based counterparts. First, I am a Westerner and consider myself better qualified to say something about Western society and the Western mindset than about Eastern society and the Eastern mindset. Second, whatever we think about the intelligibility of the notion of a universal ongoing jihad, Western society is, in comparison to, say, Iraq or Palestine, a relative low-conflict zone. Although it is open to controversy if the conflict situations in Iraq and Palestine are best described as states of war, civil war or insurgency, it is beyond debate that Iraq and Palestine are high-conflict zones. We know from experience that nasty things tend to happen in such zones – and, more generally, that when ordinary people are placed in extraordinary situations, they often make extraordinary decisions (recall Chapter 6). Prima facie at least, explaining a decision as drastic as blowing oneself up in a public place is a taller order, and more of a challenge for the academic, when it is made by what seems to be an 'ordinary' person in an 'ordinary' situation than by an 'ordinary' person in an 'extraordinary' situation.

It may seem odd, after having rejected pure psychological profiling in favour of a more multifaceted approach, to turn to insights from suicidology. After all, most people think of suicidology as a sub-branch of psychology or psychiatry. In point of fact, however, suicidology tends to have an interdisciplinary focus. This is particularly noticeable in the landmark work of the discipline's founding father, Durkheim (1951). Durkheim did not deny the psychological nature of the decision to terminate one's own life, but he clearly considered the psychology of suicide to sit atop more fundamental social causes. Durkheim was, of course, one of the fathers of modern sociology and a firm believer in the existence of collective tendencies, affecting the individual.

Durkheim categorised different types of suicide according to the social factors which allegedly unleashed them. One of the types was what he called 'altruistic suicide', a phenomenon in which individuals sacrifice themselves for the interests of the group. Durkheim viewed this type as emerging from excessive social integration and insufficient individuation, whereby individuals have dissolved their personal identity into a larger whole. When Durkheim's analysis is mentioned in the context of suicide bombings, altruistic suicide is the type that tends to be invoked (see, e.g., Gould, 2003). To be sure, such an analysis resonates well with the 'Eastern' self-concept and its potential pathologies, which I traced in Chapter 8. To revert to my earlier conceptualisation, we could say that Durkheim's 'altruistic suicide' constitutes an extreme *articulation of hyper-identity*. What is more, fieldwork in places such as Palestine and Iraq suggests that this may indeed by a plausible categorisation of much Eastern-based suicide terror (cf. Maiese, 2005; Pedahzur & Perliger, 2006; Brym & Araj, 2006). Consider a place such as Palestine, where constant struggle and the corrosive effects of fear and oppression have helped individuals' already other-entwined and culturally embedded selves to congeal into a single hyper-identity. Suicide then becomes an almost necessary tax paid by the individual to redress the group's grievances, and the prized status symbol is the ensuing martyrdom, not to mention the monetary reimbursements which typically accrue to the family after the attacker's death.

Hany Abu-Assad's feature film, *Paradise now* (2005), nominated for an Academy Award as the best foreign language film in 2006, paints a vivid picture of that scenario. Saïd and Khaled, two disgruntled car mechanics-cum-layabouts, are handpicked by the local community activists to carry out a 'martyr operation'. Toeing the community line originally, they both assume this task as a fact of life: unquestioningly and uncritically. As Saïd sees it, 'the occupation defines the resistance', and Khaled remarks that, in any case, 'under the occupation, we're already dead'. (Psychologists will call this 'dissociation'. A dissociated person may feel that he or she is already dead: 'walking dead'. It is easy to understand how dissociation may, under certain conditions, be a concomitant of hyper-identity.) Khaled eventually backs off. But for Saïd, the suicide operation that he carries out presents an opportunity to atone for the sins of his father, who was a collaborator. Talk in Durheimian terms about an individual's absorption in the whole, and there it is it in the persona of Saïd.

As apt as conceptualisations of (misplaced) altruism and hyper-identity are for an understanding of Eastern-based suicide terror in the context of the 'traditional' conception of the self, they provide scant guidance as to the motivations of Western-based suicide bombers. Why should second-generation immigrants in a country such as the UK, persons who have been educated in British schools and presumably socialised through the media and the social environment into a Western concept of the self, be susceptible to the same considerations that spur Eastern-based suicide bombers? Again, Durkheim's insights may give us some clues. Among the non-'altruistic' types of suicide he analyses are 'egoistic suicide' and suicide based on 'chronic economic anomie'. What these two latter types have in common is the long-term diminution of social integration which has eroded communal regulators without replacing them. Persons committing egoistic suicide are not sufficiently bound to social norms and values and, left with little support or guidance, suffer from a pervasive loss of meaning. I mentioned in Chapter 8 how this sort of vulnerable self in the West may find solace in (and is indeed positively encouraged to find solace in) quick external remedies of self-enhancement.

Consider, more specifically, a character type which seems to correspond to recent rudimentary profiles of Western-based suicide bombers: young Muslim men, aged 15–25, raised in Western society but not feeling totally integrated into that society. Prevailing social forces encourage them to 'leave home' and embark on a mission of self-exploration to discover their own values and to learn to express them freely. They engage in self-exploration to be sure, but whereas their non-Muslim peers start to re-enhance their selves through art, sport, hedonistic quick fixes or, if all else fails, therapy, the young Muslim men come from a family background that considers such solutions alien and unsatisfactory. This scenario chimes in well with Atran's suggestion that 'rising aspirations followed by dwindling expectations' forms a relevant background condition of suicide missions (2003, p. 11). Torn emotionally between the demands of a society that champions self-discovery and self-expression, and the norms of their tradition-based families and religion that are unsympathetic to typical Western forms of self-enhancement, those young men become easy bait for the merchants of terror, the recruiters, who promise them the best of both worlds: Western-style self-expression, glamour and self-esteem combined with a religious framework of self-respect and meaning. What a potentially lethal mixture! The recruiters penetrate to the core of loneliness in the Western self and speak to that; they goad the disenfranchised self to self-destruct and thereby – through the most aesthetically significant act imaginable – achieve lasting glory. This is, in effect, my hypothesis about the social forces breeding Western-based terror: that suicide bombers in the West are typically callow, malleable, frustrated young men targeted and groomed by terror merchants, and that their suicide missions are, first and foremost, acts of deluded, hyperbolic self-enhancement which need to be understood against the backdrops of the Western liberal versus the traditional Eastern conceptions of the self.

The term 'deluded' refers here both to the irrationality of the ultimate ends of suicide missions and the irrationality of the emotional states of the persons carrying out those missions (for an enlightening discussion of the latter point, see Elster, 2005). This is not to deny the possibility that suicide missions can be seen as rational from some other perspective of instrumental rationality (recall, for example, Pape's macro-level considerations, 2005). Nor is this hypothesis tantamount to the one, already rejected, which would consider suicide bombers to be nutcases. The point is, rather, that they are caught between two conceptions of the self, and that their actions can be located at the intersection of the most negative aspects of both. Intellectually, they are in the grip of a disorientating identity crisis. Emotionally, they are at once suspect to grief over loss of meaning as a collective, societal response and trauma or emotional numbing as a personal reaction, corresponding with a breakdown of community, which gives rise to a kind of moral solipsism (cf. Fierke, 2004). The best way to illustrate this emotional self-pathology is probably by thinking of it as diagonally opposed to the ideal of synergic bicultural integration described in Chapter 8.

Two things must be made clear at the end. First, locating psychological or social facts that underlie social trends is not the same as explaining or justifying individual actions. Violence on TV does not by itself explain, let alone excuse, an individual's decision to perform a copycat crime, for instance. That would be a miserable subterfuge. What I have tried to do is to describe the social and emotional background against which the motivations of Western-based suicide bombers become intelligible – but it is a far cry from intelligibility to moral justifiability. Second, although I do think that my hypothesis helps to make sense of available empirical data, it is not primarily the result of an empirical investigation: a detailed case study of the July 7 bombers, for instance. It is more akin to what Nietzsche would have called 'moral genealogy' – speculative moral genealogy in fact – or to Durkheim's hypotheses about the social nature of suicide.

9.3. The Case of ADD/ADHD

Consider next a certain well documented pathology of Western self-conceptions in particular: excessive medicalisation. Recent decades have seen an increasing number of life's problems conceptualised and interpreted through the prism of disease. The process by which painful experiences, aberrant behaviours and other human trials and tribulations, previously described in moral, social or religious terms, become defined as objects of medical knowledge has, since Zola (1972), been referred to as 'medicalisation'. As specified there, 'medicalisation' is a purely descriptive term, denoting a process that has taken place and is taking place, whether we like it or not. Increasingly, however, the term tends to be used in a pejorative sense, and even formally defined normatively as a process whereby non-medical problems are treated *illicitly* as medical problems (Malacrida, 2004, p. 62; Petrina, 2006, p. 504).

Loading the term 'medicalisation' with negativity from the start and thereby contracting its meaning may not be helpful. The entire history of medicine – not least psychiatric medicine – has been one of continuous medicalisation (in the descriptive sense), by which symptoms and syndromes previously poorly understood, or even ascribed to supernatural causes, have been subsumed under a medical rubric. One must be stubbornly wedded to a post-Enlightenment, anti-progressivist stance in order to reject the overall good to patients that has accrued from such medicalisation, even if sometimes achieved at a hefty price. In any case, I refer in this chapter to illicit cases of medicalisation as 'excessive medicalisation' rather than simply as 'medicalisation'.

In school contexts, medicalisation is rife with previously obscure terms from medical dictionaries such as dyslexia, ADD/ADHD, Tourette and Asperger syndromes now being routinely used to describe students. Perhaps even more importantly for present purposes, they are used by students to describe themselves, forming part of their self-concepts. I consider Attention Deficit (Hyperactivity) Disorder (ADD/ADHD) to be a useful point of departure for an exploration of this condition. It is fraught with controversy; diagnoses have proliferated in recent years; and the disorder is of unclear aetiology.

Let us start with the facts: ADD/ADHD is characterised by inattention, hyperactive motor behaviour, impetuosity and distractibility. Teachers complain that students suffering from ADD/ADHD have severe difficulty maintaining focus and staying on task. Some clinicians consider this syndrome to be the most prevalent behavioural problem affecting the school-aged population; and for up to 70% of children diagnosed with ADD/ADHD, these symptoms continue to be manifested later in life (Searight & McLaren, 1998). By the late 1970s, the use of medication to treat ADD/ADHD became standard procedure in the USA, a treatment which has since spread across the Western world. The most common drug – paradoxical as it may seem – is a stimulant: methylphenidate, better known under its trade name, *Ritalin*. The current fourth edition of the American Psychiatric Association's *Diagnostic and Statistical Manual of Mental Disorders* (DSM-IV) indicates that 3–5% of school-aged children exhibit ADD/ADHD. Yet the prevalence of diagnosed cases varies substantially among countries. Children in the UK, for instance, are 1/20 as likely to be diagnosed with this disorder as are children in the USA, where up to 10% of all children are now labelled 'hyperactive' and 10–12% of all boys are on *Ritalin*. In Canada, the rates for diagnosis and medication lie somewhere between those of the UK and USA, and are closer to the DSM-IV estimate of universal frequency (Searight & McLaren, 1998; Malacrida, 2004).

Despite the DSM-IV guidelines and criteria for diagnosis, the nature of ADD/ADHD as a putative mental disorder remains contested. Even among those who accept the existence of medically legitimate cases of ADD/ADHD, opinions about its actual prevalence fall along contentious lines of antipathy toward or enthusiasm for the diagnosis. Diagnostic difficulties are compounded by the fact that a popular conception about *Ritalin* medication – that the stimulant 'calms down' real sufferers but 'gears up' other children – has turned out to be false. In comparative studies, in fact, low doses of the drug decrease motor activity and improve attention in both 'normal' children and diagnosed ADD/ADHD sufferers. An 'appropriate' response to *Ritalin* administration, therefore, is not necessarily indicative of the existence of the disorder (Searight & McLaren, 1998; Lloyd, 2003; Malacrida, 2004).

Teachers' views on the nature and prevalence of ADD/ADHD reflect the divergence of opinion among clinicians and the diagnostic traditions of their respective countries. An additional salient variable seems to be the availability of alternative forms of social control in the classroom apart from medication. In the USA, many teachers take on trust the psy-sector's assumptions of a high prevalence of ADD/ADHD, and even initiate diagnosis themselves. In Canada, a similar story seems to be unfolding, with teachers pressing for medical treatment of unruly students with increasing vigour. In the UK – at least until recently – teachers have been more averse to the label, even to the point of claiming that 'ADHD is just another American fad that has come over here'. It remains moot if this British scepticism of student medicalisation is associated with stricter adherence to the social model of disability and the ideal of the inclusive school, or if it is positively encouraged by educational authorities as an excuse to save money and resources, as some parents suspect. There is yet another possible explanation, however: In the UK, diagnoses of ADD/ADHD are typically made on the basis of World Health Organisation criteria, rather than on DSM-IV, thereby restricting its identification to 'severe, persistent hyperactivity' (Malacrida, 2004; Phillips, 2006).

Most theorists seem to agree that the enormous cross-national differences in the registered prevalence of the syndrome reflect not only varying diagnostic criteria but also varying societal norms for accept-able behaviour and varying school measures for regulating deviant behaviour. In that case, essentially nonmedical considerations enter into the diagnosis of a putative disease. Even if one accepts the DSM-IV estimate of an average worldwide prevalence rate of 3–5% for ADD/ADHD, rather than the more moderate estimates that would follow from the World Health Organisation's criteria, one can safely divine that ADD/ADHD has – in some places at least – been excess-ively medicalised. Much of the recent literature on ADD/ADHD would support the stronger conclusion that overdiagnosis of this disorder is a widespread problem with far-reaching repercussions for health and school issues. To continue my line of argument, a weaker and less controversial conclusion will do: Too much freight has been heaped on this label in some health and school systems, overdiagnosis exists, and it constitutes a prototypical example of excessive medicalisation. The sociomorally and educationally salient questions remain, however: Why does such a tendency exist, and what can be done to stem its tide?

9.4. Medicalised Selves

Medicalisation as a general process or as one specifically germane to the school has never been without its critics (see, e.g., Illich, 1975). There are some signs that a powerful backlash is presently underway. To give a brief sampling of recent criticisms, we are being told by one theorist after another that using a medical rubric to classify socio-moral prob-lems, or even mere painful 'facts of life' (such as birth, aging, dying), (a) is both medically unwarranted and ill at ease with the Enlighten-ment value of individual accountability, (b) improperly decontextual-ises and depoliticises social issues, (c) raises unrealistic expectations of life without pain and suffering, (d) serves the unsavoury agendas of people with axes to grind, (e) contravenes the Salamanca Declaration's ideal of an inclusive school where each child is special, by patholo-gising the individual rather than the school and reproducing the divid-ing practices of old-fashioned special education, and (f) casts teachers, more or less unwillingly, in the role of sickness brokers: disease spotters and drug administrators. These dissenting voices call for a release of society in general and of the school in particular from the thralls of the medical model. How radical and life changing that necessary release is deemed to be, then, depends on the theorist in question (see, e.g., Lloyd, 2003; Malacrida, 2004; Rafalovich, 2005).

Let us leave the more radical of those misgivings aside. As we have established, however, that excessive medicalisation really does exist, in the case of ADD/ADHD for example, the most obvious question must be: Who is responsible? That is the question which crops up in various guises in much of the current 'reactionary' literature on medicalisation – a literature laden with finger-pointing at blameworthy social agents or agencies. I consider such 'blame-gaming' an unrewarding avenue for understanding the phenomenon, and suggest an alternative approach in what follows. But prior to that, I need to explain what is wrong with the blame game. The assumption underlying it is that medicalisation is as ubiquitous as it is *for a reason*. That reason has to do with axe-grinding social agents or agencies which, through medicalisation, seek to gain capital – be it symbolic capital (honour, reputation, discursive power) or hard capital (financial gain) – and which have been noticeably successful at doing so. To pave the ground for my counterargument, it is, I submit, helpful to divide the blame-game explanations into four groups with respect to two dividing variables. The first variable is whether the blameworthy actors are supposed to be the medicalised subjects themselves (explanations via 'internal reasons') or someone else (explanations via 'external reasons'). In the case of children diagnosed with ADD/ADHD, parents will act as proxies for them, so that an internal reason given for the excessive medicalisation of hyperactivity would be a reason that ascribes blame to the parents of hyperactive children. An external reason would be one which does not ascribe blame to the parents (nor obviously to the children themselves). The second variable is whether the reasons are overt or covert. By 'overt reasons' I mean reasons that are relatively uncomplicated and available to the blameworthy actors themselves; if the actors were sincere, they would admit that those actually are their reasons. By 'covert reasons' I mean reasons that are complex and not freely available to the blameworthy actors, either because the actors are self-deceived about those reasons or because the actors are not really distinct persons. This proposed classification of explanations of excessive medicalisation yields the four possibilities outlined in Table 9.1.

The adequacy of the terms I have chosen to describe those four types of explanations – conservative, existentialist, liberalist and poststructualist – will, I hope, manifest itself in the course of my discussion. The upshot of the discussion is that none of those explanations can satisfactorily account for the excessive medicalisation of ADD/ADHD. Furthermore, because they fail as explanations of a prototypical example

Table 9.1. *Explanations of Excessive Medicalisation*

	Internal Reasons	External Reasons
Overt reasons	Conservative explanations	Liberalist explanations
Covert reasons	Existentialist explanations	Poststructuralist explanations

of what they are meant to explain, they also fail as general explicatory strategies.

Let us first examine the *conservative* explanations. Conservatives consider it a major fault in dominant (liberal) political theories of the day that they offer us a reduced conception of individual responsibility. On the Rawlsian liberal account (1973), for instance, we are not really responsible for our positions in life, in respect to either nature (the distribution of natural endowments) or nurture (home environment, socioeconomic class). A number of entrenched reactive attitudes which presuppose personal responsibility, such as those embodied in the self-conscious emotion of guilt, thus lose their moral salience. This reduced conception has percolated through to the public and is, according to conservatives, the reason why so many of life's underdogs favour liberalism. It provides them with a convenient fairytale to weasel themselves out of responsibility for not having 'made it' in life, simultaneously immunising them against their own guilt and against the blame of others.

This general approach holds the key to conservative explanations of excessive medicalisation: Medicalisation is a ploy devised by medicalised or would-be-medicalised subjects to obtain benefits (emotional, social, monetary). This fact is meant to explain why it is typically the subjects themselves who incorporate the relevant diagnosis into their self-concept and are, through individual effort or grassroots campaigns, in the forefront of demands for an accepted medical label to describe their condition. Medicalisation helps them to communicate their predicament to others, gain moral sympathy and claim recognition – even strengthen their own identity (Furedi, 2004, pp. 101 and 173). In the case of ADD/ADHD, conservatives tend to view this 'disorder' with a beady eye and blame it – across the line or at least in the majority of cases – on lack of discipline and parental attention. Instead of forthrightly shouldering blame for bad parenting, as they should do, parents arguably seek solace and affirmation through the forgiving label of a medical diagnosis, thereby pinning the blame on a nonhuman agency.

Their wish to evade responsibility is father to the thought that medicalisation exonerates them from responsibility. In the good old days, people were expected to be resilient in the face of life's vicissitudes, to assume responsibility for their own mistakes and to roll up their sleeves; nowadays they cowardly pass the buck (Summerfield, 2001). Deep down, however, most parents know that they have only themselves to blame.

Conservatives may put the finger correctly on a debilitating tendency to buck-passing in modern society. Nevertheless, their pinning of blame on the medicalised subjects seems inadequate in the case of parents of hyperactive children. It is true that those parents will go to any length to clutch at a straw – but not so much the straw of guilt-evasion as the straw of finding a solution to their children's problems. The literature on ADD/ADHD is rife with vivid descriptions of parents desperately seeking any means, medical or non-medical, that offer hope of help. My own informal interviews with such parents indicate that they would be more than willing to assume full responsibility as 'bad parents' if such a self-flagellating attitude offered more hope of help than current medical labelling offers. Pressing for a medical diagnosis does tend to be the first option sought in Western societies, but this reaction may say less about parents' failure to assume responsibility than it does about their response to the reality that formal diagnosis increases the likelihood of receiving treatment.

Existentialist explanations also place the blame on medicalised subjects, but they do not suggest that the subjects themselves are aware of their evasive strategies; rather, they propose, these strategies come about through self-deceptions or 'bad faith'. As human beings we are essentially free to make choices; and even when we are coerced into doing something (such as handing our wallets to muggers who threaten our lives), we are, in principle, free to decline. However, this freedom does not constitute a pure blessing. In many cases, it bears the signs of condemnation and is a major cause of anxiety, especially for people who are contemplating doing, or have already done, something morally demeaning (such as neglecting their child's upbringing by putting work before home). A common subconscious mental strategy, then, is that of self-deception or 'bad faith' (*mauvaise foi*), a strategy by which we essentially appropriate a false notion of an unfree self – a medicalised self, for instance – which justifies our wrongdoing by making it external to the purview of personal responsibility. This surrender of self quickly becomes a self-perpetuating strategy; in order to deceive ourselves into thinking *p*, we need to avoid truth *t*, which would imply not-*p*, and by avoiding *t*, we need to avoid other truths which would unravel other painful facts about ourselves (Cumming, 1965).

As noted, existentialist explanations pin the responsibility of ADD/ADHD overmedicalisation on blame-evading parents, just as the conservative explanations did. The difference is that existentialist explanations consider the blame evasion to be a self-deceptive subconscious strategy; the putative reasons for medicalisation are covert rather than overt. Is that a defensible approach with respect to ADD/ADHD? Normally, self-deceived persons avoid potentially painful sources of truth in a systematic way. Recent literature on this disorder, however, paints a picture of parents eagerly seeking information on the Web and elsewhere, preparing information packages, bringing in specialists with varying orientations, and carefully introducing teachers to educational treatment strategies (see, e.g., Malacrida, 2004, p. 74). Such descriptions do not appear to fit parents living in a self-imposed la-la land, impervious to contravening evidence. From my own experience, affected parents generally know much more about the disorder and its connected controversies than educators do – even those who have completed university courses on special needs – and they tend to be open and hospitable to any new research findings. In so far as the existential explanations violate this fact, I consider them to hold little prospect of making sense of excessive medicalisation in general or ADD/ADHD overdiagnosis in particular.

Some (although not all) *liberals* do consider excessive medicalisation to be a problem and have their own explanations for it. Such explanations suggest that medicalisation has been openly plugged by identifiable social agents in order to obtain financial gain or power. Excessive medicalisation, by liberalist lights, is an unfortunate permutation of free-market liberalism. The chief culprits tend to be identified as medical practitioners, drug companies and politicians. Doctors and therapists – we are told – welcome a boost to their income, status and influence which comes with the conquest of any new territory of human affairs as 'medical'. They have a vested interest, therefore, in marketing medical strategies and technologies to the public and nourishing the cult of the therapeutic (Furedi, 2004, pp. 9–10). Pharmaceutical companies have a similarly clear interest in making us believe that there is a pill for every ill. Indeed, they have now embarked on a mission of organised penetration into the educational domain, unscrupulously marketing schools and students (Phillips, 2006). Last but not least, politicians have much to gain by being able to treat people as clients rather than citizens: because they are guaranteed a response whenever they say something health related, and because it helps them to wield power over wider areas of public life. Politicians are suspicious of any area of private feelings or attitudes that remains outside their gaze – outside the realm of possible political inspection, intervention and manipulation. The therapeutic ethos suits them well (Furedi, 2004). According to liberalist critics, then, these three pressure groups have been particularly clever in enlisting parents and teachers as accomplices. There is no disputing the fact that ADD/ADHD has become a 'popular' disorder through a groundswell of public support and the development of grassroots advocacy groups, for instance (Searight & McLaren, 1998). 'But', sceptical liberals will ask, 'who stands behind those groups and leads them on?' There are signs in some countries that the teaching profession has started to play a hybridised, semi-official role in the medicalisation process, acting as an extension of the medical establishment and driven by its dictates (Rafalovich, 2005).

Can the thrust of those liberalist explanations be sustained? Perhaps to some extent. I believe, however, that the stereotypes of crooked medical practitioners, drug manufactures and politicians – and of gullible parents and teachers swamped by those domineering voices – are, to a large extent, misdirected. Take doctors: As aptly noted in an editorial in the *British Medical Journal*, far from revelling in medicalisation, doctors tend to feel aggrieved by patients' constant demands for medical labels. When doctors are forced to go beyond the boundaries of the medicine they have learnt and know, 'they do not gain power or control: they suffer' (Leibovici, 2002, p. 866). Recent medical history is not one of doctors running after patients and thrusting medical labels upon them; it is story of patients in a desperate search for such labels, or for anything which gives them hope of a cure. Take drug companies: Although their influence in the public sphere should not be underestimated, research has shown that lay attitudes can be highly resistant to the authoritative tone of health-promotion materials. Drug companies do not create diseases if there is no 'demand' for them from the public. Take politicians: There seem to be equally good, if not better, reasons for politicians to resist rather than embrace the politicisation of private domains. Politicians have limited resources, and those they have will be put to better use the narrower their domain. Moreover, to depict politicians as a uniform group of sly manipulators smacks of bogus conspiracy theories. In general, as Petrina correctly observes, the history of the medicalisation process in schools has not been one of a medical or pharmaceutical (let alone a political) authority openly securing its hegemony over the jurisdiction of education. This process has occurred in much more complex and subtle ways (2006, pp. 503–505).

'Complex and subtle ways' is a neat phrase to introduce the fourth type of explanations of excessive medicalisation: the *poststructuralist* ones. Poststructuralists accuse liberals of an impoverished power discourse: of concentrating on intentional, active and overt exercises of power. Such understanding constitutes a mere one-dimensional view of power relations as observable conflict relationships between identifiable agents. Instead, we need to accommodate the insights of two- and three-dimensional views which posit that power can also be enacted by preventing certain issues to appear on the discursive agenda, and that neither the power holder nor the victim may be aware of the power relation (Lukes, 1974). In other words, power can be non-intentional, passive and covert. These general insights are then typically sharpened by poststructuralists through a Foucauldian lens. Foucault's prime example of three-dimensional power relates directly to the topic of this section: the power exerted by the 'clinical gaze' of the medical profession after the Enlightenment vis-à-vis everyone not considered normal according to bourgeois standards of reason. Hence, the massive incarcerations of the mentally ill in the eighteenth century. This 'excluding gaze', which continues to fix people in pre-regulated 'patterns of difference', serves both the need of a particular profession claiming truth authority (read: the medical profession wielding symbolic power) and the upholding of dominant capitalist power structures (Foucault, 2006). The medicalisation of a condition such as hyperactivity is, then, nothing but the extension of the general social gaze of disapproval to a particular minority group of recalcitrant outsiders who fail to conform to the behavioural values of modern society: the psychiatrisation of otherness. Nevertheless – and here lies the difference with respect to liberalist explanations of medicalisation – the medico-therapeutic ways of construing reality assume moral neutrality, and most of its practitioners are not immediately aware of their own domineering status. The culprits – if we can continue to call them that – are still basically the same as they were in the liberalist model: clinicians, drug companies, politicians. But there is no conscious conspiracy at work, no overt agendas; simply the mechanical workings of an oppressive system of social control with a monopoly on truth.

For a doctrine as chillingly grand as this one, it is based on disturbingly little empirical evidence. The 'gigantic moral imprisonment' of the eighteenth century thus never took place except in Foucault's mind (Scull, 2007). Such shortcomings notwithstanding, the more general insights of the poststructuralist explanations may still be correct. But are they? The poststructuralist project is fuelled by a sort of power fetishism. Social agencies and social actors (although the latter may not be immediately aware of it) are all driven by an urge for increased power over others, and for symbolic self-aggrandisement. The problem with that explanation is a simple one: If we revert to the particularities of the ADD/ADHD issue, what we see, more typically, are attempts at the abnegation of power rather than a quest for power. Doctors feel miserable about patients' relentless demands for the medicalisation of their sufferings; teachers (at least in the UK, see earlier) feel miserable about being cast in the role of disease brokers; parents feel miserable about the possibility that they are partly responsible for the children's predicament; politicians feel miserable over the expectation that they should come up with solutions to all human problems. One must have developed more than a modicum of insensitivity to situational particularities to see through all this the sinister workings of disciplinary power and the struggle for cultural hegemony. A dull thing to say, but probably close to the mark is that if there is any intense struggle at work in the discursive field on ADD/ADHD, it is a struggle for objective truth in the old-fashioned Enlightenment sense – the truth about what this disorder really is and what we can do about it.

The divergence of explanations for excessive medicalisation is set against a background of considerable convergence. All the explanations hold certain persons or social agencies individually or collectively blameable for the causes of such medicalisation. As noted, none of those explanations seems to bear scrutiny – when applied to the case of ADD/ADHD overdiagnosis, for instance. Let me now suggest an alternative way of understanding the phenomenon. On this proposed understanding, excessive medicalisation constitutes an historically conditioned construal – mode of thought or mindset – which rests on the Western liberal self-concept.

Recall the potential pathologies of the Western self-concept as described in Chapter 8: After 'leaving home', the self will be plagued, at least temporarily, by a sense of emotional vulnerability, disesteem, powerlessness and helplessness. Being frail, brittle and fragmented, it is potentially a self at risk (Giddens, 1991; Beck, 1992). The self is supposed to take charge of its own life; if it fails to succeed in that task, it has basically failed its life project and will be overcome by a pervasive sense of a painful emotion, shame, signalling low self-esteem.

Self-pathologies thus no longer derive from social barriers inhibiting self-realisation – as they did for the traditional self-concept – but from the demand for self-realisation itself (cf. Hammershøj, 2009). To avoid shame, we start looking high and low within ourselves for explanations of our failed self-realisation projects; and one of the avenues of our emotional despair is to medicalise our own selves – but also to offer us the hope of eventual demedicalisation through therapeutic intervention. I suggest therefore that excessive medicalisation is emblematic of a whole ideological current in contemporary Western thought: a current which considers people's selves to be essentially weak, disembedded and in need of reflexive discovery/retrieval – a current which has replaced a progressive view of human beings as active social agents with a regressive inward gaze and which has psychologised the bulk of modern life.

If we understand medicalisation in general to imply the normalisation of illness (even to the point where it becomes hip), this understanding fits well the 'objectification of human experience into the grammar of risks' and the idea of 'self-fulfilment as the promotion of self-limitation' (Furedi, 2004, pp. 7 and 21) that characterise the Western self-concept. The self needs to suffer before it can redeem itself. This suffering, if prolonged and painful enough, is characterised as a disease – either in a literal or metaphorical sense with unclear boundaries between the two – from which the self can 'learn'. Fortunately, most selves achieve 'healing and closure' in the end, either through their own efforts or through their reliance on external therapeutics. Of course, the therapy industry accentuates the emotional feebleness and fragility of the self in order to sell its remedies of continuous therapeutic interventions: 'You cannot overcome your estrangement from yourself by strengthening your ties with others – only by becoming your own best friend'. And the therapist obligingly helps the estranged self attune itself to the friend inside. Thus, modern Western culture is now correctly described as a therapy culture (cf. Furedi, 2004). Notice, however, that the industry does not *create* medicalisation; its seeds already exist, deeply embedded in the Western self-concept, waiting to be picked up in order to be used.

This conjecture of medicalisation as a *stabilising emotion-driven conduit for culturally entrenched self-beliefs* provides us, like poststructuralism, with 'covert' and 'external' reasons for excessive medicalisation. Excessive forms of medicalisation occur when the self-stabilising tendency gets the better of us: starts to misconstrue reality, dodge facts and do disservice to those involved. For instance, the excessive medicalisation of ADD/ADHD may reflect exaggerated anxieties about the impact of rapid social and technological change on children (see Searight & McLaren, 1998, p. 487). Yet, unlike poststructuralism, there is no assumption here of a power struggle at work between social structures or social agencies. To be sure, some groups benefit from medicalisation more than others do. But they are not the instigators of medicalisation.

The conjecture proposed in this section relies – just as the earlier one about suicide bombers – more on what Nietzsche would have called moral genealogy than on direct empirical evidence. Yet, such evidence may also be forthcoming. Take Furr's enlightening research on the opinions of Nepali teachers on students' misbehaviour (2004). Furr presented 276 Nepali teachers with the scenario of a troubled 12-year old girl engaging in deviant behaviour and asked them to explain the likely causes of her behaviour. The teachers' acceptance of Western and non-Western conceptions and values was also gauged. Furr's results indicated a positive correlation between Westernised attitudes entertained by teachers and the extent to which they were likely to couch explanations of misbehaviour in medical terms. Those with non-Western attitudes tended, on the other hand, to give explanations that referred to contextual factors. The ideas underlying medicalisation are, as I have suggested, shackled together with the heavy chains of cultural conditioning.

In summary, I have argued for an explanation of excessive medicalisation that locates it in certain self-stabilising tendencies of the Western liberal self-concept: tendencies that are at best self-charts, at worst self-traps. This explanation ameliorates difficulties inherent in the four types of explanations in the current literature that I have identified and criticised: conservative, existentialist, liberalist and poststructuralist. The proposed explanation makes sense, inter alia, of the eagerness of many parents and professionals to embrace the medicalisation of hyperactive behaviour as a specified disease – ADD/ADHD – an eagerness that, in some cases at least, has fuelled overdiagnosis.

9.5. The Hedonistic Self-Concept

'Only thirty years ago', Ariel Levy writes in her bestseller, *Female chauvinist pigs: Women and the rise of raunch culture* (2006), 'our mothers were "burning their bras" and picketing Playboy, and suddenly we were getting implants and wearing the bunny logo as supposed symbols of our liberation. How had the culture shifted so drastically in such a short period of time?' Levy refers to this drastic 'cultural shift' as the rise of 'raunch culture' and of such 'female chauvinist pigs' as the socialite Paris Hilton, who make sex objects of themselves in an attempt to outdo 'male chauvinist pigs' and join their frat party of pop culture (2006, pp. 3–5). A new phrase – 'Hiltonism' – has been coined in various recent Weblogs, which have begun to constitute a state-of-the-art information source on contemporary culture. This expression serves to conceptualise the popular cult surrounding the 'female chauvinist pigs' in general and the media frenzy greeting Paris Hilton's antics and imbroglios in particular. Throughout this section I avail myself of this conceptualisation to denote the social phenomenon in question.

'Raunch' is, in Levy's vocabulary at least, a term that describes the increasingly explicit and vociferous presence of sex and sexiness in today's society. With it, a tarty, rumbustious and cartoonlike version of female sexuality has become so ubiquitous that it no longer seems surprising. Levy mentions, as revealing and symptomatic of the current normalisation of raunchy concupiscence, the popular *Girls Gone Wild* series that generates an estimated $40 million a year. Some version of the sexy, scantily clad temptress has been around for ages, and there has always been a demand for smut. But smut has gradually developed from being a guilty pleasure on the margins to a mainstream phenomenon, accepted and engaged in by members of both sexes. Even avowed feminists now pride themselves in being 'sex positive' and revelling in the fun. Being objectified as a sex toy and commodified does not seem to be so bad any more, if done of one's own accord. At least it is better than seeming hopelessly 'out of touch'. Why can women not be as 'frisky' and loud as men? Why can they not also embrace the cheesy and the tacky if they want to? Is that not merely one part of the evolving story of women providing themselves with the best and the most? (Levy, 2006, pp. 5, 12, 34, 43, 63, 92, 115, 146, 173).

Levy herself does not jump on this bandwagon, however. Although there are those – academics no less than laypeople – who applaud Hiltonism as an instantiation of a groundbreaking post-feminist stance, we are told in no uncertain terms in Levy's book that the cult of the 'female chauvinist pigs' (a) contributes to an insidious pornification of mainstream culture that in the end serves only the interests of 'male chauvinist pigs'; (b) confuses sexual power with political power and self-commodification of bodies with anti-commodification; and (c) has a devastating effect on young girls who, from prepubescence, emulate the 'female chauvinist pigs' as their role models. In general, the attraction of Hiltonism – the allure of the sound of empty vessels that has become the siren song of our times – indicates for Levy the depths to which contemporary feminist culture has sunk (Levy, 2006; cf. Paul, 2005).

Levy considers raunch culture to be at best infantilising, at worst seriously damaging to women's interests. She believes that it forms part of the male-inspired 'pornification' or 'porno-isation' of contemporary society. She is not the first to make this claim: Brian McNair wrote more than a decade ago (1996) about the process of 'pornographication' evident in both art and popular culture with the proliferation of sexual texts and images – and with the iconography of pornography turning mainstream. A recent APA Task Force on the sexualisation of young girls defines 'sexualisation' in a similar vein as a process by which one's value is seen to come solely from sexual appeal: People are held to a standard that equates physical attractiveness with sexiness; they become sexually objectified and inappropriately shaped into sexual symbols. The most insidious form of contemporary sexualisation is, according to this Task Force, the self-sexualisation of girls, by which they are induced to internalise those very standards – incorporate them into their self-concepts – instead of having them imposed upon them against their overt will (APA, 2007, pp. 2–3).

The APA Task Force is specifically concerned about precocious sexualisation – the imbuing of adult sexuality upon children – and the resultant blurring of the distinction between women and girls. The recent production of 'sexy' clothing (such as thongs) in child and young teen sizes is a case in point. A recent *Newsweek* article asks if we in the West are raising a generation of 'prosti-tots' who dress and act like tarts, and makes heavy weather of children's current exposure to 'oversexed, underdressed celebrities'. *Newsweek* reporters ponder over a contemporary question: Is the new generation of 'female chauvinist pigs' making lasting mischief in the lives of the young (Deveny & Kelley, 2007)? At any rate, young girls' conceptions of self-improvement seem to have changed dramatically in the USA in the past 100 years, from being 'better mannered' to being 'more physically attractive' (APA, 2007, p. 18).

Personifying raunch culture and providing its self-concept with the designation of 'Hiltonism' is the divisive persona of the socialite and the 'it girl', Paris Hilton. Born in 1981, she is heiress to a share of the Hilton Hotel fortune. Hilton has turned up in minor roles in minor movies, has done some modelling and appeared in ad campaigns and a reality series. Apart from two video tapes of her having sex with her boyfriends, which were both conveniently leaked to the Web prior to decisive events in her 'career', Hilton is mostly 'famous for being famous': a label attached to a number of people in modernity. Hilton is constantly in the media spotlight, always doing something, being somewhere. She is not noted for what she has said but for what she has done: in particular her swashbuckling, gaudy antics. She has, in the view of many people, become a synonym for inarticulateness, parochialism, arrogance, promiscuity, exhibitionism, narcissism and pornified womanhood (Hynowitz, 2006). Contrast this character description with that of someone like Socrates (recall Section 1.1; I turn to his nemesis Callicles shortly) – his articulateness, universalism, proper pride, temperance, intellectual modesty, fortitude and unified selfhood – and the difference is striking.

As noted, Web sources have coined a term for the self-concept adopted by Paris Hilton and her admirers: 'Hiltonism'. After browsing through more than 50 Web pages found by dint of the Google search terms 'Paris Hilton' and 'Hiltonism', I have extracted from them an account of Hiltonism that can be unpacked into the three following principles: (a) There is Heaven and there is Hell on earth. Heaven is the natural beatific habitat of the rich, beautiful and famous, who know how to live their lives to the fullest. Hell is the artificially created habitat of spoilsports who do not understand what life is all about and miss out on the best that life has to offer. Somewhere between Heaven and Hell is the habitat of Heaven wannabes: Those who want to be famous rich celebs, but who lack the necessary wherewithal to achieve their aim (because they are too ugly, too fat or too poor, for instance). The middle group of 'DUFFS' (Designated Ugly Fat Friends) is, however, partly condoned by hanging out or wanting to hang out with the inhabitants of Hiltonistic Heaven. (b) The spoilsports in Hell suffer from jealousy or self-deception. Deep down, they also crave the natural and uninhibited, but they are prevented from achieving it by a misguided sense of prudishness and close-mindedness that they call 'self-respect'. They therefore miss the boat of true living. Hiltonists expend considerable energy ridiculing the self-deceivers: those uncool and uptight enough to refuse to participate in the *Girls Gone Wild* series, for example. (c) The fundamental aim in life is pleasure: having fun. The more money, the more drink, the more sex, the better, because they can be accumulated and flaunted in order to increase pleasure-inducing experiences.

Couched in alleged post-feminist terms, the unencumbered pleasure-seeking self is at once sexually liberated and personally empowered.

There seems to be a strong tendency in academic circles to link the 'female chauvinist pigs'' lusty, busty exhibitionism – as well as their alleged nouvelle raunchy post-feminism – to a playful early-postmodern self-concept. Kay Hymowitz captures this sentiment perfectly when she claims that in having programmatically offered herself to us as an 'it', a being without an inner life, a self whose only value is to be seen and known by all, Paris Hilton has become the 'total incarnation of postmodern identity', the individual who has disappeared completely and happily into her symbolic image (Hymowitz, 2006). Hymowitz's description resonates well with that of Feona Attwood's (2006) characterisation of (uncritical) postmodern sexual discourse, where irony, pastiche, excess and camp articulate our knowing relationship with sexuality, and where sexuality itself is decentred and dislocated, becoming an unstable chemistry of personal meanings.

We are also reminded here of Zygmunt Bauman's analysis of contemporary sexuality as a free-floating sensation and of the demise of the romantic 'grand passion', which has been replaced by postmodern relationships of 'liquid love' that are easy to enter and exit (2003, pp. xi–xii). Furthermore, at a more general and societal level, the characteristics of Hiltonism may seem to fit well with Lauren Langman's (2002) account of the carnivalisation and vulgarisation of postmodern society, in which entertainment values have displaced all others. Langman forges a link between 'carnivalisation' and the rise of the celebrity. The former phenomenon is, in Langman's view, not so much new and original – after all, postmodernism rejects the very notion of originality – as the resurgence of mediaeval peasant folk culture that valorised the profane, vulgar, lewd and grotesque. A natural concomitant of re-carnivalised society is the cult of the celeb – such as Paris Hilton. The emptiness of the content of fame exemplifies postmodern free-floating signification, characteristic of a Baudrillardian world where we longer assume that there is a 'reality' behind or beneath the appearance.

Apt as all those characterisations may be of what has come to be known as 'the postmodern condition', they are, in my view, essentially ill-suited to account for the principles of Hiltonism as delineated here. Recall here the self-concept of uncritical postmodernism, analysed in Section 2.2; and consider first (a) Hiltonism's distinction between the metaphorical Heaven of the liberated and the Hell of the repressed. Postmodernists are adamant in their antipathy to dualisms of this type, not least dualisms that draw a line between the natural and authentic on the one hand, and the artificial and inauthentic on the other. Moreover, they resent the term 'liberation' because it assumes the existence of a true self underneath appearances. The appeal to 'self-deceived' spoilsports in principle (b) will also ring hollow from a post-modern perspective. On the postmodern account of the self, there is, let us recall, no self-deception, for the same reason that there is no liberation. Paris Hilton's much-publicised refusal to use the toilet during her prison stay in 2007, for fear that guards would photograph her, demonstrates a spectacularly un-postmodern self-concept. One of the presumed personal consequences of postmodern carnivalisation is, after all, the demise of shame (Langman, 2002, p. 522) – for shame presupposes discrepancy between an actual self and an ideal possible self (for postmodernists, an outdated conceptualisation). Consider, finally, Hiltonism's valorisation of pleasure as the ultimate goal in life (c). To be sure, following Barthes, postmodernists also place considerable stock in pleasure *qua* bliss or *jouissance* (see, e.g., Gallop, 1984). They carefully distinguish it, however, from ordinary pleasure (*plaisir*). Whereas the latter is comfortable, ego-assuring, recognised and legitimated by mainstream culture, *jouissance* is shocking, ego-disruptive and in conflict with the canons of culture. Specifically, this embellished postmodern sense of fun is an unsettling reaction, typically felt in response to provocative texts. It signifies the breakdown of self rather than its idyllic maintenance. It does not require an extended study of the Hiltonists' descriptions of the fun they allegedly enjoy in life to realise that their idea of pleasure is much closer to the mundane, ego-assuring and authenticity-preserving one of *plaisir* than to that of *jouissance*.

Levy does not directly discuss or adjudicate on the postmodern hypothesis in her book. However, the tenor of her criticism indicates that she views Hiltonistic 'post-feminism' as a late-modernist aberration of real feminism rather than the manifestation of a radically new, postmodern self-concept. 'Raunch culture' is, for her, essentially conservative and commercial rather than progressive: a backlash and rebellion against the values of feminism proper. She even likens the 'female chauvinist pigs' to the protagonist in *Uncle Tom's Cabin*: Uncle Tom, who upholds the stereotypes assigned to his marginalised group in the interest of getting on with the dominant group (Levy, 2006, pp. 29, 44, 105). In her view, Hiltonists and their supporters simply try to disguise folly by giving it a fine name: post-feminism. Although I agree with Levy that there is little that is post-this or post-that in the principles of

Hiltonism, there is no denying the fact that its advent must be understood against the backdrop of a modern pluralistic society in a state of flux. If Levy had given more attention to that fact, she might have been more adept at diagnosing the appeal of raunch culture, rather than merely dismissing it.

If the self-concept of Hiltonists is not a postmodern one, is it simply that of old-fashioned hedonists, as thousands of Web pages suggest? The word 'hedonism' is derived from the Greek *hēdonē*, which means pleasure, enjoyment or delight. Hedonism is the doctrine that pleasure is the highest good. The point of living is to enjoy life, and the best life is the most pleasurable one. Hedonism can assume the form of a psychological doctrine (what really motivates us is pleasure), a normative doctrine (what really *should* motivate us is pleasure) or both. The normative doctrine catches within its net distinct theses, varying as to what we believe involves true pleasure and whether we understand hedonism egoistically (such that only our own pleasure has value for ourselves) or non-egoistically. Furthermore, there are prudential hedonists who seek to maximise pleasure in the general course of their lives, as well as indiscriminate hedonists who follow a policy of satisfying all their occurrent desires. Different schools of hedonism had already evolved in antiquity, with the Cyrenaics, for instance, holding that only the gratification of our sensual desires for food, drink, sex and the like constituted true pleasure, whereas Epicureans equated pleasure with the absence of pain and focused on life's quieter enjoyments. A widely discussed form of hedonism in modernity is classical (Millian) utilitarianism, which distinguishes higher from lower pleasures (as qualitatively superior, irrespective of quantity) and encourages the maximisation of the pleasure of the greatest number of sentient beings.

All these subtle philosophical distinctions notwithstanding, what the general public – including most of the authors of the thousands of Web pages linking Hiltonism with hedonism – understand by 'hedonism' is probably closest to the Cyrenaic type: egoistically driven satisfaction of felt sensual desires. A prototype of the hedonist on this understanding is Callicles, Socrates' unforgettable interlocutor in the dialogue *Gorgias*. Callicles – not a relativist sophist like most of Socrates' other opponents – appears to be a self-made businessman who is concerned exclusively with the satisfaction of his own sensual pleasures, constantly pouring scorn on Socrates' moralism. Callicles holds that any action or object, in so far as he *feels* an appetite for it, is intrinsically desirable for him. The pleasant is nothing but the satisfying of such felt appetites (see Rudebusch, 1999, chap. 4). It is salutary for our present concerns to analyse Callicles's doctrine in greater detail.

First, Callicles draws a sharp distinction between nature and convention, which he claims are 'antagonistic to each other'. Socrates' fault is to espouse 'the general conventional view' of morality. According to Callicles, Socrates' moralism embraces only 'what is fine and noble, not by nature, but by convention'. But, in Callicles's view, conventional morality is, in fact, created by 'the weaker folk, the majority' controlling the naturally strong, the minority. Nature, especially the animal kingdom, makes it plain 'that it is right for the better to have advantage over the worse, the more able over the less'. The 'better' on this understanding comprise those more daring and 'competent to accomplish their intentions', whatever those intentions may be: those ready to shake off all artificial legal and moral controls and 'break loose'. Second, the majority of people are a 'rabble of slaves', 'nondescripts' and 'simpletons'. Not all of them are naturally weak, however; some are 'exceptionally gifted' but are unfortunately misguided and self-deceived about their real interests and 'deserve a whipping'. They have been persuaded to or socialised into 'living the life of a stone' and acting like miserable toothless lions, although deep down they have the capacity to become high achievers. Third, 'luxury and intemperance and license, when they have sufficient backing, are virtue and happiness, and all the rest is tinsel, the unnatural catchword of mankind'. More specifically, true pleasure consists of allowing one's appetites 'the fullest possible growth' without curbing them, and in procuring 'satisfaction for them from whatever source' through courage and cleverness (Plato, 1973, pp. 264–76 [481b–494b]).

It will not have escaped readers' attention how similar Callicles's doctrine is to that of the Hiltonists. Indeed, the three aspects of his hedonism – the nature-convention distinction, the self-deception thesis and the characterisation of uninhibited sensual pleasure as the true human good – correspond fully to the 'three principles' of Hiltonism delineated previously (and obviously clash not only with Socrates' doctrines but also blatantly with the brief character description of the historic Socrates that I presented in Section 1.1). Those writers who link Hiltonism with late-modernist hedonism rather than early-postmodern carnivalisation, let alone late-postmodern regionalism, seem to be on the right track. Consider, for instance, John O'Shaughnessy and Nicholas J. O'Shaughnessy's lucid analysis of the hedonism inherent in modern consumer society (2002). They see nothing radically new in consumerism, except that more people than ever before are able to indulge. Being a famous celebrity is a scarce and exclusive product, hence highly valued. The hedonistic pleasure satisfied through belonging to the Hiltonistic Heaven is the satisfaction of the need to be socially admired and envied, and to maintain a sense of connection with others of the same ilk. Furthermore, the understanding of sex as fun is linked to a broader ideological condition of modernism: the injunction to be authentic, spontaneous and involved – a sensation-seeker who leaves behind the security of 'home' and creates his or her own values. This modernist framework explains why the sexual antics of the Hiltonists seem distinctly more Marie Antoinettish than Andy Warholish. At the same time, they are inspired by the modernist call for the re-enhancement and redemption of a vulnerable self, freed from deception, rather than the postmodern one for the continuing splitting of the individual into ever more fragmented self-investments.

Why does the kind of hedonism identified in the Hiltonists count as a self-pathology? To explain that, I can do no better than to quote Charles Taylor who notes that 'our normal understanding of self-realization presupposes that some things are important beyond the self, that there are some goods or purposes the furthering of which has significance for us and which hence can provide the significance a fulfilling life needs'. A 'total and fully consistent subjectivism' – as embodied, for instance, in Hiltonistic hedonism – tends, however, 'towards emptiness: nothing would count as fulfilment in a world in which literally nothing was important but self-fulfilment' (Taylor, 1989, p. 507). Such hedonism threatens to undermine the kind of *emotional depth and complexity* that gives human being their unique moral and emotional standing. Although the present study is not a self-help manual, I return to this particular self-pathology as well as the other two test cases that I have dissected in this chapter in Section 10.5, in order to offer some remedial suggestions.

10. Self-Change and Self-Education

10.1. Conceptual Preliminaries

It is almost a truism that all education is about change: changed patterns of knowing, feeling, conceptualising and perceiving. Someone may want to say that all education is consequently self-changing: If you teach a group of students the names of the capitals in Africa, then one aspect of their selves has changed when they leave the classroom. This use of the term 'self', however, would be considerably broader than allowed by the commonsense view of the self on which I rely in this study. Although the commonsense view acknowledges that selves gradually develop and change over time, the notion of a sudden self-change or self-transformation cannot – given the restrictive sense of selfhood embodied in this view – be taken that lightly.

Yet there is, on the commonsense view, a profound sense in which some education can be considered self-changing. 'That course in philosophy I took really changed my life', someone might say, or 'I came back from the field trip to Africa a completely changed person'. A woman described how joining the feminist movement changed her: 'I feel as if I woke up one morning to find myself completely different [...] I am just not the same person I was three months ago. I look back and cannot believe that I was her' (Goodman, 1979, p. 69). We know what such utterances mean; reports of life-changing experiences are well documented in biographies, films and novels. Some of us have undergone such experiences ourselves. Few theorists would go as far as to claim that what is at issue in those experiences is our selfhood as a fundamental metaphysical entity; indeed, there is every reason to believe that transformations of our commonsense moral self can be understood only against the backdrop of the basic stability of

218

our metaphysical self – although I have, for reasons of methodological parsimony, decided to remain agnostic on the exact nature of the latter in this book. In other words, despite the change of the everyday self in such transformations, there will still be enough similarity between the pre-transformation self and the transformed one to say that they are numerically identical (see Gunnarsson, 2002). James (1890) would probably want to go further and claim that even behind changes in the 'barometric' part of the everyday self – say when an anti-feminist turns into a feminist – there will still remain a 'baseline' everyday self that has not changed (cf. Harter, 1999, p. 327; Elster, 1986, p. 14). Be that as it may, there is no denying the radicality of some self-transformations – and it is on the nature of those that I focus in what follows.

A popular, if a tad hackneyed, literary theme is that of the engaged, charismatic teacher who successfully challenges students to leave behind their hidebound, ossified selves and 'suck the marrow out of life'. Take Jaime Escalante in the film *Stand and Deliver*, John Keating in *Dead Poets Society* or Jean Brodie in *The Prime of Miss Jean Brodie*. Escalante builds from scratch a calculus programme, rivalled only by a handful of exclusive academies, in a poor, under-achieving US public high school. Keating inspires boys at a conservative and autocratic prep school to reinvigorate their lives of conformity through the passionate reading of poetry and literature. Brodie imbues her students in a 1930s traditional Edinburgh school for girls with her passion for art, beauty and truth. Let us use these examples as test cases of radical self-change and utilise the opportunity to explore the educational ramifications of such changes.

To be sure, the general relationship between 'the charismatic teacher' and students' self-change is more complex than depicted in those three sources. Psychologically, some such teachers may be accused of a degree of superficiality, and the self-change they bring about in students can turn out to be shallow and short-lived. Morally, the motives of some such teachers may be considered suspect. For instance, the self-change that Jean Brodie enacted upon the 'Brodie girls' was evidently not done with their interests primarily in mind, but rather to satisfy the narcissistic need of projecting her own dreams and values onto others (see Katz, 2006, for a debunking diagnosis of Brodiean self-change). Be that as it may, Escalante, Keating and Brodie all seem to turn their students' self-conceptions – and arguably also their actual full selves – upside down.

We must obviously avoid treating fiction as providing empirical evidence of facts. It should be noted, however, that *Stand and Deliver* is based on a true story (albeit considerably spiced up in the film). Moreover, the explicit inspiration for the Keating character in *Dead Poets Society* was a certain Connecticut English professor, and the depiction of the influential teacher in *The Prime of Miss Jean Brodie* is said to be modelled upon one of Muriel Spark's former teachers. More important than those clues about the actual provenance of the relevant characters is the fact that, cliché-ridden as they are, those representations strike a chord with us as viewers and readers. It is not unlikely that this is the case precisely because they exemplify what we take to be familiar realities or realistic possibilities. In any case, I assume in what follows that transformations of the kind depicted in these three sources do, from time to time, take place in classroom settings, and that they can be distinguished from the more ordinary (gradual/incremental) personal development and growth – the bread and butter of all education.

The addiction and counselling literature is rife with discussions of radical self-change, not to mention the plethora of popular accounts churned out by the self-help industry. Mainstream educational discourse seems, however, to be relatively silent on this issue, with the exception of the adult education literature, in which education for self-change tends to be unashamedly promoted (see Tennant, 2000). In order to throw light on radical self-change and its educational ramifications, I suggest that it may once again be helpful to pursue a scholarship of blurred genres. So in what follows I subject some psychological writings on self-change to philosophical scrutiny and elicit their educational implications. Notice, however, that the sociological literature is also replete with references to radical self-change. A classic introductory text from 1924 discusses 'the sudden mutation of life attitudes' (Park & Burgess, 1924, p. 309). Since then, various sociologists have tried to dissect the radical reorientation of selfhood that a profound self-change involves, and the characteristic series of stages through which an individual progresses while configuring a new selfhood. A common assumption in those writings is that self-change is 'drastic and abrupt' and that it culminates in 'social segregation': the gravitation to a new social group which embraces the subject's reshaped identity (Athens, 1995). The reason for this shared assumption seems to be that the majority of the sociological writings is focused on self-change *qua* religious conversion. They therefore pay scant attention to types of self-change which – although cumulatively profound – are less 'dramatic', more drawn-out and do not necessarily involve the self's redirection toward a new reference group of shared identities.

To gauge the educational ramifications of self-change, we have more to learn, I submit, from the psychological literature. I have chosen for consideration three semi-popular books, by Kenneth J. Gergen, Carol S. Dweck and William B. Swann Jr., which all tell us stories – albeit quite different stories – of the self and its possible reconfigurations. All contain explicit theorisations concerning the nature of self and its capacity for change; and they also carry significant implications, either explicit or implicit, for the issue of the pedagogical practices required for self-change. Before beginning my inquiry, however, four caveats are in order. *First*, these three texts obviously do not exhaust the range of psychological accounts of self-change. Nevertheless, they do cover a relatively broad spectrum, and serve as a good place to start. I singled out Dweck's work because it is already being taught in a number of education and psychology courses around the world; I chose Swann because of the broad range of psychological background theories that he brings to bear in his research; and I added Gergen to the mix because of the exhilarating – if unsettling – radicality of his suggestions and because some of those have already been subjected to critical scrutiny in this book. *Second*, there are no direct inter-citations among the texts; they do not belong to a single discourse within psychology. That is not tantamount to saying, however, that they are not competing or that it is not instructive to try to juxtapose them. The authors' apparent lack of awareness of each other's works is simply one more example of a lamentable lack of rapport not only among academic disciplines but also among different factions within the same disciplines. *Third*, none of the authors distinguishes clearly between profound self-change and self-change as ordinary personal growth. We can nonetheless ask how well each theory would account for the profound self-change, and use that as a salient measure of the theory's general plausibility. *Fourth*, of the three authors, only Dweck explicitly elicits the lessons to be learnt from her theory for pedagogical practice. It is not difficult, however, to tease out the educational implications of the two other theories as well.

10.2. The Crystallised Self

Kenneth J. Gergen's *The Saturated Self* (1991) is the oldest of the three books and also the most radical. It offers a semi-popular, sweeping and deconstructive account of modernist conceptions of the self – in many ways picking up the historical thread where Charles Taylor left it off in his much-read *Sources of the Self* (1989) – although Taylor's name does not appear in the index – and offers us the antidote of a postmodernist conception. Gergen has continued to write and edit books relevant to conceptions of self and self-change in times of postmodernity.

(a) *Theoretical assumptions* – (b) *Self-theory.* Gergen's main method-ological assumptions of ontological anti-realism and epistemological perspectivism have already been fleshed out in Section 2.2, and I simply refer back to them here. Those assumptions have, in any case, become familiar from recent postmodern discourse: Our perspectives are driven by power structures that define (Foucauldian) 'rituals of truth', each with its own incompatible 'truth effects'. There is no object-ive truth in the world, and there is no truth about individuals that can be revealed by gazing at their alleged core of being. The modernist icon of a self, which 'leaves home' in adolescence in order to 'find itself' and then fights a continuous emotional battle against alienation, presup-poses the existence of a true self from which a person's less authentic self can become alienated and in which the liberating process of 'find-ing oneself' refers to a reunification of the two. A constant refrain in Gergen's book, however, is that no such true self exists. The common-sense view of the self is thus a mere sham. Once the idea of a true self has been put under erasure, what replaces it? Recall that Gergen refers to the deconstructive self-process of postmodernity as 'crystallisation'; the new self he depicts and recommends is therefore best described as the *crystallised self.* Crystals grow, change and alter, and the more facets they display, the more beautiful and complex they are (cf. Tracy, 2005, p. 186). Early uncritical postmodernists revelled in eclecticism; late critical postmodernists, like Gergen, forge temporary social identit-ies – mutually irreconcilable relationships and alliances – without mis-taking any of them as revealing 'the truth' about their selves.

(c) *Educational implications.* Gergen's aspirations, at least in his 1991 book, are not primarily those of a pedagogue. Yet if one looks closely, his text is rife with educational advice. The early postmodern concep-tion was that of a 'restless nomad' – clearly not one to be encouraged in students. At the beginning of the critical stage of postmodernism, however, its 'positive potentials' begin to unfold. An educator who understands the nature of the late-postmodernist relational self will encourage students to 'complicate themselves' – to try out a multi-plicity of self-understandings and self-commitments ('the serious stu-dent', 'the light-hearted student', 'the politically engaged student', 'the nerdy student', etc.) – but discourage a commitment to any of those accounts as standing for the final truth of the self. More specifically, educators should help students learn how to develop intense relationships quickly and how to let go equally quickly: to enter groups of symbolic, fractional relationships and to leave such groups. The fractured individual derives pleasure from gazing in wonderment at the possible diversity of human patterning, and as the separation between self and others becomes diminished, warfare between temporary tribes of selves becomes nonsensical. If peace on earth is one's goal, then an insight into the crystallisation of the self is a way of achieving it (Gergen, 1991, pp. 173–254; cf. Tennant, 2000; Tracy, 2005).

(d) Pros and cons. Beginning with the pros, Gergen paints a vivid picture of the challenge to any fixed self-accounts in post-Enlightenment times. The plurality of values and the plurality of options available to us (post)moderns can easily lead to an identity crisis (although Gergen would resent that term). But Gergen takes his illustrations of the postmodern condition to absurd extremes in his deconstruction of the self. To be sure, denials of the existence of a metaphysical self are no novelty in mainstream philosophy. Gergen, however, wants to dethrone the everyday moral self. The radicality of his postmodern anti-self-realism must not be underappreciated therefore. Admittedly, the idea of the relational nature of the self is not, in itself, radical – witness Mead's symbolic interactionism, for instance. But Meadians criticise postmodernists not so much for socialising and decentring as for completely eliminating the self. Despite overtures to the social, postmodernist self-talk remains entrapped in an abstract language game, making the human potential for shared understandings ultimately mystifying (Dunn, 1997).

One of the problems with Gergen's account – as with many of the postmodern ilk – is that it reads at times as little more than a collection of pretentious metaphors. Rejections of truth, even of the simple there-is-a-cat-on-the-mat type, are perhaps most charitably passed over, especially because they undermine any truth claims subsequently made by Gergen – when the poacher turns gamekeeper, so to speak – about the superiority of postmodern self-accounts over modernist ones. Sarah Tracy (2005) wonders why on earth people still talk routinely in terms of 'real' and 'fake' selves rather than in the correct postmodern terms of fragmented, conflictual, discursively constituted and crystallised selves. Why have people not heeded Gergen and his colleagues? As the predicted collapse of the modernist self does not seem to be transpiring spontaneously, Tracy takes it upon herself to hurry things along. It does not seem to have crossed her mind that the postmodern conception may not have percolated through to the public precisely because it sets ordinary human experience utterly at naught.

On Gergen's account, self-change is constantly taking place as we configure new relationships, new fractional identities, choosing to display one facet of the self's crystal rather than another. Not only does this account fall afoul of ordinary experiences of a relatively stable self with relatively stable emotional dispositions, it trivialises the idea of radical self-change by obscuring the difference between radical change and minor personal changing and chopping. Gergen will be at a loss to explain what happened *specifically* to the students of Keating, Escalante and Brodie, because his account is so permissive as to consider radical self-changes to be unproblematically possible, at one's will, at every living moment. The few individuals who do seem to make Gergen's self-changing decisions regularly are, in fact, suffering from psychological disturbances of a serious nature (self-loss or split personality). Gergen's postmodernism trivialises self-change and pedestrianises what would more realistically be understood as pathological conditions of the self. By normalising the dysfunctional, it leads to counter-intuitive conclusions bordering on the absurd; and by collapsing the distinction between aimless drift and guided development, it dissolves the foundations of any scientific study of human development (cf. Modood, 1998; Chandler, 1999; Illeris, 2003; Schwartz, 2006).

10.3. The Incremental Self

Carol S. Dweck's book *Self-Theories* (1999) provides a semi-popular synthesis of 30 years of extensive research conducted with colleagues and students. It is an engaging read, particularly for educators. Unfortunately, her 2006 book *Mindsets* adds little more than anecdotal evidence to her earlier account.

(a) Theoretical assumptions. Underlying Dweck's work is a social-cognitive approach to motivation and self-regulation, according to which people's beliefs and values create meaning systems ('implicit theories'), within which people define themselves and operate, leading different individuals to react in radically different ways to identical situations. In particular, people's beliefs about the extent of their ability to control situations and personal capacities influence their motivations to engage in personal change. Some of those meaning systems may be

psycho-socially adaptive, others maladaptive (Dweck, 1999, pp. xi, 138, 144; Tamir, John, Srivastava & Gross, 2007). More generally, Dweck's methodological framework is part of attribution research in psychology which assumes that people act in accordance with the attributes they consider themselves to be possessing. (I mentioned attributionism in Section 2.2 as a type of psychological soft anti-self-realism.)

(b) *Self-Theory*. Dweck's repeated findings indicate that one can divide people into two groups according to the 'implicit theories' they embrace. People with an 'entity view' consider their personal attributes to be fixed, stable and resistant to change. People with an 'incremental view', on the other hand, consider their attributes to be relatively malleable and amenable to change. 'Incremental theorists' relish challenges and are 'mastery-oriented'; they like to master tasks that are one increment more difficult than the ones they have accomplished so far. 'Entity theorists' are, in contrast, saddled with a disabling self-view that feeds on a diet of easy successes. They are constantly worried about the level of their fixed positive attributes and need repeated verifications of their abilities. They are 'performance-oriented': like to repeat earlier performances over and over again, but are suspicious, if not positively scared, of new challenges. The entity view thus creates emotional vulnerability and learned helplessness. Dweck has designed various self-report instruments that are meant to determine to which of the two categories individuals belong. She has found out that some people are not global entity theorists or global incremental theorists. Rather, they can hold an entity view in one domain (say, intelligence) and an incremental view in another (say, moral character). Nevertheless, for each specific domain, the number of people who show a helpless entity response and those who show a mastery-oriented incremental response turns out to be approximately equal, with a small group (maybe 15%) falling somewhere in the middle. This result applies to individuals of all ages, even as young as $3^1/_2$ years (Dweck, 1999, pp. 2–7, 96).

The bulk of Dweck's empirical research has focused on intelligence. Entity theorists consider intelligence to be a fixed trait and their own IQ scores to be carved in stone. If given the option, they choose repetitive performance goals over learning goals. Moreover, they withhold effort when they confront difficult tasks. If they do badly, they can at least preserve the belief that they would have done well had they applied themselves. They are IQ-validation seekers. Entity theory is thus self-handicapping (1999, chaps. 4–6). Incremental theorists consider intelligence to be dynamic and progressive (depending on the effort they expend in cultivating it). They prefer learning goals to performance goals, even when the former are slightly beyond their reach. They are IQ-growth seekers.

Dweck and her colleagues have recorded similar results in the areas of personality, intimate relationships and emotions. Entity personality theorists prefer, from early childhood onwards, to court status and approval and avoid rejection, whereas incremental personality theorists like to take risks and start new friendships. In romantic relationships, the former type seeks validation from partners, whereas the latter aims at mutual growth. Furthermore, implicit theories of emotion have crucial long-term implications for socio-emotional functioning, especially during challenging transitional periods such as entering college – when those who believe in the possibility of emotional self-regulation thrive and those who do not flounder (Dweck, 1999, chaps. 10 and 18; Tamir et al., 2007). The 'implicit theories' or beliefs that Dweck describes penetrate to the very core of an individual's being; they are self-shaping. Couched in the terms of this chapter, we can say that according to her research, only people possessing an incremental self are capable of radical self-change – because in order to modify one's self, one must believe that it is, indeed, modifiable.

(c) Educational implications. Dweck's findings have aroused considerable interest among educators and in the public media (see, e.g., Bronson, 2007). Most parents and teachers think it is important to praise children. Dweck puts a damper on the valorisation of praise. What we need to do is to praise effort rather than ability. If we praise ability – by telling children that they are talented or gifted, for instance, or even worse, by offering vacuous unsubstantiated praise – we inculcate in them an entity theory: 'Try to appear smart, do not risk making mistakes.' Instead, praise should be specific and directed at mastered tasks. This is, in Dweck's view, particularly true in the case of girls, who already get too much approval for just being 'good'; boys are by nature more risk-oriented and receive more praise for effort – which helps them later in life. Similar to praise, criticism should be item-specific, for if you criticise children for global characteristics, you instil in them a sense of contingent self-worth (1999, chaps. 15 and 16). Using praise and blame constructively is thus a major factor in cultivating an incremental self, amenable to positive self-change. Dweck suggests another route: exposing young people to stories of individuals who have succeeded in life through effort rather than inborn ability. She has recorded a significant change in subjects' self-theories after such exposure, but admits that it may be short lived (1999, pp. 23–26).

(d) Pros and cons. This summary does not do justice to the scope of Dweck's research and theorising. She seems to succeed in good measure in proving her point that one's view of self can either facilitate or hinder – even block completely – one's capacity for self-change. Nevertheless, I have a number of difficulties with her account. One concerns her strict dichotomies. It beggars belief that people, in every domain, fall so neatly and evenly into two distinct categories. She admits in her latest book that she has posited a simple either–or 'for the sake of simplicity' (2006, p. 46); yet her research findings record strict and consistent divisions. When I ask my own students if they think intelligence or personality can be changed, I rarely get such either–or answers. Her questionnaires (Dweck, 1999, pp. 175–86) seem to be tailored so as to catch exaggeratedly divisive responses. Similarly, her strict dualism on praising sounds impractical and unrealistic. The exact *phrasing* of the praise cannot matter as much as the more general educational context. A child will not necessarily understand 'You are great' to mean 'You are great, no matter what' any more than a child will necessarily understand 'You have done really well on this' to mean 'You have done well for now but it does not tell us anything about how good you are in general'. It is no wonder that some parents find Dweck's advice here artificial, if not downright corny (Bronson, 2007).

Unlike Gergen, Dweck does not explicitly reject objective truth. She places little stock, however, in the difference between fact and fiction when analysing our attributes; what matters is how we *perceive* of them (as static or dynamic). She has no patience with the fact that one's IQ score is, as a matter of fact, relatively stable and reliable; or that personality traits, such as those explored in Big Five research, and self-constituting emotional dispositions tend to show little fluctuation. If one expresses those truths in response to her questionnaires (see, e.g., Dweck, 2006, pp. 12–13), one will simply be deemed to have a maladaptive mindset. In general, she does not distinguish clearly between the view that some of our attributes are difficult to change (which is no doubt true) and that some of them are impossible to change (which is probably false). Both views will fall under the rubric of a damaging 'entity theory'.

Dweck correctly points out that her theory assigns a central role to self-development and even to life-transforming self-change (1999, pp. 137, 154). Her pedagogical insights are at best underdeveloped, however, and at worst paradoxical. She stresses that self-theory (or mindset) change is not easy – it may be difficult 'to let go of something that has felt like your "self" for many years' (2006, p. 219). Nevertheless, she asserts, you *can* change, but only if you have an incremental view of self. Did all the students taught by Keating, Escalante and Brodie (and their counterparts in the real world) then happen to start with such a view? Are entity theorists simply stuck with their mindsets (which would make radical self-change paradoxical)? Not necessarily, it seems, for a radical change of mindsets is also described as possible along Dweckian lines, more radical even than the results of contemporary cognitive therapy (2006, p. 210). The problem is that we are given scant clues about what could produce such a transformation. Apart from trite messages about the correct phrasing of praise, and a reference to a successful eight-session-long workshop on the 'growth-mindset', the details of which are left unexplained (2006, p. 215), little of substance is said about how to move beyond a fixed mindset. Indeed, this advice is so meagre that an educator without other resources would starve on it.

10.4. The Homeostatic Self

Like Dweck's book, William B. Swann's *Self-Traps* (1996) synthesises and popularises years of research on the self. He has continued to pursue similar lines of inquiry in subsequent works, some of which I also cite below.

(a) *Theoretical assumptions*. The assumptions fuelling Swann's research are varied. One source is the attribution tradition, within which people like Dweck work. Swann wants to delve further, however, and explain persistent self-attributions by appealing to a cognitive motive to find oneself explicable and predictable. There he takes his cue inter alia from Prescott Lecky's early work on the need for self-coherence to maintain self-comprehension (cf. Velleman, 2006, chap. 10). Swann (2005) also considers himself to be working within the general Meadian tradition of symbolic interactionism and Heiderian balance theories (of the consistency motive as a drive toward psychological balance), although he also claims to transcend the work of Heider. Finally, Swann mentions approvingly the work by psychoanalyst Harry Stack Sullivan on people's deep-seated desire for self-stability (Swann, 1996, p. 31).

(b) *Self-theory*. Swann has conducted a number of psychological experiments which demonstrate that people tend to pay attention to, seek, believe, value and retain feedback that confirms their present self-concept, whether that self-concept is positive or negative. These findings contradict the well-entrenched assumption that people in general are self-enhancement seekers and praise junkies: consumed by an overwhelming desire to think well of themselves and always on the lookout for responses that show them in a positive light. The assumption that Swann challenges is implicit in two well-known theories of self-motives: *self-enhancement theory* and *self-expansion theory*. According to self-enhancement theory, people are driven by a fundamental desire to maintain or increase the positivity of their self-concept, manifested, for instance, through self-serving attributions by which positive outcomes are attributed to their own responsibility but negative ones are attributed to factors beyond their control. Self-expansion theory, on the other hand, contends that people possess a central motivation for self-expansion – a motive to increase their physical and social resources – by developing potentially 'useful' relationships, for instance (see Leary, 2007a). Both theories see in the self something like a totalitarian regime that revises history in order to portray itself in a positive light, and continually tries to expand its territory.

In contrast to those theories, Swann's studies suggest that once people have incorporated a given characteristic – however negative – firmly into their self-concept, they seek feedback that verifies that characteristic, even if it brings them intense pain. In other words, we like to seek out others who see us as we see ourselves, or we like to persuade them to do so, and we tend to flee contexts in which such self-verifying evaluations are not forthcoming. Swann refers to this tendency as 'self-traps': stubborn impediments to higher self-esteem. Swann does not reject the view that we also have a desire for positive feedback, but he suggests that people with a negative self-concept are deeply torn and ambivalent emotionally; they want both a favourable and an unfavourable evaluation, and are therefore caught in a self-trap. The underlying motive, Swann hypothesises, is the desire for self-stability and self-cohesion: the desire for a *homeostatic self*. When people find that fundamental aspects of their self-concept are being jeopardised, they feel as anxious as if the ground were being cut from beneath their feet; they experience an emotional sense of loss and hollowness, just like that described by adults who have been blind from birth and are finally given a sight-restoring operation (Swann, 1996, pp. 10–14, 23–25, 51; Swann, 2005; Swann & Bosson, 2008).

Swann's *self-verification theory* becomes a powerful tool in explaining various puzzling social phenomena, such as why the victims of bullying often like to hang out with the bullies who mistreat them, and why battered women often seem to end up with another violent partner. Some of Swann's most engaging studies revolve around dating and marriage rituals. They reveal that people with positive self-views are most intimate with partners who evaluate them favourably, but those with negative self-views are most intimate with – and directly seek – partners who evaluate them unfavourably (1996, chaps. 4 and 5). A profound self-change is, by Swann's evaluation, an extremely difficult and painful process. One may even wonder why it ever takes place.

(c) Educational implications. How can we educate people out of their self-traps? Swann suggests that by far the best way is to prevent them from ever forming negative self-views in the first place. This is why he explores child-rearing practices closely and stresses the importance of positive and responsive caregivers (1996, chap. 7). But he does not stop there; he also proposes ways to raise low self-esteem. This may come as something of a surprise, given that Swann's book was meant to explain, among other things, why the quest for boosted self-esteem has proved to be so elusive – and because his research is generally seen as a threat to the self-esteem industry. Swann readily agrees that global self-esteem has scant predictive value; nor is he optimistic that people's general self-views can be changed at the drop of a hat. What he does believe, however, is that the specificity of predictors and criteria must be matched in psychological research. Although students' global self-esteem says little about their forthcoming maths results, for instance, their domain-specific self-esteem as maths students may. This is fully in line with earlier observations in Chapter 5. People cannot be magically charmed into possessing high global self-esteem, but Swann suggests that there are various small steps that educators can take to raise domain-specific self-esteem (Swann, Chang-Schneider & McClarty, 2007). For instance, people with low global self-esteem almost invariably possess some positive domain-specific or item-specific views of themselves. This fact raises the possibility for educators (or therapists) to help them to think in terms of strengthening those views rather than of losing their global view. In simpler terms, educators can, via a mixed diet of self-confirming and favourable evaluations, encourage people to place more weight on their strengths and less on their weaknesses, thereby gradually tipping the balance of the homeostatic self (Swann, 1996, pp. 148–49).

(d) Pros and cons. Swann explains in empirically grounded, convincing terms the stubborn character of our selves: how resistant we are to radical self-change. We take great comfort and security from viewing and acting in the same way as 'we always have'; and we defend our self-citadels as strenuously as a bird defends its nest. To borrow

Dweck's terminology, it seems from Swann's research that people tend to be 'entity theorists' not only in a descriptive sense but also in a normative sense; they not only *believe* in the static, they positively *value* it. Yet radical self-change does take place from time to time, where we learn to see our lives in a new light, and I am not sure that Swann's strategy of domain-specific small steps can really explain what occurs during such a change. Does it explain what happens to the students of teachers such as Keating, Escalante and Brodie?

From an educational perspective, Swann's writings contain disturbingly little reference to the psychology of learning. Greater illumination would have been gained for educational purposes had he devoted more space to the processes at work when our 'conservative impulse' is seriously challenged and a new homeostasis that is more than a minor modification of the earlier one is formed within the self. Also off-putting – for self-realists at least – is the fact that Swann's theory is only about self-concept change or, better put, about the subjective resistance of preforged self-views and self-identities to change. He does not mention possible changes in the objective full self, probably because his soft anti-self-realism does not acknowledge the existence of such a self.

To recap, I have now explored three psychological self-theories from the perspective of their ability to account for radical self-change and its educational repercussions. My overall conclusion is that whereas all three theories provide some enlightening insights, none of them gives a fully satisfying account. Gergen's theory of the crystallised self offers a provocative account of how self-views have become problematised in a postmodern age of flux. The philosophical assumptions he introduces are controversial, however, if not light-weight, and his theory constitutes a hyperbolic reaction which ultimately trivialises and pedestrianises self-change. Dweck's theory of the incremental self focuses persuasively on the effects of external reinforcement on the psychological conditions of self-change, but her account is too divisive and makes the conditions for self-change seem to be 'all in the head'. Swann's theory of the homeostatic self provides a solid explanation of people's resistance to radical self-change, but makes the overcoming of such resistance seem emotionally undermotivated and mystifying.

The failure to provide a fully satisfying account of self-change should, I believe, prompt moves in other directions: directions which I have already indicated with my defence of self-realism in Chapter 2. Animating any such realism, be it Aristotle's 'hard' or Hume's 'soft' one – but conspicuously missing from their modern psychological counterparts – is the presupposition that what matters in the end is not how one conceives of oneself, but whether or not one's self-conceptions are truthful. What is the actual full self beneath all the 'identities'? How can we bring our 'mindsets' or 'identities' into line with objective moral truth about ourselves and about the world in which we live?

I wonder why the emotional allure of objective truth – of truth as a 'turn-on' if you like – has been lost on contemporary psychologists. Arguably, the best description of what took place in the classes conducted by our fictional teachers, Keating, Escalante and Brodie, was the *awakening of truth*, inspired by the *emotion of intellectual curiosity* that had been elicited in them by their teachers. The students realised that their self-conceptions were not only static and maladaptive; they were objectively false in the sense of fostering falsehoods about the students' potentialities. By either rejecting objective truth or relegating it to a side-issue compared with 'self-perceptions', psychologists foreclose a distinctively classical avenue of understanding, and I believe they do so at their peril. For thinkers of a 'post-Enlightenment' bent, this may sound like a noxiously obsolete suggestion. Those who still believe in the Enlightenment project, however, will carry on undaunted in their quest.

10.5. Conclusion – and Some Educational Implications

As this book draws to a close, let me now, by way of conclusion, offer a summary of the 'alternative' self-paradigm that I have developed throughout – and then end on a practical note with some educational implications of this paradigm.

The main methodological assumption behind the development of the 'alternative' self-paradigm was that self research has been and cannot avoid to continue being informed by moral theorising – and that further progress will not be made unless traditional fences between disciplines (especially philosophy and psychology, but also including sociology and education) are more unhesitatingly and systematically crossed (see Chapter 3). I hope that enough has been said both to explain the meaning of this assumption and to justify it.

The 'alternative' paradigm takes as its starting point the common-sense view of the self as the set of one's core commitments, traits, aspirations and ideals. While remaining agnostic on the metaphysical status of this self, the 'alternative' paradigm posits that such a self exists, in an everyday realist sense, as the object of moral evaluation and the locus of moral agency. Rather than being identical to constructed self-concept or identity, moral selfhood is understood as the target object of self-concept. Self-understanding refers to the successful targeting of selfhood by self-concept. Whereas complete self-understanding may be a *de facto* impossibility for finite beings like us – given that many of our inner processes are unconscious and ultimately hidden from view – we should aim at approaching as accurate a self-understanding as possible. Despite being conceptually distinct from the self, self-concept matters for two reasons: morally, because knowledge of who we are empowers us, and epistemologically, because self-views are themselves part of the actual full self that they target (see Chapter 2).

The self essentially comprises – and is even originally produced by – emotion. Our core emotional dispositions are self-constituting; some are also self-comparative in that they involve the self as a necessary reference point. Particularly noteworthy are the self-conscious emotions such as pride and shame, because they are simultaneously part of the actual full self (and as such can be essentially hidden from view) and about the self (have that actual full self as their intentional object). Self-conscious emotions, like all emotions, embody a cognitive element – and the traditional dichotomy of one's cognitive self versus one's non-cognitive affective life is misplaced (see Chapter 4).

Two of the main ingredients in self-concept, self-esteem and self-confidence, are best understood as constituted by so-called background emotions. Having high self-esteem, for instance, is not so much about having particular beliefs as it is about possessing the emotions of pride and self-satisfaction as background concerns. Although global self-esteem has turned out to have little socio-moral relevance, domain-specific self-esteem and self-confidence are vital ingredients in the good life. So-called implicit self-esteem is also important for providing us with an emotional ballast of self-worth, but, contrary to ordinary self-esteem, it is not part of self-concept but only of the target self (see Chapter 5). Human behaviour is, to a certain extent, context-sensitive: The more unusual the situations are that we get into and the less time we have to think about what to do, the less predictable our actions become. Emotions – especially *qua* reactive attitudes – are more stable, and tell us more about a person's moral worth (see Chapter 6). In order to understand self-respect, an objective feature of our actual full self that provides it with moral worth, we must therefore understand our moral emotions (see Chapter 7).

Self-concepts differ among cultures, even systematically between the 'traditional' East and the 'liberal' West. Incompatible as some of the underlying beliefs and emotions are, no good reason has emerged for seeing them as being incommensurable and irreconcilable. In contrast, successful 'synergic bicultural integration' seems to be possible, operating in much the same way as Aristotle's *phronesis* adjudicates between the demands of different values and emotions (see Chapter 8). Nevertheless, un-reconciled emotional conflicts between the Eastern and Western self-concepts do contribute to some of the most debilitating self-pathologies of the day. Other such pathologies are caused by emotional tensions that are internal to the Western self-concept (see Chapter 9). Self-realism helps to explain what happens when selves change radically. Radical self-change is not best seen as an existential jump or an irrational epiphany, but rather as an emotion-driven search for objective truth and meaning (see Chapter 10).

In 1935, Scottish philosopher John Macmurray wrote: 'The emotional life is not simply a part or an aspect of human life. It is not, as we often think, subordinate or subsidiary to the mind. It is the core and essence of human life' (1935, p. 75). Translated into today's jargon about selfhood, this quotation pretty much sums up the 'alternative' self-paradigm: *Emotions are not simply a part or an aspect of the self. They are not subordinate or subsidiary to some other cognition-dependent processes. Rather, emotions are the core and essence of the self.* I said in Section 1.1 that my aim was to show how emotions are implicated in selfhood in all its manifestations and at all levels of engagement. I hope this has now been achieved, both for the actual full self and for self-concept. The *actual full self* is emotion-grounded; our *moral self-system* is a single system of cognition and emotion; *self-esteem and self-confidence* (making up *self-concept*) are constituted by background emotions; *moral character* is best gauged via emotions; *self-respect* is both constituted by emotional virtues and protected by an emotion (pridefulness); integrated *multicultural selfhood* requires emotional harmony; *self-pathologies* manifest themselves as emotional dissonances or tensions; *self-change* is typically guided by emotions. How true, then, is the complaint that the rift between self- research and emotion research has hurt and continues to hurt both fields.

In my quest to elicit some of the educational implications of the 'alternative' self-paradigm, Macmurray can also provide initial guidance: 'The failure to develop the emotional life will [...] result in abstraction and division; in a failure to see life steadily and as a whole'

(1935, p. 77). It is almost as if Macmurray were forestalling the claims of the two systems self-view that I criticised in Chapter 4. When he said that there was 'an increasing recognition in educational circles of the urgent need for a proper training of the emotions' (1935, p. 67), he was mainly engaging in wishful thinking. Such recognition, however, really did emerge half a century later, with the resurgence of cognitive approaches to emotion and of an Aristotle-inspired call for emotion education. As an educator, it worries me to think of the impact that the two-systems self-view, with its impoverished notion of the affective, might have for the burgeoning practice of such education. I have written at some length on previous occasions (Kristjánsson 2002, 2006, 2007) about its nature and contours and do not wish to repeat myself here. Notice simply that two of the most popular trends in moral education succeeding Kohlberg's developmentalism are emotion-grounded and avowedly Aristotelian in origin: *character education*, based broadly on the tenets of virtue ethics, and *social and emotional learning*, derived from the concept of emotional intelligence. Devout Aristotelians may grumble that those trends have deviated too much from their original source. Character educationists seem at times to be overly concerned with the inculcation of a body of set traits but concerned too little with the development of critical moral wisdom (*phronesis*), and EQ theorists typically fail to heed Aristotle's warning that emotional competence without moral depth is the mere calculated cleverness of a knave. Nevertheless those two approaches have unleashed an unprecedented interest in methods of moral coaching that include emotion education as an essential element.

When Macmurray wrote about the need for proper training of young people's emotions, he referred to it is the 'development of sensuous discrimination and co-ordination': the 'refinement of sensuality' (1935, p. 71). Macmurray realised, just as Aristotle did, that the parent–child and teacher–child relationships have an enormous influence on this process of sensitisation. This is why Aristotle has aptly been called 'the founder of the ethics of care' (Curzer, 2007). One could also, for the same reason, call him the founder of attachment theory. Aristotle famously foregrounds behavioural strategies of habituation in early childhood, which teach children to feel the right things at the right times towards the right people. Yet it is clear that the eventual aim of emotional habituation is to help the young gradually actualise their own *phronesis*, in order to re-evaluate and possibly revise the emotional dispositions with which they were originally inculcated, and to infuse those dispositions with moral value (see further in Kristjánsson, 2007, chap. 5).

This Aristotelian picture of emotion education may seem to be compatible with Lapsley and Hill's account, discussed in Chapter 4, of the education of 'System 1' processes (namely our intuitive, experiential, automatic and tacit ones) as 'the outcome of repeated experience, of instruction, intentional coaching and socialisation' (2008, pp. 324–25). Yet three things must be borne in mind. *First*, Aristotelian habituation is not invoked as a method to train only intuitive and automatic mental processes, but all processes. Every disposition we have, to act as well as to react, is seen as the outcome of original habituation. *Second*, the idea of the policing by one system (e.g., rational) of another (e.g., irrational) is entirely foreign to Aristotle's moral ideals. Virtuous agents have no emotions to 'control' any more, as their emotions are already reason-infused. *Third*, equally foreign to Aristotle is the idea that 'hot' emotions need 'cool' moral principles to lend them moral worth, and that when exploring young people's moral selves, we need to concentrate on pure cognitive constructions of their 'sense of purpose' (see, e.g., Stanford Center on Adolescence, 2003) rather than their affective dispositions. All in all, there is no hint in Aristotle of any 'two systems' at work, be they complementary or competing. The emotional life is once again not 'another' or 'alien' aspect of human life. It is at the very core of our single moral system. This Aristotelian insight is part and parcel of the 'alternative' self-paradigm.

In Chapter 4, I also discussed the controversy surrounding the alleged moral-self versus moral-emotion dichotomy. Beyond the theoretical deconstruction of that false dichotomy lies an acute practical issue: For Kohlbergians, moral education is primarily a *rational* quest, best attained via the training of critical faculties of judgement. For Blasi and the moral-self theorists, moral education is primarily an *existential* quest in which a fundamental role is played by role-model education (the emulation of moral exemplars) and the existential what-kind-of-person-do-I-want-to-be questions of adolescence. For the moral-emotion theorists, moral education is primarily a *conditioning* process of emotional sensitisation in which children are made to internalise proper reactions to diverse situations through early parent–child interaction, subsequent service learning and other guided activities. Although Hume's soft realist account of the moral self is more streamlined than is Aristotle's hard realist one, the practical message to be drawn from it is basically the same. These methods are not *alternatives*. They are *complementary* ways of providing children with moral motivation: of bridging the gap between cognition and action. What we need is a plurality of methods. Moral education is constant work in progress, which should start from the person's earliest age. Most importantly, moral education in early years not only fosters childhood antecedents of the moral self; it nourishes the moral self as it develops and grows.

The 'alternative' self-paradigm' has various other educational implications apart from the emphasis of emotion education. One of them will be the retrieval of the notion of *self-understanding* as an educational value. When people learn to understand themselves, according to the 'alternative' realist self-paradigm, they discover objective truths that have hitherto eluded them. Such discoveries are characterised by a sense of accomplishment. When people understand themselves according to the 'dominant' anti-realist paradigm, they choose or re-choose their identities: re-determine themselves (see, e.g., Walker, 2005). Self-understanding is then characterised by unexpected or unforced shifts in our understanding (Hogan, 2005) or by non-rational existential jumps into the unknown. As there is no 'real' self to be understood, what can be understood is only one's self-construct which may be chosen and polished.

Although self-understanding, in the realist sense, is a good thing, it is not necessarily pleasant. We may learn things about ourselves and our relationships with others that shame and embarrass us (which also harmonises with the Socratic conception, mentioned in Section 1.1, of self-understanding as the realisation of one's own ignorance). Only for the ideally perfect moral person will self-understanding be wholly pleasant. In the SEAL programme for developing 'the social and emotional aspects of learning', which is now being piloted in English primary schools, the focus is exclusively on the enhancement of 'comfortable feelings': pleasant emotions (see critiques by Miller, 2008, and Cigman, 2008). The SEAL programme is under the spell of the dogmas of currently fashionable positive psychology. Positive psychologists consider the main criterion of a successful self-change to be pleasure and psychological adaptiveness. This does not mean that the change itself is pleasant – the discovering self is, after all, according to the 'standard' self-paradigm which nourishes positive psychology, an emotionally vulnerable self – but that the final destination is characterised by 'positive emotions', which simply means 'pleasant emotions'. So ingrained is this understanding in many contemporary theorists that even those who would not be counted as positive psychologists are held firmly in its grip. Take an article in which the Gadamerian notion of 'being pulled up short' (undergoing experiences of disorientation and the realisation of one's limitations) is seen as a 'challenge' to the idea of self-understanding as a focus of teaching and learning (Kerdeman, 2003). Far from being a challenge to self-understanding according to the 'alternative' self-paradigm, the experience of being frequently pulled up short would constitute a prototypical example of self-understanding, however disorientating and unsettling it may feel. Moreover, a well-known Aristotelian insight, which informs the 'alternative' self-paradigm, is that what needs to be 'enhanced' are not only pleasant emotions, but also painful ones that contribute to the good life: emotions such as compassion with undeserved suffering and righteous indignation over wrongdoings – even proper shame over one's own failures as a moral learner.

Although few educators would take exception to the claim that self-understanding is a fundamental educational value, we should recall that this claim is not incontestable. Renowned writers such as Henrik Ibsen and Eugene O'Neill have toyed with the idea of self-deceptions and unrealistic pipe-dreams as 'vital lies' that enable us to avoid self-contempt and existential despair. Like blinders on a horse, self-deceptions may help us to move forward unhampered by distress (see Martin, 1985, p. 7). Philosopher Amélie Rorty has also praised selective uses of self-deception, claiming that, like programmes for completely eradicating the vices, 'attempts at doing away with self-deception would damage habits that are highly adaptive' – 'habits' which include romantic love and unswerving loyalty (Rorty, 1975, p. 22). And in an influential article, social psychologists Taylor and Brown (1994) argue that a vast body of empirical research in social and cognitive psychology suggests that most people harbour certain mildly positive illusions about themselves, and that contrary to conventional wisdom, these illusions are promoters rather than contraveners of mental health and happiness.

There may be some truth in the Rousseauean dictum that an educator has no more right to tell students what they do not want to hear than not to tell them what they want to hear. I would argue, however, that the general point about people's need for self-deception underestimates the enticement and value of objective truth (cf. Carr, 2003), as well as people's capacity to cope with distress when truth turns out to be unsettling. It is no coincidence that informed consent and truth telling have become ground rules in the health sector. Even John Stuart Mill, that uncompromising advocator of happiness as the ultimate moral goal, wrote a long chapter in *On Liberty* (1972) entirely in praise of truth and its value in human life – and the disvalue of trying to suppress it. It is true that young children are not always ready to hear the truth about everything, including themselves. Witness, for instance, Cigman's well-taken point, raised in Chapter 5, about toddlers' need for abundant – even unrealistic – assurances of their self-worth. That does not change the general truth that self-deceptions are disabling – however 'pleasant' they may at times be – because they undermine the self-transformative value of objective truth, which is conducive to human *eudaimonia*.

Philosopher Neera Badhwar (2009) has argued convincingly for the relationship between realistic self-understanding and *eudaimonia*. She claims that people who possess such self-understanding have 'rich factual knowledge about human nature' and 'rich procedural knowledge about ways of dealing with life problems'. Although knowledge of some facts *can* create sorrow so great that it leads to a decrease of overall happiness, such sorrow does not typically come from knowledge of the truth per se, but from the untimeliness of the discovery. Like surgical procedures, unpleasant truths may need a certain prep time. She notes that Taylor and Brown (1994) regard happiness as a purely subjective state, whereas she is talking about happiness as *eudaimonia*. (For philosophers, it is no news that a satisfied pig experiences more subjective happiness than a disgruntled Socrates!) She goes even further, however, by suggesting that self-deceptions do not enhance subjective happiness either, at least not in the long run. The appearance that they do may stem from the fact that when social psychologists study correlations between illusions and pleasure, the subjects of their studies are typically first-year college students. But those are not exactly representative of the population at large. Given their youth and inexperience, we should expect students to be particularly susceptible to illusions of control and to exaggerated optimism.

According to the 'alternative' self-paradigm, the ultimate goal of self-understanding is the appreciation of truths about the self, and the emotional maturity of a self that has learnt to respect itself as the possessor of such truths. Notice, however, that the method of *self-reflection* may not always be the most appropriate one to achieve self-understanding. It is not only the case that there may be absolute psychological constraints on the degree of reflective self-comprehension that finite beings such as ourselves can achieve (cf. Flanagan, 1991, p. 144; Jopling, 2000, pp. 62 and 137), psychological studies have shown that encouraging self-reflection can sometimes lessen accuracy in self-understanding by prompting rationalisation and slanted intellectualising. Couples who analyse their relationships extensively, instead of simply getting on with the business of being together, are more likely to break up, for example (Wilson, 1985), and in general, excessive self-focus is associated with depression (Gasper & Robinson, 2004, p. 147). Perhaps these findings provide evidence for the Aristotelian insight that the best way forward for self-understanding is not through an inward gaze and 'self-work' but through sustained serious engagement with others.

This insight chimes in nicely with Thomas Ziehe's observations about the role of the school in contemporary society. Recall from Section 1.1 that Ziehe considers the chief characteristic of today's students in Western societies to be their excessive self-focus and subjectivism. Just as Western society has embraced 'The Age of the Self', so the excesses of today's subjectivisation have entered the texture of young people's self-conceptions. A common assumption in reformist educational theories is that in order for effective learning to take place, the practices of the school must be in line with the prevailing *habitus* of the students' homes and that of society at large: If self-work is the order of the day in the popular media and the day-to-day *habitus* of students, for example, then self-work must also be the order of the day in schools. Ziehe (2000) rejects this assumption. He suggests, rather, that the school should offset an emphasis on the exploration of one's inner world of values, forging instead a 'normative relationship of difference'. The aura of the school must differ from that of society. In contrast to the deformalised and in many ways trivialised practices of the outside world, the school should symbolise respect, ritual, theoretical contemplation and the concept of 'asceticism': a pattern of mentality which demands of young people to hold back their own needs in favour of school norms and their long-term life plans. Only if students see in the school an institution with its own logic – a radically alternative territory with initially alienating elements – will they come to feel emotionally attached to its alternative way of being. Underlying Ziehe's suggestion seems to be the same ideal of the best-of-both-worlds synergic identity – applied here to the school and society rather than to independent and interdependent self-concepts – that I championed in Chapter 8. And I welcome it.

Some further comments are in order about the impact of the self-esteem fallacy on education. Although much has been made – and a good deal of it, no doubt, rightly – of the corrosive effect that the ideal of global self-esteem has had on educational standards, some of the misgivings aired in Chapter 5 about alleged partners in crime may on closer inspection turn out to be unfounded. Smith (2006, p. 51) is, for example, concerned that the ideal of individualised education – as *personalised learning* – most touted nowadays in the UK, may have been infected by the self-esteem mantra. De Waal (2005) airs similar concerns about the *differentiation* version of individualised education that has been gaining ground in the USA. She believes that differentiation devotees have psychologised education in order to serve the unsavoury agenda of political correctness, and that they primarily pursue what should be education's secondary goal: student self-esteem. If ideas of individualised education are really ripples in the same wave that drove the self-esteem movement, should individualised education then fall by the wayside too?

In the UK, *personalised learning* has the backing of the government as the way forward in education. Smith (2006, p. 51) specifically mentions the UK-government-sponsored Website on this method, and other Internet material linked from that site, as promulgating views in line with the self-esteem orthodoxy (that students do not flourish at school when learning tasks are pitched dauntingly high, for instance). There is a great deal of political rhetoric on those Web pages, especially long-winded speeches by the minister responsible for school standards. Yet precisely those speeches provide us with considerable enlightenment about the philosophy behind personalised learning. Personalised learning means 'building the organisation of schools around the needs, interests and aptitudes of individuals pupils; it means shaping teaching around the way different youngsters learn; it means taking the care to nurture the unique talents of every pupil'. Special emphasis is placed on the needs of the gifted learner, who – no longer ostracised as a smart-alec – will thrive in a school celebrating individual success and challenging the culture of low aspirations. All in all, personalised education promises to lay the foundation of an educational system moulded around the child, not of a child moulded around the system (Personalised Learning Website, 2006). Contrary to Smith, I find no indication on this Website or in the linked material to suggest that personalised learning has any special truck with the self-esteem movement. There is no mention of the word 'self-esteem' or the danger of too daunting challenges. By contrast, there is a warning against allowing students to 'coast at their preferred pace of learning' and there are exhortations about giving students the 'confidence and skills to succeed' (Personalised Learning Website, 2006).

Consider next the (originally US-based) educational approach of differentiated instruction. Its founder and current guru is Carol Ann Tomlinson, and I have studied two of her canonical works (Tomlinson, 1995, 1999). One-size-for-all instruction will sag or pinch, she says (given student variances in readiness, interest and learning styles), exactly as single-size clothing would. In contrast, differentiating instruction means '"shaking up" what goes on in the classroom so that students have multiple options for taking in information, making sense of ideas, and expressing what they learn' (Tomlinson, 1995, pp. 2–3). Differentiation becomes a new way of thinking about teaching and learning: a 'philosophy' (Tomlinson, 2000, p. 6). As an educational philosophy, differentiation is defined as an approach to teaching in which teachers proactively modify curricula, teaching methods, resources and learning activities in order to maximise the learning opportunities for individual students. Is Tomlinson's primary goal, as De Waal has suggested (2005), to boost students' self-esteem? And does that goal then carry the possibility of lowered standards and a curriculum pitched exactly at the students' current levels of aptitude in order not to hurt their feelings? I have tried but altogether failed to find either this goal or its implications in Tomlinson's work. She recommends that teachers create tasks that are a chunk more difficult that one believes students can accomplish. Thus students are encouraged to 'work up', not down (Tomlinson, 1995, pp. 17, 45) – advice that also applies to the most gifted students. In sum, classrooms are supposed to be places of 'rigorous intellectual requirements', 'zones of proximal development', where simply reducing expectations in order to achieve plain sailing is proscribed. If this were not unambiguous enough, Tomlinson emphatically forswears self-esteem as a goal of teaching, but recommends self-efficacy (or self-confidence) instead: 'Self-esteem is fostered by being told that you are important, valued, or successful. Self-efficacy, by contrast, comes from stretching yourself to achieve a goal that you first believed was beyond your reach' (Tomlinson, 1995, p. 15).

In sum, then, there is no freight heaped on students' self-esteem in the official UK material on personalised learning, and the guru of differentiation goes out of her way to reject self-esteem as an educational goal. This does not mean that the self-esteem movement may not have had a pernicious influence on various strands in educational thought in the 1980s and 1990s – influence that now needs to be wound down. It simply means that the dismissal of one-size-fits-all instruction, implicit in the concept of individualised education, emerges unscathed from any encounter it may have once had with the now-discarded global self-esteem fallacy.

I next offer a couple of terse suggestions about possible practical – political and educational – reverberations of the paradigm of synergic bicultural integration proposed in Chapter 8. Multicultural politics and multicultural education are, of course, buzzwords of the day, and it may seem obvious that the above paradigm can provide positive input into discussions of multicultural co-existence in our quickly evolving 'glocal' (global + local) world. We must be careful, however, not to jump to conclusions about the unity of psychological and political issues. Coordinating the conflicting conceptions and emotions of a single self is one thing; coordinating the conflicting conceptions of many distinct selves under a common denominator is quite another. Nevertheless, it is reasonable to assume that people actively and sincerely engaged in negotiating the conflicts of contemporary multicultural society are people simultaneously engaged in a project of selfhood: a project aimed at personal development and self-adaptation (see van der Merwe & Jonker, 2001). Given that understanding, the paradigm of synergic bicultural integration should help to pull us away from ideas of postmodern or ultra-pluralist liberal multiculturalism, which emphasise difference, and towards essentialist conceptions of multiculturalism, which emphasise human similarities (see, e.g., Nussbaum, 1992). 'If we are lucky', one sceptic of multicultural fusion says, 'there is coexistence and the different racial groups become good neighbours, but a symbiosis is hardly conceivable' (Luzzati, 2005, p. 109). The possibility of synergic bicultural integration goes some distance in moving the burden of proof from the believers in such societal symbiosis towards its detractors.

Educational problems loom large, however: Should multicultural education aim at the credo 'integration while maintaining one's identity'? Spiecker, Steutel and de Ruyter (2004) question its feasibility. They argue that development into a good citizen in a Western liberal democracy cannot be combined with the full preservation of an interdependent self-concept in Markus and Kitayama's (1991) sense of the term. For instance, the liberal core virtue of respect for individual rights presupposes that bearers of this virtue are able to comprehend themselves and

244 The Self and Its Emotions

others as independent persons – but it is 'highly doubtful' if someone with an interdependent self-concept can do so. Hence, the liberal state has a duty to educate such a self-concept out of students (Spiecker, Steutel & de Ruyter, 2004, pp. 168 and 173). This argument rests on the premise that the well-rounded possession of an interdependent self-concept in a liberal society runs afoul of Flanagan's often-mentioned principle of psychological realism. That is a psychological claim rather than a moral claim. It also admits, then, of empirical refutation. If the paradigm of synergic bicultural integration holds good, as I argued in Chapter 8, the suggestion that an interdependent self-concept needs to be completely educated out of students may turn out to be too drastic. Perhaps we should, instead, help them to cultivate *phronesis*, to enable them to re-evaluate the content of both their interdependent and independent self-conceptions, and, when necessary, to adjudicate between them in cases of conflict.

Finally I turn to the three test cases of self-pathologies explored in Chapter 9, and offer some remedial educational suggestions. If my hypothesis on suicide terrorism succeeds, there is a world of difference – social, ideological, psychological – between Eastern-based and Western-based suicide terror. Similarly, if we ask about possible educational interventions – what can be done, for example, through systematic moral education to stem the tide of terror – we will, in fact, be asking about different malaises and different measures. Given the absorption of the individual into the whole, which underlies Eastern-based terrorism, the educational issue there must be addressed at the level of the extended group of selves rather than the individual self. Tellingly, in the movie *Paradise Now* (Abu-Assad, 2005), Khaled is finally persuaded to cancel his plans for a suicide mission by the young Palestinian woman, Suhu, who uses arguments that are internal to the Palestinian cause: Suicide terror is detrimental to the interests of the Palestinian people – indeed, to the interests of all people.

As suggested, the Western liberal notion of an emotionally vulnerable self that needs to re-enhance itself plays into the hands of recruiters who offer malleable young Western Muslims an 'easy' route to self-redemption. How can we disarm their temptation to fall prey to the siren song of the terrorists' fix-it-all: the deluded self-enhancement more immediately harmful even than the quick fixes offered by Western hedonism and therapy culture? Perhaps we cannot do anything about it unless we win release from that very liberal self-concept which permeates Western society. That, for many, would be a sobering thought – for others one bordering on the naïve. For those who exclude the possibility that the Western conception of the self can be radically changed through moral education or other forms of consciousness-raising, it may be worth recalling, however, the historical recency of this conception. The 1980s–1990s idea that the main purpose of primary schooling is to boost self-esteem would, for instance, have sounded outlandish to most people only a few decades earlier. A change of compass in schooling from self-esteem to self-respect is surely not a practical impossibility (recall Chapter 7).

A deeper question remains: Do we really want to renege on the Western liberal conception of the self and return to the embrace of a traditional conception? I simply note here, in line with the paradigm of synergic bicultural integration, that the choice may not be 'either–or'. We may not need to choose between the emotional straitjacket of hyper-identity and the excessive anomie of a shrunken self in need of healing. Giving up on those items of the liberal self that make it most vulnerable to abuse does not require us to consign Western liberalism and individualism to the scrapheap. Quite the contrary, it may help us to resolve the very paradox at the heart of the liberal self-concept: that it is at once a socio-cultural construction and the source of moral solipsism. Consider John Stuart Mill's brand of expansive liberalism, espoused in such classic works as *Utilitarianism* and *On Liberty* (1972). His clarion call for liberal freedoms of speech, conscience and individual development is combined with 'strong evaluations' (in Charles Taylor's sense): an acceptance of nonsubjective essential goods, including the universal moral virtues, and substantive moral demands to further those goods. A system of moral education that ceased to be neutral with regard to different conceptions of essential goods may give young people in the West the sense of rootedness so badly lacking in their current self-conceptions – without falling back on the holism of the traditional self-concept – and help some of our most emotionally vulnerable individuals to resist the allure of the 'merchants of happiness', be they dope peddlers, spin-doctors, quack therapists or terrorist recruiters.

Many of the same considerations apply in response to the self-pathology of excessive medicalisation discussed in Section 9.4. If, as I claimed there, no single agent or agency is responsible for the Western self-concept, however, is it then incumbent on anyone to remedy it? Notice that although no individual may be held responsible for the imposition of an obstacle (whether a landslide that blocks our path or a culturally conditioned self-concept amenable to perversion), this does not mean that no one can be held responsible for the removal of the obstacle (see Kristjánsson, 1996, chap. 4). To take one small example, research into the effects of teachers' attitudes towards medicalisation (Malacrida, 2004) seems to indicate that teachers can be effective in stemming the tide of excessive medicalisation, if only by refusing to act as disease franchisees. Perhaps Willy Brandt's old dictum of 'the policy of the small steps' can be enacted successfully by teachers fighting excessive medicalisation, allowing the school to be become – just as Thomas Ziehe envisages – a vehicle for cultural change.

Finally, why do so many people baulk at raunch culture in general and the Hiltonistic self-concept in particular? As noted in Section 9.5, one of the main reasons is fear of the effects of raunch culture on young people, particularly girls. The powerful message emanating from the Hiltonists is commonly considered to be a lesson in immorality: Not only do young girls like to dress like Paris Hilton (or Lindsay Lohan or Britney Spears); they may also try to emulate their lives of smoking, drinking, drugs and sexual promiscuity. The APA Task Force considers precocious sexualisation to be a broad and increasing problem, linked to the most common emotional problems of girls and women, including eating disorders and depression (2007, p. 24). Deveny and Kelley (2007) wonder if the cult of the Hiltonists signals something even more ideologically profound: a coarsening of our culture and a devaluation of sex, love and lasting commitment. They allude to a recent *Newsweek* poll finding: 77% of Americans believe that Paris Hilton, Lindsay Lohan and Britney Spears have too much influence on young girls.

This belief does not seem to concur with the scientific evidence, however. When today's young are asked about their role models, parents and other relatives continue to be mentioned most often, as they have always been. Much to the surprise of Yancey, Siegel and McDaniel (2002), their survey of 12- to 17-year-old Los Angeles adolescents showed parents to be their most common role models, and demonstrated that nearly 75% of adolescents choose a role model of their own gender and ethnic group. Now we may, of course, suspect that some of the respondents in such self-report questionnaires are less than forthright in their answers. A girl might have deceptively or self-deceptively presented her mother as her role model, when it was actually a scantily clad Paris Hilton. But such suspicions are merely conjectural. In fact, it could easily work the other way around, for it would be considered cooler for a teenage girl to present Paris Hilton as her role model, although it was in fact, more mundanely, her mother. We must remember that fascination is not the same as emulation (see Kristjánsson, 2007, chap. 7). Moreover, recent findings indicate that in the USA at least, teen pregnancy, drinking and drugs are on the decline, and there is no evidence that girls are having intercourse at a younger age (Deveny & Kelley, 2007).

Throughout the ages, people have always had someone to remind them of the lures of lustful living and the horrors of a worsening world. Important as it is to remain level-headed and to consider the actual scientific data, the APA warns against too cavalier an attitude toward the recent raunch culture. Although its effects might not yet have become evident in statistical figures or self-report questionnaires, it could be subject to a gradual, subtle osmosis. The authors refer to the tenets of *cultivation theory*, according to which exposure to consistent themes *over time* leads viewers to adopt a particular – in this case harmful – perspective on the world. They are particularly concerned by what they see as processes of self-objectification in young girls, whereby they learn to think of and treat their bodies as objects of others' desires, and then incorporate this construal into their self-concept. They claim that there is ample evidence that such self-objectification is becoming common and can be linked to diminished emotional health (APA, 2007, pp. 4, 18, 21, 26). It is probably right to take the authors of the APA report on trust and try to remain vigilant against the possible effects of the Hiltonistic self-concept on young people. Being 'born into porn' and unbridled hedonism may well lead to emotional desensitisation, not least in matters sexual. It is natural to expect this concern to be addressed in values education, formal as well as informal.

If the Hiltonistic self-concept is, as I argued in Section 9.4, fuelled by hedonism, and Hiltonism is deemed to have harmful emotional and socio-moral consequences, including lack of emotional depth and complexity, this truth may prompt moves to unseat the underlying hedonism – a tall order. Many normative hedonists are psychological hedonists as well, and tend to believe that it is a necessary truth that all people seek pleasure; they will find any injunctions to the contrary to be meaningless. Instead of encouraging Calliclesian hedonists to relinquish their doctrine and embrace a Socratic ideal of unmitigated self-respect, it would be more feasible to try to persuade them that limited, prudential and qualitatively discriminating hedonism (perhaps of the classical Millian type) is preferable to the Calliclesian type that Hiltonists tend to espouse. There is nothing original about the observation that the satisfaction accompanying short-term sensual pleasure is a diet that easily wearies one. Some observations in Levy's book seem to attest to the truth of that dictum: how bored and uninterested Paris Hilton seems to look in her own sex tapes, and Hilton's grumblings about her boyfriends' claims that she is 'sexy but not sexual'. Levy ascribes these facts to the Hiltonistic emphasis on performance over real pleasure: on quantity over quality (Levy, 2006, pp. 168 and 183). She might also have mentioned the old Aristotelian-cum-Millian truisms that pleasure typically lies in unimpeded activity rather than in a special sensation aimed for by the activity, and that it is likely to be counter-productive to seek pleasure systematically and directly.

It must be admitted, however, that moral philosophers and moral educators tend to be overly sanguine about the way in which people's preferences can be transformed through rational persuasion – and at the same time unduly insensitive to cultural factors that provide the backdrop to those preferences. All effective persuasion must tap right into the target audience's emotions – no easy matter – and people's self-concepts seem, according to Swann's research at least, hard nuts to crack. It is one thing to nourish the fond hope that Hiltonism can some-how be countered at the moral and educational level, it is quite another to let that hope translate into effective action. The recent rise of Hilton-istic hedonism and the other self-pathologies traced in Chapter 9 may speak less to a long-standing failure of moral educators than it speaks to the challenge of creating more favourable societal conditions for the construction of young people's self-concepts – as well as the general development of their emotion-grounded full selves – in late modernity.

References

Abu-Assad, H. (2005). *Paradise now* (feature film). Warner Bros Entertainment Inc.

Ainslie, D. C. (1999). Scepticism about persons in Book II of Hume's Treatise. *Journal of the History of Philosophy*, 37(3), 469–492.

American Psychological Association Task Force on the Sexualization of Girls (APA). (2007). *Report of the APA Task Force on the sexualization of girls*. Washington, D. C.: American Psychological Association. Retrieved July 21, 2007, from http://www.apa.org/pi/wpo/sexualization.html

Árdal, P. S. (1989). Hume and Davidson on pride. *Hume Studies*, 15(2), 387–394.

Aristotle. (1985). *Nicomachean ethics*, trans. T. Irwin. Indianapolis: Hackett Publishing.

Aristotle. (1991). *On rhetoric*, trans. G. A. Kennedy. Oxford: Oxford University Press.

Arndt, J., Schimel, J. & Cox, C. R. (2007). A matter of life and death: Terror management and the existential relevance of self-esteem. In C. Sedikides & S. J. Spencer (Eds.), *The Self* (pp. 212–234). Hove: Psychology Press.

Athanassoulis, N. (2001). A response to Harman: Virtue ethics and character traits. *Proceedings of the Aristotelian Society*, 100(2), 215–221.

Athens, L. H. (1995). Dramatic self-change. *The Sociological Quarterly*, 36(3), 571–586.

Atran, S. (2003). The strategic threat from suicide terror. *Aei-Brookings Joint Center Publications*, December.

Attwood, F. (2006). Sexed up: Theorizing the sexualization of culture. *Sexualities*, 9(1), 77–94.

Ausubel, D. P. (1968). *Educational psychology: A cognitive view*. New York: Holt, Rinehart & Winston.

Badhwar, N. K. (2009). Is realism really bad for you? A realistic response. Retrieved March 4, 2009, from: http://www.ou.edu/ouphil/faculty/badhwar/Realism.RevisedJP.Footnotes.doc

Bandura, A. (1997). *Self-efficacy: The exercise of control*. New York: W. H. Freeman & Co.

Barrett, L. F. (2006). Emotions as natural kinds? *Perspectives on Psychological Science*, 1(1): 28–58.

Bauman, Z. (2003). *Liquid love: On the fragility of human bonds*. Cambridge: Polity Press.

Baumeister, R. F., Campbell, J. D., Krueger, J. I. & Vohs, K. D. (2003). Does high self-esteem cause better performance, interpersonal success, happiness, or healthier lifestyles? *Psychological Science in the Public Interest*, 4(1), 1–44.

Beck, U. (1992). *Risk society: Towards a new modernity*. London: Sage.

Benet-Martínez, V., Leu, J. & Lee, F. (2002). Negotiating biculturalism: Cultural frame switching in biculturals with oppositional versus compatible cultural identities. *Journal of Cross-Cultural Psychology*, 33(5), 492–516.

Ben-Ze'ev, A. (2000). *The subtlety of emotions*. Cambridge, MA: MIT Press.

Berger, R. (1997). Adolescent immigrants in search of identity: Clingers, eradicators, vacillators and integrators. *Child and Adolescent Social Work Journal*, 14(4), 263–275.

Bergman, R. (2004). Identity as motivation: Toward a theory of the moral self. In D. K. Lapsley & D. Narvaez (Eds.), *Moral development, self, and identity* (pp. 21–46). Mahwah, NJ: Lawrence Erlbaum.

Blasi, A. (1980). Bridging moral cognition and moral action: A critical review of the literature. *Psychological Bulletin*, 88(1), 1–45.

Blasi, A. (1990). How should psychologists define morality? Or, the negative side effects of philosophy's influence on psychology. In T. Wren (Ed.) *The moral domain: Essays on the ongoing discussion between philosophy and the social sciences* (pp. 38–70). Cambridge, MA: MIT Press.

Blasi, A. (1993). The development of identity: Some implications for moral functioning. In G. G. Noam & T. E. Wren (Eds.), *The moral self* (pp. 99–122). Cambridge, MA: MIT Press.

Blasi, A. (1999). Emotions and moral motivation. *Journal for the Theory of Social Behaviour*, 29(1), 1–19.

Blasi, A. (2004). Moral functioning: Moral understanding and personality. In D. K. Lapsley & D. Narvaez (Eds.), *Moral development, self, and identity* (pp. 335–348). Mahwah, NJ: Lawrence Erlbaum.

Blasi, A. (2005). Moral character: A psychological approach. In D. K. Lapsley & D. Narvaez (Eds.), *Character psychology and character education* (pp. 67–100). Notre Dame: University of Notre Dame Press.

Bosma, H. A. & Kunnen, E. S. (Eds.). (2001). *Identity and emotion: Development through self-organization*. Cambridge: Cambridge University Press.

Bosson, J. K. & Prewitt-Freilino, J. L. (2007). Overvalued and ashamed: Considering the role of self-esteem and self-conscious emotions in covert narcissism. In J. L. Tracy, R. W. Robins & J. P. Tangney (Eds.), *The self-conscious emotions: Theory and research* (pp. 407–425). New York: Guilford Press.

Branden, N. (1969). *The psychology of self-esteem: A new concept of man's nature*. Los Angeles: Nash Publishing.

Bronson, P. (2007). How not to talk to your kids: The inverse power of praise. New York Magazine, February 19. Retrieved June 1, 2007, from http://nymag.com/news/features/27840/

Brown, D. & Hooper, M. (2008, August 9). Hume's pride: Agency, attention and self-individuation. 35th Annual Hume Society Conference, University of Akureyri. Iceland. Retrieved January 25, 2009, from http://www.rit.edu/cla/ethics/Brown.pdf

Brown, J. D. & Marshall, M. A. (2001). Self-esteem and emotion: Some thoughts about feelings. *Personality and Social Psychology Bulletin*, 27(5), 575–584.

Bruner, J. (2004). Life as narrative. *Social Research*, 71(3), 691–710.

Brym, R. J. and Araj, B. (2006). Suicide bombing as strategy and interaction: The case of the second Intifada. *Social Forces*, 84(4), 1969–1986.

Calhoun, C. & Solomon, R. C. (1984). *Introduction*. In C. Calhoun & R. C. Solomon (Eds.), *What is an emotion?* (pp. 3–40). Oxford: Oxford University Press.

Carr, D. (1986). Narrative and the real world: An argument for continuity. *History and Theory*, 25(2), 117–131.

Carr, D. (2002). Moral education and the perils of developmentalism. *Journal of Moral Education*, 30(1), 5–19.

Carr, D. (2003). Rival conceptions of practice in education and teaching. *Journal of Philosophy of Education*, 37(2), 253–266.

Carr, D. (2007). Moralized psychology or psychologized morality? Ethics and psychology in recent theorizing about moral and character education. *Educational Theory*, 57(4), 389–402.

Casey, K. (1995). The new narrative research in education. *Review of Research in Education*, 21, 211–253.

Chandler, M. (1999). Stumping for progress in a post-modern world. In E. Amsel & K. A. Renninger (Eds.), *Change and development: Issues of theory, method, and application* (pp. 1–26). Mahwah, NJ: Lawrence Erlbaum.

Chandler, M. (2000). Surviving time: The persistence of identity in this culture and that. *Culture & Psychology*, 6(2), 209–231.

Chandler, M. J., Lalonde, C. E., Sokol, B. W. & Hallett, D. (2003). Personal persistence, identity, and suicide: A study of native and non-native American adolescents. *Monographs for the Society for Research in Child Development*, 68(2), 1–130.

Chappell, T. (2006). The variety of life and the unity of practical wisdom. In T. Chappell (Ed.), *Values and virtues: Aristotelianism in contemporary ethics* (pp. 136–157). Oxford: Oxford University Press.

Chazan, P. (1998). *The moral self*. London: Routledge.

Christopher, J. C. (1999). Situating psychological well-being: Exploring the cultural roots of its theory and research. *Journal of Counseling and Development*, 77(2), 141–152.

Christopher, J. C. & Hickinbottom, S. (2008). Positive psychology, ethnocentrism, and the disguised ideology of individualism. *Theory & Psychology*, 18(5), 563–589.

Cigman, R. (2001). Self-esteem and the confidence to fail. *Journal of Philosophy of Education*, 35(4), 561–576.

Cigman, R. (2004). Situated self-esteem. *Journal of Philosophy of Education*, 38(1), 91–105.

Cigman, R. (2008). Enhancing children. *Journal of Philosophy of Education*, 42(3–4), 539–557.

Colby, A. & Damon, W. (1992). *Some do care: Contemporary lives of moral commitment*. New York: The Free Press.

Cooley, C. H. (1902). *Human nature and the social order*. New York: Scribner.

Cumming, R. D. (1965). *The philosophy of Jean-Paul Sartre*. New York: Vintage Books.

Curzer, H. J. (2005). How good people do bad things: Aristotle on the misdeeds of the virtuous. *Oxford Studies in Ancient Philosophy*, 28(1), 233–256.

Curzer, H. J. (2007). Aristotle, founder of the ethics of care. *Journal of Value Inquiry*, 41(2–4), 221–243.

Damon, W. (1981). The development of justice and self-interest during childhood. In M. J. Lerner & S. C. Lerner (Eds.), *The justice motive in social behavior: Adapting to times of scarcity and change* (pp. 57–72). New York: Plenum Press.

Damon, W. (1988). *The moral child: Nurturing children's natural moral growth*. New York: Free Press.

Damon, W. (1995). *Greater expectations: Overcoming the culture of indulgence in our homes and schools*. New York: Free Press.

Darley, J. M. & Batson, C. D. (1973). From Jerusalem to Jericho: A study of situational and dispositional variables in helping behavior. *Journal of Personality and Social Psychology*, 27(1), 100–119.

D'Arms, J. & Jacobson, D. (2000). The moralistic fallacy: On the 'appropriateness' of emotions. *Philosophy and Phenomenological Research*, 61(1), 65–90.

Davidson, D. (1989). *Essays on actions and events*. Oxford: Clarendon Press.

De Sousa, R. (2001). Moral emotions. *Ethical Theory and Moral Practice*, 4(2), 109–126.

De Waal, A. (2005). When kindness kills standards. Retrieved October 10, 2006, from http://www.civitas.org.uk/blog/2005/03/when_kindness_kills_standards.html

Dennett, D. (1976). Conditions of personhood. In A. Rorty (Ed.), *The identities of persons* (pp. 175–196). Berkeley: University of California Press.

Dennett, D. C. (1992). The self as the center of narrative gravity. In F. S. Kessel, P. M. Cole & D. L. Johnson (Eds.), *Self and consciousness: Multiple perspectives* (pp. 103–115). Hillsdale, NJ: Lawrence Erlbaum.

Deonna, J. & Teroni, F. (2008). Shame's guilt disproved. *Critical Quarterly*, 50(4), 65–72.

Deonna, J. & Teroni, F. (2009). The self of shame. In M. Salmela & V. Mayer (Eds.), *Emotion, Ethics, and Authenticity* (pp. 35–50). Amsterdam: John Benjamins.

Deveny, K. & Kelley, R. 2007. Girls gone bad. Retrieved July 21, 2007, from http://www.msnbc.msn.com/id/16961761/site/newsweek/page/0/

Dewhurst, D. W. (1991). Should teachers enhance their pupils' self-esteem? *Journal of Moral Education*, 20(1), 3–11.

Diener, E. & Diener, M. (1995). Cross-cultural correlates of life satisfaction and self-esteem. *Journal of Personality and Social Psychology*, 69(5), 851–864.

Doris, J. (1998). Persons, situations, and virtue ethics. *Noûs*, 32(4), 504–530.

Doris, J. (2002). *Lack of character: Personality and moral behavior*. Cambridge: Cambridge University Press.

Doris, J. M. & Stich, S. P. (2003). As a matter of fact: Empirical perspectives on ethics. In F. Jackson & M. Smith (Eds.), *The Oxford companion to contemporary philosophy* (pp. 114–152). Oxford: Oxford University Press.

DuBois, D. L., Felner, R. D., Brand, S., Phillips, R. S. C. & Lease, A. M. (1996). Early adolescent self-esteem: A developmental-ecological framework and assessment strategy. *Journal of Research on Adolescence*, 6(4), 543–579.

Dunn, R. G. (1997). Self, identity, and difference: Mead and the poststructuralists. *The Sociological Quarterly*, 38(4), 687–705.

Dunne, J. (1993). *Back to the rough ground: 'Phronesis' and 'techné' in modern philosophy and in Aristotle*. Notre Dame: University of Notre Dame Press.

Durkheim, E. (1951). *Suicide: A study in sociology*. Glencoe: The Free Press.

Dweck, C. S. (1999). *Self-theories: Their role in motivation, personality, and development*. Philadelphia: Psychology Press.

Dweck, C. S. (2006). *Mindset: The New Psychology of Success*. New York: Random House.

Elster, J. (1986). Introduction. In J. Elster (Ed.), *The multiple self* (pp. 1–34). Cambridge: Cambridge University Press.

Elster, J. (2005). Motivations and beliefs in suicide missions. In D. Gambetta (Ed.), *Making sense of suicide missions* (pp. 233–258). Oxford: Oxford University Press.

Emler, N. (2001). *Self-esteem: The costs and causes of low self-worth*. York: Joseph Rowntree Foundation.

Ferkany, M. (2008). The educational importance of self-esteem. *Journal of Philosophy of Education*, 42(1), 119–132.

Fierke, K. M. (2004). Whereof we can speak, thereof we must not be silent: Trauma, political solipsism and war. *Review of International Studies*, 30(4), 471–491.

Flanagan, O. (1991). *Varieties of moral personality: Ethics and psychological realism*. Cambridge, MA: Harvard University Press.

Flanagan, O. (1996). *Self-expressions: Mind, morals, and the meaning of life*. Oxford: Oxford University Press.

Fleming, D. (2006). The character of virtue: Answering the situationist challenge to virtue ethics. *Ratio*, 19(1), 24–42.

Foster, R. M. P. (1996). The bilingual self: Duet in two voices. *Psychoanalytic Dialogues*, 6(1), 99–121.

Foucault, M. (2006). *The history of madness*, trans. J. Murphy & J. Khalfa. London: Routledge.

Fox, R. (2001). Constructivism examined. *Oxford Review of Education*, 27(1), 23–35.

Frankfurt, H. G. (1971). Freedom of the will and the concept of a person. *The Journal of Philosophy*, 68(1), 5–20.

Frimer, J. A. & Walker, L. J. (2008). Towards a new paradigm of moral personhood. *Journal of Moral Education*, 37(3), 333–356.

Funder, D. C. (1999). *Personality judgment: A realistic approach to person perception*. San Diego: Academic Press.

Furedi, F. (2004). *Therapy culture: Cultivating vulnerability in an uncertain age.* London: Routledge.

Furr, L. A. (2004). Medicalization in Nepal: A study of the influence of Westernization on defining deviant and illness behavior in a developing country. *International Journal of Comparative Sociology,* 45(1–2), 131–142.

Gallop, J. (1984). Beyond the jouissance principle. *Representations,* 7, 110–15.

Gasper, K. & Robinson, M. D. (2004). Locating the self in the stream of emotions: Promises and problems. *Psychological Inquiry,* 15(2), 145–149.

Gergen, K. J. (1991). *The saturated self: Dilemmas of identity in contemporary life.* New York: Basic Books.

Giddens, A. (1991). *Modernity and self-identity: Self and society in the late modern age.* London: Polity Press.

Goetz, J. L. & Keltner, D. (2007). Shifting meanings of self-conscious emotions across cultures: A social-functional approach. In J. L. Tracy, R. W. Robins & J. P. Tangney (Eds.), *The self-conscious emotions: Theory and research* (pp. 153–173). New York: Guilford Press.

Goldberg, L. R. (1993). The structure of phonotypic personality traits. *American Psychologist,* 48(1), 26–34.

Goldie, P. (2004). *On personality.* London: Routledge.

Goodman, E. (1979). *Turning points: How people change, through crisis and commitment.* New York: Doubleday.

Gould, H. (2003). Suicide as a weapon of mass destruction: Emile Durkheim revisited. Retrieved May 21, 2007, from http://www.counterpunch.org/gould11282003.html

Greer, S. (2003a). Self-esteem and the de-moralized self: A genealogy of self research and measurements. In D. Hall & M. Krall (Eds.), *About psychology: Essays at the crossroads of history, theory, and philosophy* (pp. 89–108). Albany, NY: SUNY Press.

Greer, S. (2003b). On the disciplining of esteem in psychological research: Three objections from Foucault, Rogers, and Luther. *History and Philosophy of Psychology Bulletin,* 15(1), 2–9.

Greer, S. (2007). Is there a 'self' in self research? Or, how measuring the self made it disappear. In A. C. Brock & J. Louw (Eds.), *History of Psychology and Social Practice. Special issue of Social Practice/Psychological Theorizing.* Retrieved March 1, 2008, from http://sppt-gulerce.boun.edu.tr.html

Gunnarsson, L. (2002). What is constituted in self-constitution? In C. Kanzian, J. Quitterer & E. Runggaldier (Eds.), *Personen: Ein interdiziplinärer Dialog* (pp. 76–78). Kirchberg: Austrian Wittgenstein Society.

Haidt, J. (2001). The emotional dog and its rational tail: A social intuitionist approach to moral judgment. *Psychological Review,* 108(4), 814–834.

Hall, S. (1996). Who needs 'identity'? In S. Hall & P. Du Gay (Eds.), *Questions of cultural identity* (pp. 1–17). London: Sage.

Hammershøj, L. G. (2009). The social pathologies of self-realization: A diagnosis of the consequences of the shift in individualization. *Educational Philosophy and Theory,* 41(5), 507–526.

Harding, E. & Riley, P. (1986). *The bilingual family: A handbook for parents.* Cambridge: Cambridge University Press.

Hardy, S. A. & Carlo, G. (2005). Identity as a source of moral motivation. *Human Development*, 48(4), 232–256.

Hardy, S. A. (2006). Identity, reasoning, and emotion: An empirical comparison of three sources of moral motivation. *Motivation and Emotion*, 30(3), 207–215.

Harman, G. (1999). Moral philosophy meets social psychology: Virtue ethics and the fundamental attribution error. *Proceedings of the Aristotelian Society*, 99(3), 315–331.

Hart, D. & Fegley, S. (1995). Prosocial behaviour and caring in adolescence: Relation to self-understanding and social judgment. *Child Development*, 66(5), 1346–1359.

Hart, D. & Fegley, S. (1997). Children's self-awareness and self-understanding. In U. Neisser & D. A. Jopling (Eds.), *The conceptual self in context: Culture, experience, self-understanding* (pp. 128–153). Cambridge: Cambridge University Press.

Hart, D., & Matsuba, M. K. (2007). The development of pride and moral life. In J. L. Tracy, R. W. Robins & J. P. Tangney (Eds.), *The self-conscious emotions: Theory and research* (pp. 114–133). New York: Guilford Press.

Harter, S. (1999). *The construction of the self: A developmental perspective*. New York: Guilford Press.

Hartshorne, H. & May, M. A. (1928). *Studies in the nature of character (Vol. 1: Studies in deceit)*. New York: Macmillan.

Haslam, N. (2007). *Introduction to personality and intelligence*. London: Sage.

Haste, H. & Abrahams, S. (2008). Morality, culture and the dialogic self: Taking cultural pluralism seriously. *Journal of Moral Education*, 37(3), 377–394.

Heider, F. (1958). *The psychology of interpersonal relations*. New York: Wiley.

Higgins, E. T. (1987). Self-discrepancy: A theory relating self and affect. *Psychological Review*, 94(3), 319–340.

Hoffman, M. L. (2000). *Empathy and moral development: Implications for caring and justice*. Cambridge: Cambridge University Press.

Hogan, P. (2005). The politics of identity and the epiphanies of learning. In W. Carr (Ed.), *The RoutledgeFalmer reader in philosophy of education* (pp. 83–96). London: Routledge.

Hong, Y.-y., Wan, C., No, S. & Chiu, C.-y. (2007). Multicultural identities. In S. Kitayama & D. Cohen (Eds.), *Handbook of cultural psychology* (pp. 323–345). New York: Guilford.

Hume, D. (1972). *Enquiries concerning the human understanding and concerning the principles of morals*. Oxford: Clarendon Press.

Hume, D. (1978). *A treatise of human nature*. Oxford: Clarendon Press.

Hursthouse, R. (1995). Applying virtue ethics. In R. Hursthouse, G. Lawrence & W. Quinn (Eds.), *Virtues and reasons: Philippa Foot and moral theory* (pp. 57–75). Oxford: Clarendon Press.

Hymowitz, K. S. (2006). The trash princess. *City Journal*, Autumn. Retrieved July 21, 2007, from http://www.city-journal.org/html/16_4_urbanities-paris_hilton.html

Illeris, K. (2003). Learning, identity and self-orientation in youth. *Young: Nordic Journal of Youth Research*, 11(4), 357–376.

Illich, I. (1975). *Medical nemesis*. London: Calder & Boyars.

Irwin, T. (2000). Ethics as an inexact science: Aristotle's ambitions for moral theory. In B. Hooker & M. O. Little (Eds.), *Moral particularism* (pp. 100–129). Oxford: Oxford University Press.

Isen, A. M., & Levin, P. F. (1972). The effect of feeling good on helping: Cookies and kindness. *Journal of Personality and Social Psychology*, 21(3), 384–388.

James, W. (1890). *The principles of psychology* (Vol. 1). New York: Henry Holt.

Jopling, D. A. (1997). A 'self of selves'? In U. Neisser & D. A. Jopling (Eds.), *The conceptual self in context: Culture, experience, self-understanding* (pp. 249–267). Cambridge: Cambridge University Press.

Jopling, D. A. (2000). *Self-knowledge and the self*. London: Routledge.

Kagitçibasi, Ç. (1996). The autonomous–relational self. *European Psychologist*, 1(3), 180–186.

Kamtekar, R. (2004). Situationism and virtue ethics on the content of our character. *Ethics*, 114(3), 458–491.

Kant, I. (1967). Groundwork of the metaphysic of morals. In H. J. Paton (Trans.), *The Moral Law*. New York: Barnes & Noble.

Katz, M. S. (2006). Trust, trustworthiness, narcissism and moral blindness: An examination of *The prime of Miss Jean Brodie*, PESGB conference paper. Retrieved June 1, 2007, from: http://www.philosophy-of-education.org/pdfs/Saturday/Katz.pdf

Kawakami, K., Dunn, E., Karmali, F. & Dovidio, J. F. (2009). Mispredicting affective and behavioral responses to racism. *Science Magazine*, 323(5911), 276–278.

Keller, H. (2008). Culture and biology: The foundation of pathways of development. *Social and Personality Psychology Compass*, 2(2), 668–681.

Keller, M. & Edelstein, W. (1993). The development of the moral self from childhood to adolescence. In G. G. Noam & T. E. Wren (Eds.), *The Moral Self* (pp. 310–336). Cambridge, MA: MIT Press.

Kenny, A. (1963). *Action, emotion and will*. London: Routledge and K. Paul.

Kerdeman, D. (2003). Pulled up short: Challenging self-understanding as a focus of teaching and learning. *Journal of Philosophy of Education*, 37(2), 293–306.

Keshen, R. (1996). *Reasonable self-esteem*. Montreal: McGill-Queen's University Press.

Killen, M. & Wainryb, C. (2000). Independence and interdependence in diverse cultural contexts. *New Directions for Child and Adolescent Development*, 87(1), 5–21.

Kinsella, E. A. (2005). Constructions of self: Ethical overtones in surprising locations. *Journal of Medical Ethics; Medical Humanities*, 31(2), 67–71.

Kohlberg, L. (1981). *Essays on moral development*, I-III. New York: Harper Row.

Koole, S. L. & DeHart, T. (2007). Self-affection without self-reflection: Origins, models, and consequences of implicit self-esteem. In C. Sedikides & S. J. Spencer (Eds.), *The Self* (pp. 21–49). Hove: Psychology Press.

Korsgaard, C. M. (1996). From duty and for the sake of the noble: Kant and Aristotle on morally good action. In S. Engstrom & J. Whiting (Eds.),

Aristotle, Kant, and the Stoics: Rethinking happiness and duty (pp. 203–236). Cambridge: Cambridge University Press.

Kristjánsson, K. (1996). *Social freedom: The responsibility view*. Cambridge: Cambridge University Press.

Kristjánsson, K. (1998). Liberating moral traditions: Saga morality and Aristotle's *megalopsychia*. *Ethical Theory and Moral Practice*, 1(4), 397–422.

Kristjánsson, K. (2002). *Justifying emotions: Pride and jealousy*. London: Routledge.

Kristjánsson, K. (2006). *Justice and desert-based emotions*. Aldershot: Ashgate.

Kristjánsson, K. (2007). *Aristotle, emotions, and education*. Aldershot: Ashgate.

Kundera, M. (1987). *Life is elsewhere*. London: Faber and Faber.

Ladyman, J., Ross, D., Spurrett, D. & Collier, J. (2007). *Every thing must go: Metaphysics naturalized*. Oxford: Oxford University Press.

Lagattuta, K. H. & Thompson, R. A. (2007). The development of self-conscious emotions: Cognitive processes and social influences. In J. L. Tracy, R. W. Robins & J. P. Tangney (Eds.), *The self-conscious emotions: Theory and research* (pp. 91–113). New York: Guilford Press.

Lamarque, P. (2004). On not expecting too much from narrative. *Mind & Language*, 19(4), 393–408.

Langman, L. (2002). Suppose they gave a culture war and no one came: Zippergate and the carnivalization of politics. *American Behavioral Scientist*, 46(4), 501–534.

Lapsley, D. & Hill, P. L. (2008). On dual processing and heuristic approaches to moral cognition. *Journal of Moral Education*, 37(3), 313–332.

Lapsley, D. & Narvaez, D. (Eds.). (2004). *Moral development, self, and identity*. Mahwah, NJ: Lawrence Erlbaum.

Lapsley, D. & Narvaez, D. (2005). Moral psychology at the crossroads. In D. Lapsley & D. Narvaez (Eds.), *Character psychology and character education* (pp. 18–35). Notre Dame: University of Notre Dame Press.

Lapsley, D. & Narvaez, D. (2008). 'Psychologized morality' and its discontents, or, do good fences make good neighbours? In F. Oser & W. Veugelers (Eds.), *Getting involved: Global citizenship development and sources of moral value* (pp. 279–292). Rotterdam: Sense Publishers.

Lazarus, R. S. (1994). The stable and the unstable in emotion. In P. Ekman & R. J. Davidson (Eds.), *The nature of emotions: The fundamental questions* (pp. 79–85). Oxford: Oxford University Press.

Leary, M. R. (2007a). Motivational and emotional aspects of the self. *Annual Review of Psychology*, 58, 317–344.

Leary, M. R. (2007b). How the self became involved in affective experience: Three sources of self-reflective emotions. In J. L. Tracy, R. W. Robins & J. P. Tangney (Eds.), *The self-conscious emotions: Theory and research* (pp. 38–52). New York: Guilford Press.

Leary, M. R. & Baumeister, R. F. (2000). The nature and function of self-esteem: Sociometer theory. *Advances in Experimental Social Psychology*, 32, 1–62.

Lee, F., Hallahan, M. & Herzog, T. (1996). Explaining real life events: How culture and domain shape attributions. *Personality and Social Psychology Bulletin*, 22(7), 732–741.

Leibovici, L. (2002.) Medicalisation: Peering from inside medicine. *British Medical Journal*, 324, 866.

Lewis, M. (2000). Self-conscious emotions: Embarrassment, pride, shame, and guilt. In M. Lewis & J. M. Haviland-Jones (Eds.), *Handbook of emotions* (2nd ed., pp. 623–636). New York: Guilford Press.

Lewis, M., Sullivan, M. W., Stranger, C. & Weiss, M. (1989). Self-development and self-conscious emotions. *Child Development*, 60(1), 146–156.

Levy, A. (2006). *Female chauvinist pigs: Women and the rise of raunch culture.* London: Simon & Schuster.

Lloyd, G. (2003). Inclusion and problem groups: The story of ADHD. In J. Allan (Ed.), *Inclusion, participation and democracy: What is the purpose?* (pp. 105–115). Dordrecht: Kluwer.

Lu, L. & Yang, K.-S. (2006). Emergence and composition of the traditional–modern bicultural self of people in contemporary Taiwanese societies. *Asian Journal of Social Psychology*, 9(3), 167–175.

Lukes, S. (1974). *Power: A radical view.* London: Macmillan.

Luzzati, C. (2005). Matters of identity. *Ratio Juris*, 18(1), 107–119.

McDowell, J. (1996). Deliberation and moral development in Aristotle's ethics. In S. Engstrom & J. Whiting (Eds.), *Aristotle, Kant, and the Stoics: Rethinking happiness and duty* (pp. 19–35). Cambridge: Cambridge University Press.

MacIntyre, A. (1981). *After virtue.* Notre Dame: University of Notre Dame Press.

McKinnon, C. (2005). Character possession and human flourishing. In D. Lapsley & D. Narvaez (Eds.), *Character psychology and character education* (pp. 36–66). Notre Dame: University of Notre Dame Press.

McLaughlin, T. H. & Halstead, J. M. (1999). Education in character and virtue. In J. M. Halstead & T. H. McLaughlin (Eds.), *Education in morality* (pp. 132–164). London: Routledge.

Macmurray, J. (1935). *Reason and emotion.* London: Faber and Faber.

Macmurray, J. (1958). *The self as agent.* London: Faber and Faber.

McNair, B. (1996). *Mediated sex: Pornography and postmodern culture.* London: Arnold.

Maiese, M. (2005). Suicide bombers. Retrieved May 21, 2007, from http://www.beyondintractability.org/essays/suicide_bombers/

Malacrida, C. (2004). Medicalization, ambivalence and social control: Mothers' descriptions of educators and ADD/ADHD. *Health: An Interdisciplinary Journal for the Social Study of Health, Illness and Medicine*, 8(1), 61–80.

Markus, H. R. & Kitayama, S. (1991). Culture and self: Implications for cognition, emotion, and motivation. *Psychological Review*, 98(2), 224–253.

Marsh, H. W. & Craven, R. G. (2006). Reciprocal effects of self-concept and performance from a multidimensional perspective: Beyond seductive pleasure and unidimensional perspectives. *Perspectives on Psychological Science*, 1(2), 133–163.

Marsh, H. W., Trautwein, U., Lüdtke, O., Köller, O. & Baumert, J. (2006). Integration of multidimensional self-concept and core personality constructs: Construct validation and relations to well-being and achievement. *Journal of Personality*, 74(2), 403–456.

Martin, J. (2006). Self research in educational psychology: A cautionary tale of positive psychology in action. *The Journal of Psychology*, 140(4), 307–316.

Martin, M. W. (1985). General introduction. In M. W. Martin (Ed.), *Self-deception and self-understanding* (pp. 1–27). Lawrence: University Press of Kansas.

Martin, R. & Barresi, J. (2006). *The rise and fall of soul and self: An intellectual history of personal identity.* Columbia: University of Columbia Press.

Maslow, H. A. (1970). *Motivation and personality.* New York: Harper & Row.

Massey, S. J. (1983). Is self-respect a moral or a psychological concept? *Ethics*, 93(1), 246–261.

Matsumoto, D. (1999). Culture and self: An empirical assessment of Markus and Katayama's theory of independent and interdependent self-construals. *Asian Journal of Social Psychology*, 2(3), 289–310.

Maxwell, B. (2008a). *Professional ethics education: Studies in compassionate empathy.* Dordrecht: Springer.

Maxwell, B. (2008b, October 2). Kohlberg's error? Psychologizing morality without ethical theory. Paper delivered at Metro Université de Montréal Philosophy Seminar, Montreal, Canada (unpublished).

Maxwell, B. (2009). A review of Kristján Kristjánsson, 2006: *Justice and desert-based emotions. Studies in Philosophy and Education*, 28(1), 51–71.

Mesquita, B. & Karasawa, M. (2004). Self-conscious emotions as dynamic cultural processes. *Psychological Inquiry*, 15(2), 161–166.

Milgram, S. (1974). *Obedience to authority.* New York: Harper.

Mill, J. S. (1972). *Utilitarianism, liberty, representative government.* New York: E. P. Dutton & Co.

Miller, A. (2008). A critique of positive psychology – or 'the new science of happiness'. *Journal of Philosophy of Education*, 42(3–4), 591–608.

Miller, C. (2003). Social psychology and virtue ethics. *The Journal of Ethics*, 7(4), 365–392.

Miller, P. J., Wang, S.-h., Sandel, T. & Cho, G. E. (2002). Self-esteem as folk theory: A comparison of European American and Taiwanese mother's beliefs. *Parenting: Science and Practice*, 2(3), 209–239.

Mills, J. (2001). Being bilingual: Perspectives of third generation Asian children on language, culture and identity. *International Journal of Bilingual Education and Bilingualism*, 4(6), 383–402.

Modood, T. (1998). Anti-essentialism, multiculturalism and the 'recognition' of religious groups. *The Journal of Political Philosophy*, 6(4), 378–399.

Montada, L. (1993) Understanding oughts by assessing moral reasoning or moral emotions. In G. G. Noam & T. E. Wren (Eds.), *The moral self* (pp. 292–309). Cambridge, MA: MIT Press.

Moshman, D. (2004). False moral identity: Self-serving denial in the maintenance of moral self-conceptions. In D. K. Lapsley & D. Narvaez (Eds.), *Moral development, self, and identity* (pp. 83–110). Mahwah, NJ: Lawrence Erlbaum.

Mulligan, K. (2009). Moral emotions. Retrieved March 4, 2009, from http://www.philosophie.ch/preprints/56_Moral_emotions.pdf

Narvaez, D. & Vaydich, J. L. (2008). Moral development and behaviour under the spotlight of the neurobiological sciences. *Journal of Moral Education*, 37(3), 289–312.

Neisser, U. (1988). Five kinds of self-knowledge. *Philosophical Psychology*, 1(1), 35–59.

Neisser, U. (1997). Concepts and self-concepts. In U. Neisser & D. A. Jopling (Eds.), *The conceptual self in context: Culture, experience, self-understanding* (pp. 3–12). Cambridge: Cambridge University Press.

Nesbitt, W. (1993). Self-esteem and moral virtue. *Journal of Moral Education*, 22(1), 51–53.

Nguyen, A.-M. D., & Benet-Martínez, V. (2007). Biculturalism unpacked: Components, individual differences, measurement, and outcomes. *Social and Personality Psychology Compass*, 1(1), 101–114.

Nucci, L. (2004). Reflections on the moral self-construct. In D. K. Lapsley & D. Narvaez (Eds.), *Moral development, self, and identity* (pp. 111–132). Mahwah, NJ: Lawrence Erlbaum.

Nussbaum, M. C. (1992). Human functioning and social justice: In defence of Aristotelian essentialism. *Political Theory*, 20(4), 202–246.

Nussbaum, M. C. (1996). Aristotle on emotion and rational persuasion. In A. O. Rorty (Ed.), *Essays on Aristotle's Rhetoric* (pp. 303–323). Berkeley: University of California Press.

Nussbaum, M. C. (2001). *Upheavals of thought: The intelligence of emotions*. Cambridge: Cambridge University Press.

Oatley, K. (2007). Slings and arrows: Depression and life events. *The Psychologist*, 20(4), 228–230.

O'Shaughnessy, J. & O'Shaughnessy, N. J. (2002). Marketing, the consumer society and hedonism. *European Journal of Marketing*, 36(5/6), 524–547.

Oser, F. K., Althof, W. & Higgins-D'Alessandro, A. (2008). The just community approach to moral education: System change or individual change? *Journal of Moral Education*, 37(3), 395–416.

Pape, R. (2005). *Dying to win: The strategic logic of suicide terrorism*. New York: Random House.

Park, R. & Burgess, E. (1924). *Introduction to the science of sociology*. Chicago: University of Chicago Press.

Paul, P. (2005). *Pornified: How pornography is transforming our lives, our relationships, and our families*. New York: Times Books.

Pedahzur, A. & Perliger, A. (2006). The changing nature of suicide attacks: A social network perspective. *Social Forces*, 84(4), 1987–2008.

Personalised Learning Website (2006). Retrieved October 10, 2006, from http://www.teachernet.gov.uk/management/newrelationship/personalisedlearning

Petrina, S. (2006). The medicalization of education: A historiographic synthesis. *History of Education Quarterly*, 46(4), 503–531.

Phillips, C. B. (2006). Medicine goes to school: Teachers as sickness brokers for ADHD. *PLoS Medicine*, 3(4), 182.

Phillips, D. C. (1994). Telling it straight: Issues in assessing narrative research. *Educational Psychologist*, 29(1), 13–21.

Plato. (1973). *Gorgias*, trans. W. D. Woodhead. In E. Hamilton and H. Cairns (Eds.), *The collected dialogues of Plato* (pp. 229–307). Princeton: Princeton University Press.

Polkinghorne, D. (1988). *Narrative knowing and the human sciences*. Albany: State University of New York Press.

Postman, N. (1985). *Amusing ourselves to death: Public discourse in the age of show business*. Harmondsworth: Penguin.

Prinz, J. J. (2007). *The emotional construction of morals*. Oxford: Oxford University Press.

Pugmire, D. (2005). *Sound sentiments: Integrity in the emotions*. Oxford: Oxford University Press.

Puka, B. (2004). Altruism and character. In D. K. Lapsley & D. Narvaez (Eds.), *Moral development, self, and identity* (pp. 161–188). Mahwah, NJ: Lawrence Erlbaum.

Purviance, S. M. (1997). The moral self and the indirect passions. *Hume Studies*, 23(2), 195–212.

Rafalovich, A. (2005). Relational troubles and semiofficial suspicion: Educators and the medicalization of 'unruly' children. *Symbolic Interaction*, 28(1), 25–46.

Rawls, J. (1973). *A theory of justice*. Oxford: Oxford University Press.

Reddy, W. M. (2009). Historical research on the self and emotions, *Emotion Review*, 1(4), 302–315.

Reed, D. C. (2008) A model of moral stages. *Journal of Moral Education*, 37(3), 357–376.

Reynolds, P. (2006). Seeking out the suicide bombers. Retrieved May 21, 2007 from http://news.bbc.co.uk/2/hi/uk_news/4958314.stm

Ricouer, P. (1992). *Oneself as another*, trans. K. Blamey. Chicago: University of Chicago Press.

Roberts, R. C. (2003). *Emotions: An essay in aid of moral psychology*. Cambridge: Cambridge University Press.

Roland, C. E. & Foxx, R. M. (2003). Self-respect: A neglected concept. *Philosophical Psychology*, 16(2), 247–288.

Rorty, A. O. (1975). Adaptivity and self-knowledge. *Inquiry*, 18(1), 1–22.

Rorty, A. O. & Wong, D. (1990). Aspects of identity and agency. In O. Flanagan & A. O. Rorty (Eds.), *Identity, character and morality* (pp. 19–35). Cambridge, MA: MIT Press.

Rose, N. (1996). *Inventing our selves: Psychology, power, and personhood*. Cambridge: Cambridge University Press.

Rosenberg, M. (1965). *Society and the adolescent self-image*. Princeton: Princeton University Press.

Rudd, A. (2009). In defence of narrative. *European Journal of Philosophy*, 17(1), 60–75.

Rudebusch, G. (1999). *Socrates, pleasure, and value*. Oxford: Oxford University Press.

Russell, D. (2005). Aristotle on the moral relevance of self-respect. In S. M. Gardiner (Ed.), *Virtue ethics, old and new* (pp. 101–121). Ithaca: Cornell University Press.

Ryle, G. (1949). *The concept of mind*. New York: Barnes and Noble.
Ryle, G. (1954). *Dilemmas*. Cambridge: Cambridge University Press.
Sabini, J. & Silver, M. (2005). Lack of character? Situationism critiqued. *Ethics*, 115(2), 535–562.
Sachs, D. (1981). How to distinguish self-respect from self-esteem. *Philosophy and Public Affairs*, 10(4), 346–360.
Schapp, W. (1953). *In Geschichten verstrickt*. Frankfurt am Main: Vittorio Klostermann.
Schechtman, M. (1996). *The constitution of selves*. Ithaca: Cornell University Press.
Scheff, T. (1997). *Emotions, the social bond, and human reality*. Cambridge: Cambridge University Press.
Schmitter, A. (2009). Making an object of yourself: On the intentionality of the passions in Hume. In J. Miller (Ed.), *Topics in Early Modern Philosophy of Mind* (pp. 223–240). Dordrecht: Springer.
Schwartz, S. J., Montgomery, N. J. & Briones, E. (2006). The role of identity in acculturation among immigrant people: Theoretical propositions, empirical questions, and applied recommendations. *Human Development*, 49(1), 1–30.
Schwarzer, R. & Jerusalem, M. (1995). Generalized self-efficacy scale. In J. Weinman, S. Wright & M. Johnston (Eds.), *Measures in health psychology: A user's portfolio* (pp. 35–37). Windsor: NFER-Nelson.
Schwitzgebel, E. (2008). The unreliability of naive introspection. *Philosophical Review*, 117(2), 245–273.
Scull, A. (2007, March 23). Scholarship of fools: The frail foundations of Foucault's monument. *Times Literary Supplement*, 3–4.
Searight, H. R. & McLaren, A. L. (1998). Attention-deficit hyperactivity disorder: The medicalization of misbehaviour. *Journal of Clinical Psychology in Medical Settings*, 5(4), 467–494.
Seigel, J. (2005). *The idea of the self: Thought and experience in Western Europe since the seventeenth century*. Cambridge: Cambridge University Press.
Seligman, M. E. P. (1995). *The optimistic child*. New York: Houghton Mifflin.
Sharpe, M. (2006, February 23). The psychological profile of the Islamic terrorist. Security in the City Conference, London, UK (unpublished).
Smith, R. (2002). Self-esteem: The kindly apocalypse. *Journal of Philosophy of Education*, 36(1), 87–100.
Smith, R. (2006). On diffidence: The moral psychology of self-belief. *Journal of Philosophy of Education*, 40(1), 51–62.
Snævarr, S. (2007). Don Quixote and the narrative self. *Philosophy Now*. Retrieved August 29, 2008, from http://www.philosophynow.org/issue60/60snaevarr.htm
Solomon, R. C. (1999). *The joy of philosophy: Thinking thin versus the passionate life*. Oxford: Oxford University Press.
Solomon, R. C. (2002). 'Back to basics': On the very idea of 'basic emotions'. *Journal for the Theory of Social Behaviour*, 32(2), 115–144.
Sorabji, R. (2006). *Self: Ancient and modern insights about individuality, life, and death*. Chicago: University of Chicago Press.

Spiecker, B., Steutel, J. & de Ruyter, D. (2004). Self-concept and social integration: The Dutch case as an example. *Theory and Research in Education*, 2(2), 161–175.

Spiro, M. E. (1993). Is the Western conception of the self peculiar within the context of the world cultures? *Ethos*, 21(2), 107–153.

Stanford Center on Adolescence. (2003). Exploring the nature and development of purpose in youth. Retrieved January 15, 2009, from http://www.stanford.edu/group/adolescent.ctr/Conference/2003/marconfindex.html

Statman, D. (1993). Self-assessment, self-esteem and self-acceptance. *Journal of Moral Education*, 22(1), 55–62.

Stout, M. (2000). *The feel-good curriculum: The dumbing down of America's kids in the name of self-esteem*. Cambridge, MA: Da Capo Press.

Strawson, G. (1997). 'The self'. *Journal of Consciousness Studies*, 4(5–6), 405–428.

Strawson, G. (2004). Against narrativity. *Ratio*, 17(4), 428–452.

Suh, E. M. & Oishi, S. (2002). Subjective well-being across cultures. In W. J. Lonner, D. L. Dinnel, S. A. Hayes & D. N. Sattler (Eds.), *Online readings in psychology and culture*. Retrieved March 1, 2008, from http://www.ac.wwu.edu/~culture/Suh_Oishi.htm

Summerfield, D. (2001). The invention of post-traumatic stress disorder and the social usefulness of a psychiatric category. *British Medical Journal*, 322, 95–98.

Sutherland, S. R. (1975). Hume on morality and the emotions. *The Philosophical Quarterly*, 26(102), 14–23.

Swann, W. B., Jr. (1996). *Self-traps: The elusive quest for higher self-esteem*. New York: W. H. Freeman & Co.

Swann, W. B. Jr. (2005). The self and identity negotiation. *Interaction Studies*, 6(1), 69–83.

Swann, W. B. Jr., Chang-Schneider, C. & McClarty, K. L. (2007). Do people's self-views matter? Self-concept and self-esteem in everyday life. *American Psychologist*, 62(2), 84–94.

Swann, W. B. Jr. & Bosson, J. K. (2008). Identity negotiation: A theory of self and social interaction. In O. John, R. Robins & L. Pervin (Eds.), *Handbook of personality psychology: Theory and research* (pp. 448–471). New York: Guilford Press.

Tangney, J. P., Stuewig, J. & Mashek, D. J. (2007). What's moral about the self-conscious emotions? In J. L. Tracy, R. W. Robins & J. P. Tangney (Eds.), *The self-conscious emotions: Theory and research* (pp. 21–37). New York: Guilford Press.

Tamir, M., John, O. P., Srivastava, S. & Gross, J. J. (2007). Implicit theories of emotion: Affective and social outcomes across a major life transition. *Journal of Personality and Social Psychology*, 92(4), 731–744.

Taylor, C. (1967). Neutrality in political science. In P. Laslett & W. G. Runciman (Eds.), *Philosophy, politics and society* (Vol. III, pp. 25–57). Oxford: Basil Blackwell.

Taylor, C. (1989). *Sources of the self: The making of modern identity*. Cambridge, MA: Harvard University Press.

Taylor, S. & Brown J. (1994). Positive illusions and well-being revisited: Separating fact from fiction, *Psychological Bulletin*, 116(1), 21–27.

Telfer, E. (1995). Self-respect. In R. S. Dillon (Ed.), *Dignity, character, and self-respect* (pp. 107–116). London: Routledge.

Tennant, M. (2000). Adult learning and self work, AERC conference paper. Retrieved June 1, 2007, from http://www.edst.educ.ubc.ca/aerc/2000/tennantm1-web.htm

Teroni, F. & Deonna, J. (2008). Distinguishing shame from guilt. *Consciousness and Cognition*, 17(4), 725–740.

Tomlinson C. A. (1995). *How to differentiate instruction in mixed-ability classrooms*. Alexandria, VA: Association for Supervision and Curriculum Development.

Tomlinson, C. A. (1999). *The differentiated classroom: Responding to the needs of all learners*. Alexandria, VA: Association for Supervision and Curriculum Development.

Tracy, J. L. & Robins, R. W. (2004) Putting the self into self-conscious emotions: A theoretical model. *Psychological Inquiry*, 15(2), 103–125.

Tracy, J. L. & Robins, R. W. (2007a). The self in self-conscious emotions: A cognitive appraisal approach. In J. L. Tracy, R. W. Robins & J. P. Tangney (Eds.), *The self-conscious emotions: Theory and research* (pp. 3–20). New York: Guilford Press.

Tracy, J. L. & Robins, R. W. (2007b). Self-conscious emotions: Where self and emotion meet. In C. Sedikides & S. J. Spencer (Eds.), *The self: Frontiers of social psychology* (187–209). New York: Psychology Press.

Tracy, J. L. & Robins, R. W. (2007c). The nature of pride. In J. L. Tracy, R. W. Robins & J. P. Tangney (Eds.), *The self-conscious emotions: Theory and research* (pp. 263–282). New York: Guilford Press.

Tracy, S. J. (2005). Fracturing the real-self <-> fake-self dichotomy: Moving toward 'crystallized' organizational discourse and identities. *Communication Theory*, 15(2), 168–195.

Uchida, Y., Norasakkunkit, V. & Kitayama, S. (2004). Cultural constructions of happiness: Theory and empirical evidence. *Journal of Happiness Studies*, 5(3), 223–239.

Valentine, J. C. (2001). *The relation between self-concept and achievement: A meta-analytic review*. Unpublished doctoral dissertation, University of Missouri-Columbia.

Van Der Merwe, W. L. & Jonker, C. (2001). Liberalism, communitarianism and the project of self. *South African Journal of Philosophy*, 20(3), 270–289.

Velleman, J. D. (2006). *Self to self: Selected essays*. Cambridge: Cambridge University Press.

Vleioras, G. (2005). *Identity and emotions: An overlooked link*. Groningen: Stichting Kinderstudies.

Vollmer, F. (2005). The narrative self. *Journal for the Theory of Social Behaviour*, 35(2), 189–205.

Walker, J. C. (2005). Self-determination as an educational aim. In W. Carr (Ed.), *The RoutledgeFalmer reader in philosophy of education* (pp. 74–82). London: Routledge.

Walker, L. J. (2004). Gus in the gap: Bridging the judgment–action gap in moral functioning. In D. K. Lapsley & D. Narvaez (Eds.), *Moral development, self, and identity* (pp. 1–20). Mahwah, NJ: Lawrence Erlbaum.

Wang, Q. & Chaudhary, N. (2006). The self. In K. Pawlik & G. d'Ydewalle (Eds.), *Psychological concepts: An international historical perspective* (pp. 325–358). Hove: Psychology Press.

Waters, E., Merrick, S., Treboux, D., Crowell, J. & Albersheim, L. (2000). Attachment security in infancy and early adulthood: A twenty-year longitudinal study. *Child Development*, 71(3), 684–689.

Webber, J. (2006). Virtue, character and situations. *Journal of Moral Philosophy*, 3(2), 193–213.

Welchman, J. (2005). Virtue ethics and human development: A pragmatic approach. In S. M. Gardiner (Ed.), *Virtue ethics, old and new* (pp. 142–155). Ithaca: Cornell University Press.

Wickline, V. B. (2003). Ethnic differences in the self-esteem/academic achievement relationship: A meta-analysis. Retrieved May 24, 2006, from http://userwww.service.emory.edu/~vwickli/SEAAeric.doc

Williams, B. (1993). *Shame and necessity*. Berkeley: University of California Press.

Wilson, T. D. (1985). Self-deception without repression: Limits on access to mental states. In M. W. Martin (Ed.), *Self-deception and self-understanding* (pp. 95–116). Lawrence: University Press of Kansas.

Winch, C. (2005). Autonomy as an educational aim. In W. Carr (Ed.), *The RoutledgeFalmer reader in philosophy of education* (pp. 65–73). London: Routledge.

Wittgenstein, L. (1958). *Philosophical investigations*, trans. G. E. M. Anscombe. London: Basil Blackwell.

Wolf, S. (2007). Moral psychology and the unity of the virtues. *Ratio*, 20(2), 145–167.

Wren, T. & Mendoza, C. (2004). Cultural identity and personal identity: Philosophical reflections on the identity discourse of social psychology. In D. Lapsley & D. Narvaez (Eds.), *Moral development, self, and identity* (pp. 239–266). Mahwah, NJ: Lawrence Erlbaum.

Wright, C. (2002). What could anti-realism about ordinary psychology possibly be? *Philosophical Review*, 111(2), 205–233.

Yancey, A., Siegel, J. & McDaniel, K. (2002). Role models, ethnic identity, and health-risk behaviors in urban adolescents. *Archives in Pediatrics & Adolescent Medicine*, 156(1), 55–61.

Zahavi, D. (2007). Self and other: The limits of narrative understanding. In D. D. Hutto (Ed.), *Narrative and understanding persons* (pp. 179–201). Cambridge: Cambridge University Press.

Ziehe, T. (2000). School and youth – a differential relation. *Young: Nordic Journal of Youth Research*, 8(1), 54–63.

Zola, I. (1972) Medicine as an institution of social control. *Sociological Review*, 20(4), 487–504.

Index